Carrick, County Wexford

Carrick, County Wexford

Ireland's first Anglo-Norman stronghold

Denis Shine, Michael Potterton, Stephen Mandal
& Catherine McLoughlin

EDITORS

FOUR COURTS PRESS

Typeset in 10.5pt on 13.5pt AdobeGaramondPro by
Carrigboy Typesetting Services for
FOUR COURTS PRESS LTD
7 Malpas Street, Dublin 8, Ireland
www.fourcourtspress.ie
and in North America for
FOUR COURTS PRESS
c/o IPG, 814 N Franklin St, Chicago, IL 60610.

A catalogue record for this title is available
from the British Library.

ISBN 978-1-84682-796-9

SPECIAL ACKNOWLEDGMENT

This volume derives from the *Digging the Lost Town of Carrig Project* as part of a series of
eight-hundred-and-fiftieth anniversary commemorative events. The project is a partnership
between the Irish Archaeology Field School and the Irish National Heritage Park,
supported by Wexford County Council.

Printed in Spain
by GraphyCems, Navarra.

Contents

Illustrations

FIGURES

TABLES

Abbreviations

A	alluvial sediments
AD	Anno Domini
AIA	Archaeological Institute of America
AMS	accelerator mass spectrometry
BAR	British Archaeological Reports
cal.	calibrated
Carb.	Caribbean
CIRCLE	A Calendar of Irish Chancery Letters, *c.*1224–1509
cm	centimetre(s)
comp.	compiler/compiled by
CR	close rolls
CW	curtain wall
ed.	editor/edited by/edition
EMI	electromagnetic induction
ESRI	The Economic and Social Research Institute
EU	European Union
fl.	*floruit*
G	gravels
GPR	ground-penetrating radar
GPS	global positioning system
GSI	Geological Survey Ireland
IAFS	Irish Archaeology Field School
IFR	Institute for Field Research
INHP	Irish National Heritage Park
ITM	Irish Transverse Mercator
km	kilometre(s)
Lidar	Light Detection and Ranging
m	metre(s)
n	number
n.d.	no date (given)
NGR	national grid reference
NIAH	National Inventory of Architectural Heritage
NLI	National Library of Ireland
NMS	National Monuments Service
NUI	National University of Ireland
OD	ordnance datum

OPW	Office of Public Works
ORS	old red sandstone
OS	Ordnance Survey
OSI	Ordnance Survey of Ireland
pers. comm.	personal communication
PR	patent roll
Rck	rock
RMP	Record of Monuments and Places
RUC	Royal Ulster Constabulary
s	second
s.	*shilling*
s.a.	*sub anno*, under the year
SA	Structure A
SB	Structure B
TCD	Trinity College Dublin
TD	Teachta Dála (member of Dáil Éireann)
td	townland
Tq	tills from quartzite
Ts	tills from shales
UCD	University College Dublin
UN	United Nations
UVF	Ulster Volunteer Force
WCC	Wexford County Council
WX	Wexford county

Contributors

TERRY BARRY is Fellow Emeritus of Trinity College Dublin, a Fellow of the Society of Antiquaries of London and a Fellow of the Royal Historical Society. He has published widely on the archaeology of medieval Ireland, including several papers relating to Wexford.

FIONA BEGLANE is a zoo-archaeologist and lecturer at the Institute of Technology, Sligo, specialising in the analysis of animal bones from excavations. Her research focuses mainly on medieval archaeology, hunting and the use of scientific techniques in archaeology. She has published extensively on these topics.

ISABEL BENNETT is an Enniscorthy native who was the first archaeologist to dig at Carrick, in 1984. She works as a museum curator on the Dingle Peninsula, Co. Kerry, and is the editor of www.excavations.ie.

RYAN BOURICIUS is a physicist and former researcher with Ithaca College, New York, who has partnered with the IAFS on a range of 3D scanning projects in Ireland.

RAN BOYTNER is the founding executive director of the Institute for Field Research. He earned his PhD in archaeology from University of California, Los Angeles in 1998 and has worked extensively on archaeological excavations in Peru, Ecuador, Chile, Israel and the US.

RICHARD CLUTTERBUCK is a project archaeologist with Archaeological Management Solutions. His MLitt thesis (1996) looked at medieval settlement and architecture in Tipperary, and his PhD (2015) examined the landscape archaeology of improvement in later historic Ireland.

BILLY COLFER, a graduate of St Patrick's College, Drumcondra, completed his doctoral research on medieval Wexford at Trinity College Dublin. His career as a teacher was spent in the Christian Brothers School, Wexford. Billy published extensively on medieval Wexford, before his passing in 2013.

NIALL COLFER is an archaeologist with Dublin City Council, having previously worked as an archaeological consultant. He completed his doctoral research on post-medieval milling at University College Dublin in 2016.

IAN W. DOYLE is an archaeologist and head of conservation at the Heritage Council of Ireland.

ASHELY GREEN is a geophysicist and PhD candidate with the University of Bournemouth. Ashely graduated with an MSc from the Department of Archaeology, Anthropology and Forensic Science in Bournemouth University in 2015.

MADELEINE HARRIS works with the Irish Archaeology Field School. Madeleine graduated from UCLA with a BA in history in 2017, and is currently completing her MA at University College Dublin, assessing the educational benefits of field schools.

CHRISTOPHER HAYES is the park manager of the Irish National Heritage Park. He is a native of Co. Wexford, with a long-standing interest in the county's cultural and natural heritage.

STEPHEN MANDAL is a founding director of the Irish Archaeology Field School and a founding partner of the *Digging the Lost Town of Carrig Project*.

CATHERINE McLOUGHLIN is a Wexford-based archaeologist and heritage professional who is particularly interested in medieval landscapes and built heritage conservation.

DEREK O'BRIEN works with the Irish National Heritage Park. Derek has a BA in archaeology and history, and an MPhil in archaeology from University College Cork.

RONAN O'FLAHERTY is an archaeologist and heritage consultant based in Wexford. He is a graduate of University College Dublin and a former CEO of the Discovery Programme and former principal officer in the Department of Agriculture. His research interests extend from Bronze Age combat to the 1798 Rebellion.

MICHAEL POTTERTON is a lecturer in the Department of History at Maynooth University. He has published widely on the archaeology and history of medieval Ireland.

RICHARD REID is the senior site supervisor with the Irish Archaeology Field School. Richard is a director of Concept Development Solutions, a heritage consultancy business.

MICHAEL 'BODHI' ROGERS is a professor of physics and astronomy at Ithaca College, New York. He has led several 3D scanning projects in Ireland.

DENIS SHINE is a director of the Irish Archaeology Field School and a founding partner of the *Digging the Lost Town of Carrig Project*.

EMMET STAFFORD is an archaeologist and heritage professional. A native of Co. Wexford, he is particularly interested in maritime archaeology and heritage interpretation and presentation.

DANNY ZBOROVER is the academic director of the Institute for Field Research and a Mesoamerican historical archaeologist. He currently co-directs archaeological field schools in Mexico and Peru.

Foreword

It is hard to underestimate the importance of Carrick Castle, either historically or archaeologically. Situated a few kilometres to the north-west of Wexford town, it has always been thought that this was one of the first Anglo-Norman constructions designed to assist in holding down their newly conquered lordship. The most recent excavation, in 2018, cleared the site of undergrowth, and located the outlines of the cuttings from earlier excavations. This will assist with future excavations by the Irish Archaeology Field School, employing both overseas and Irish students. These will concentrate on a large external ditch and bank with post-holes, and in the interior two stone buildings, possibly the ruinous hall and chapel mentioned in the inquisition of 1324. They will also help to integrate Carrick better within the Irish National Heritage Park, especially as it is the only known authentic archaeological site within its bounds.

It is not possible in this brief foreword to cover all twelve instructive chapters, and so I will simply give a flavour of the book. One of the chapters discusses another unique 'archaeological' construction built in the centre of Carrick Castle in the middle of the nineteenth century. This is the 'early medieval' round tower, almost 25m tall, commemorating the Wexford men who died in the Crimean War. It is a real pity that the names of the fallen were not carved on the stone tower itself. Indeed, this war, in which several thousand Irishmen lost their lives, has largely been forgotten within the context of Ireland in the nineteenth century.

On a personal level, it is sad to read the impressive introductory chapter on Anglo-Norman colonisation written by the late Billy Colfer, who probably knew more about the history and archaeology of Wexford than anyone else. The sadness is more than mitigated by the other author, his son Niall Colfer, who is also an archaeologist and who facilitated the incorporation of Billy's text within this volume. There are also chapters that investigate the broader landscape of Carrick utilising digital methods, such as laser scanning, which really prove the efficacy of these systems for future research here. The use of 3D visualisation software will create a reconstruction of Carrick and its landscape that will be of inestimable help at home and in the classroom.

I must congratulate the team led by Denis Shine, Michael Potterton, Stephen Mandal and Catherine McLoughlin in producing such a comprehensive volume. Not only is the archaeology discussed, but the monument is contextualised within its surrounding landscape, both archaeological and historical, as well as the wider area. And so, the reader gets a very complete picture.

In conclusion, this book is an excellent example of how best to critically examine a complex archaeological landscape, and is a model that should be followed by similar studies in the future. It is one of the first, if not the first, archaeological and historical studies in the whole of Ireland to critically examine an important medieval castle within its broader landscape. The contributors and all the students should be proud to have taken part in such a ground-breaking research project.

TERRY BARRY
Trinity College Dublin
29 July 2019

Preface

INTRODUCTION

In January of 2018 the *Digging the Lost Town of Carrig Project* commenced at Carrick ringwork in the Irish National Heritage Park (INHP), Ferrycarrig, Co. Wexford. The project, established as a partnership between the Irish Archaeology Field School (IAFS) and the INHP (with support from Wexford County Council), aims to assess one of the most historically significant, but lesser known, medieval sites in Ireland. The Carrig project is centred on a major research excavation of the ringwork, which hopes to draw the site into the park as a 'key attraction', in the process providing added economic and amenity value to the local community. Crucially, through heritage engagement and education initiatives, the project aims to bring the site into public consciousness both locally and nationally.

The site, founded in the winter of 1169 by Robert Fitz Stephen, was the first Anglo-Norman stronghold in the country, being constructed the year before the main Anglo-Norman landing party disembarked at Baginbun. A stone castle, medieval borough and deer park developed close to (or on) the site of the ringwork in the thirteenth century. Despite the historical importance of the ringwork, its location within a heritage park and the occurrence of excavations at the site in the 1980s, the site does not feature heavily in public memory. This volume is an important step in establishing Carrick's rightful place in the medieval histories of Co. Wexford, Ireland and Britain.

The 2018 excavations initiated a 'soft launch' for the project, with a recognition from the outset of the importance of the impending eight-hundred-and-fiftieth anniversary of both the Anglo-Norman landing and the Carrick site in 2019, when the official project launch takes place. Progress in 2018 exceeded expectations, with the groundwork laid in terms of excavation, non-invasive survey, historical research and academic collaboration to produce this volume just a year after the project start.

CARRICK

While the site is commonly referred to as Ferrycarrig, Carrick ringwork is in fact located in the townland of Newtown (named after Carrick's medieval borough, a 'Newtown' to Wexford) on the southern side of the River Slaney approximately 4km west of Wexford town. The site is situated at the head of a 'promontory' of land that falls dramatically in a sheer escarpment towards the river.

There is no clear archaeological evidence for occupation at the site before its 1169 foundation date (see ch. 5 for a discussion), although a collared-urn burial is located within Newtown townland, *c.*200m south-east of the site. The historical importance of Carrick in the medieval period is, however, well documented and it features in both the *Expugnatio Hibernica* and *The song of Dermot and the earl.*

In May 1169 a force of approximately 500 to 600 Anglo-Normans led by Robert Fitz Stephen and Maurice de Prendergast landed at Bannow Bay on the south coast of Wexford (see ch. 1 for a discussion on the coming of the Anglo-Normans and ch. 3 for a summary of their archaeological legacy). They were joined by Diarmait Mac Murchada with a force of 500 men, before marching and capturing the Hiberno-Norse town of Wexford. Lands, including the town of Wexford, were granted to Fitz Stephen and Maurice Fitz Gerald, with the former fortifying his new grant by constructing a ringwork castle on top of a large rock at Ferrycarrig (or Carrick). Carrick was attacked by Domhnall, son of Diarmait Mac Murchada, with a purported force of three thousand men in 1171, forcing Fitz Stephen to surrender. Accounts of the siege indicate that in 1171 the site consisted of a bank and fosse, with a wooden palisade (as well as a presumably wooden castle and potentially a wooden gatehouse).

The site, along with Wexford town, was given to Strongbow in 1173, passing to Strongbow's daughter Isabella de Clare upon his death in 1176. A stone castle at the site was almost certainly constructed between 1189 and 1231 when Carrick was under the control of the Marshal family (see ch. 1). Certainly, the first reference to a castle of Carrick is recorded at the time of William Marshal II's death in 1231 (ch. 4). Carrick was established as a borough at some stage during the early thirteenth century, as an inquisition in 1307 records a borough with *c.*111 houses; the borough is now understood to have grown up to the east of the ringwork (see ch. 6), having since been separated from the ringwork and stone castle in the modern landscape by the construction of the main N11 road in the 1980s (ch. 6; see also ch. 9 for a reconstruction of the landscape prior to the road construction). A deer park, one of a handful of recorded examples in Ireland and perhaps one of the earliest, was also established at the site by the mid-thirteenth century (ch. 7).

By the early fourteenth century, Carrick was recorded as ruinous (a ruined hall and chapel are documented within the enclosure at this time). The decline of the town in the fourteenth century mirrors the experience of the Anglo-Norman colony in much of Co. Wexford and Ireland in general. The manor of Carrick, and a number of land sales, continued to be recorded in the fifteenth and sixteenth centuries, with the castle last noted as 'still remaining' as late as 1587 (ch. 4). The final destruction of the castle is likely to have resulted from quarrying in the eighteenth or nineteenth century, for use in buildings such as Wexford Bridge in the 1790s or Belmont House (*c.*1km from the site) in *c.*1800. Stone from the castle was also used during the construction of a replica early medieval round tower, built as a Crimean War memorial in the middle of the ringwork in 1857/8 (ch. 9).

In 1987, following the construction of the N11, the landscape surrounding the site was established as the INHP, a fourteen-hectare outdoor museum that depicts nine-thousand years of re-created Irish history within natural forestry and wet woodlands (ch. 10). Covering prehistoric through to Anglo-Norman periods and featuring various buildings and structures typical of each period, the INHP has been educating the general public on Irish heritage for over thirty years. Despite the Carrick ringwork being the only authentic archaeological site within the park, it did not feature heavily as an attraction. To encourage public understanding of the site and to increase tourist footfall to this area of the park, the INHP invited the IAFS to undertake an archaeological research and teaching excavation at the site in 2018, and the *Digging the Lost Town of Carrig Project* was founded. This was spearheaded by an international field school, a concept that has grown exponentially in popularity in recent years as a complement to traditional campus-based third-level education (ch. 11).

EXCAVATIONS

Archaeological excavations have been undertaken at Carrick ringwork on three occasions prior to the IAFS, in 1984, 1986/7 and 2015. The first occurred when several cuttings, including one through the ringwork, were excavated by Isabel Bennett in advance of the construction of the INHP. Further excavations were undertaken at the site by Claire Cotter in 1986 and 1987, when six cuttings were dug through the ditch and a further four were excavated on the interior of the site. Finally, keyhole excavations were undertaken by Emmet Stafford at the base of the Crimean War monument (round tower), to facilitate the placement of lightning-conductor mats for the monument in 2014.

In January 2018, the IAFS commenced archaeological excavations at the site under licence from the National Monuments Service (licence 17E0318). The main agenda for initial excavation and associated works was to ready the project for its official launch in 2019. These works included: a) clearing the site of vegetative overgrowth, to define the monument's form; b) re-exposing the 1980s cuttings, before undertaking a selective programme of excavation and environmental sampling, in advance of radiometric dating; and c) incorporating the dig into a full programme of historical and archaeological research, so that Carrick might be better understood within its wider landscape. This programme of research included commissioning high-resolution geophysical surveys and 3D scans in partnership with the University of Bournemouth and Ithaca College respectively (chs 5, 6, 8). A geological assessment of the masonry remains on the site and the round tower was also undertaken (ch. 5).

In the inaugural year, the three internal cuttings that contained archaeology in the 1980s were re-exposed and re-recorded. An additional new cutting was opened (ch. 5). These excavations helped assess the original twelfth-century defences, twelfth-century structures and thirteenth-/fourteenth-century masonry buildings, as well as their overlying deposits.

The twelfth-century defences include a large external ditch (*c.*2m in depth by 5m+ in width) and a *c.*2m-high bank; a large possible defensive wall, or a wall of a defensive structure (1.8m wide and 10.2m long), was also found crowning a part of the bank. The ephemeral remains of twelfth-century wooden structures were recorded on the ringwork interior, overlain by a charcoal layer dating to 1040–1210 cal. AD (with a 57.8 per cent probability of dating from AD1120 to 1210). These post-holes are likely to represent some of the very first Anglo-Norman structures in the country. Two stone buildings were documented during the excavation, each consisting of three surviving walls, typically only one or two courses in height. While the excavation of these buildings is in its infancy, it is tempting to associate them with the ruinous hall and chapel located within the 'enclosure' (or *classum*) of Carrick, as recorded in an inquisition in 1324 (ch. 4).

CONCLUSION

The excavation in 2018, while a great success, was only the first step of a fifteen-plus-year research project. This excavation in time will lead to a greater understanding of the Carrick ringwork and subsequent stone castle, as well as comparable sites. The dig will add to our understanding of the rest of the medieval settlement of Carrick (outside the confines of the INHP), where future non-invasive survey and, hopefully, targeted excavation is planned. As important as the excavations themselves is the integration of the archaeological work into the consciousness of the local community and historical dialogues on the coming of the Anglo-Normans to Co. Wexford and Ireland at large. The *Digging the Lost Town of Carrig Project*, facilitated by a third-level research dig, is an opportunity for all to understand in a richer and experiential way what happened in the south-east of Ireland eight-hundred-and-fifty years ago when the first wave of Anglo-Normans landed on Wexford's coast. While this event may have been overlooked or misrepresented in the past (ch. 12), remembering shared histories and commonalities seems to take on even greater importance as the years go by.

ACKNOWLEDGMENTS

We would like to thank each of the contributors for their work in researching and preparing their chapters. This was not an easy undertaking, considering the tight turnaround required for this volume to appear in tandem with the eight-hundred-and-fiftieth anniversary of the construction of the Carrick site. Each author was asked for timely submissions and replies to editors' comments, and we thank them for their patience and efficiency in this regard. On the subject of patience and efficiency, we are very grateful indeed for the hard work and commitment of the team at Four Courts Press, especially Martin Fanning, Martin Healy and Anthony Tierney. We thank Michael Ann Bevivino for compiling the index.

The funding provided by Wexford County Council was essential to all the 'Carrick 850' commemorative events, including the preparation of this volume and the conference that followed. The council members have been a great support to the *Digging the Lost Town of Carrig Project* and we are exceptionally thankful for the faith they have shown in this venture.

The following institutions are thanked for their permission to reproduce illustrations: Royal Irish Academy; National Library of Ireland; Ordnance Survey of Ireland; and National Museums Northern Ireland. The staff in each of those institutions were efficient and helpful with our requests for all images and maps. We would like to thank Riccardo Conway for supplying a series of site photographs taken by drone, and Richard Reid for his help in sourcing other illustrations. Catherine McLoughlin would like to acknowledge Emmet Stafford's work in preparing some of the illustrations for Chapter 4.

Michael Potterton would like to thank the following for their assistance with illustrations in his chapter: Michael Ann Bevivino (University College Dublin); Michela Bonardi (British Museum); Keith Busby; Niall Colfer; David Collins (Maynooth University); Christiaan Corlett (National Monuments Service); Katherine Daly (Discovery Programme); James Harte (National Library of Ireland); Grace Fegan (Medieval Mile Museum, Kilkenny); Michael Harpur (eOceanic); Paul Johnson (The National Archives, UK); Valerie J. Keeley (VJK Ltd); Ann Lynch; Cóilín Ó Drisceoil (Kilkenny Archaeology); Katie D. Potterton; Tony Roche (National Monuments Service); Robert Shaw (Discovery Programme); Brian Sherwood (British Library); Emma Ward (Maynooth University); Marysia Wieckiewicz-Carroll (Royal Society of Antiquaries of Ireland); Cressida Williams (Canterbury Cathedral).

We would like to thank the Colfer family for allowing us to reproduce the late Billy Colfer's work from *Wexford castles: landscape, context and settlement* (2013, 23–36), as well as several of the illustrations. Niall Colfer would like to acknowledge the support of Mike Collins of Cork University Press and Matthew Stout and Kevin Whelan (as well as F.H.A. Aalen), editors of the Wexford trilogy written by his father.

This book largely derives from the Carrig project and excavation in the Irish National Heritage Park (INHP), which was founded in 2018 on the principle of partnership. The key partners of the excavation are the Irish Archaeology Field School (IAFS) and the INHP. Denis Shine and Stephen Mandal of the IAFS would like to thank everyone at the park who has helped make the vision of Carrick a reality, especially the park manager, Chris Hayes (who initiated the project), and general manager, Maura Bell. The staff have been very supportive, from the outdoor park staff who maintain the site and its facilities to Alan Boland who has steadfastly supported the promotion of the project and this volume with his digital-media and graphic-design skills.

The wider Carrig project, and this volume, would not have happened without the fantastic third-level students and partner organisations who populate the excavation each year. Your hard work and enthusiasm at the excavation site has ultimately contributed to this book; we told you your trowelling was important to more than just context sheets!

Finally, the editors would like to thank their families for allowing us the time to complete this book. Each of us has a day job meaning publications like these eat away at time with our partners and children. Thank you for your support, patience and understanding.

THE EDITORS
1 May 2019

CHAPTER ONE

The Anglo-Norman colonisation of Wexford

BILLY COLFER & NIALL COLFER

PRELUDE

It can be argued strongly that the arrival of the Anglo-Normans in south-west Wexford in 1169 constitutes the principal historical occurrence in the county, one which helped shape the landscape and people into the unique entities they are today. It could also be maintained that any study of the Anglo-Normans in the south-east would be incomplete without reference to the research undertaken by my father, Billy Colfer.

Having grown up on the Hook Peninsula within sight of the thirteenth-century lighthouse built by William Marshal to control Waterford Harbour, as well as Baginbun, the original landing place for the second fleet of the Anglo-Normans, a thirst for an understanding of the Anglo-Norman conquest of the south-east occupied much of his adult life.

When I was approached by the editors of this book to contribute a chapter focusing on the arrival of the Anglo-Normans in Wexford I felt that, rather than present a piece under my name based on my father's various publications (see Murphy 2016 for a full bibliography), it was more appropriate for his own work to be included verbatim. This was for a variety of reasons. First, his book *Arrogant trespass* (Colfer 2002), which had its origins as a PhD thesis for Trinity College Dublin in the mid-1980s, remains the seminal work on the subject. Second, as evidenced in his publications, he understood the importance of Carrick as the first permanent settlement established by the first knight to land, Robert Fitz Stephen. Third, my father was involved in the founding of the Irish National Heritage Park (INHP) and there is little doubt that the current excavations and rekindling of enthusiasm surrounding Carrick are something in which he would have been involved and of which he would have approved whole-heartedly.

This is a chapter focusing on the arrival of the Anglo-Normans, replicated with minor amendments from that published in *Wexford castles: landscape, context and settlement* (Colfer 2013). This book was the last in a trilogy on Wexford, all published by Cork University Press, with *The Hook Peninsula* (Colfer 2004) and *Wexford: a town and its landscape* (Colfer 2008) constituting the earlier publications. The chapter on Anglo-Norman colonisation in *Wexford castles* provides a succinct synopsis of years of research. In relation to Carrick, it details the background leading to the establishment of the fort on a steep rock on the right bank of the River Slaney by Fitz Stephen, who possibly feared a revolt by the Norse from Wexford, 4km down-river. The subsequent arrival of Strongbow and William Marshal, two names synonymous with the Anglo-Norman feudalisation of Wexford, is also discussed.

I would like to thank Mike Collins of Cork University Press for allowing the editors and publishers of the current book to use a chapter first presented in *Wexford castles: landscape, context and settlement*. Thanks are also due to Matthew Stout and Kevin Whelan (along with Fred Aalen), editors of the Wexford trilogy written by my father, for their approval of the reuse of the chapter below and for the happy memories of listening to those scholars in both serious and jovial consultation in my father's study in Slade on the Hook Peninsula. The maps are designed by Matthew Stout.

INTRODUCTION

By the early twelfth century, profound economic, social, military and cultural advances had so transformed the English, that their Celtic neighbours were regarded as inferior and barbaric. This attitude resulted in an incipient imperialism, four centuries earlier than is generally supposed, providing a convenient moral pretext for the anglicisation of Ireland, Scotland and Wales (Gillingham 1992). Political events in Ireland facilitated the initiation of this process. In 1166, Diarmait Mac Murchada, deposed king of Leinster and Uí Chennselaig, determined to regain his former power, fled overseas in search of foreign aid (Orpen 1892, line 140). Mac Murchada succeeded in enlisting the aid of a disparate group in south Wales, spearheaded by Anglo-Norman knights who agreed to serve him as mercenaries (for a full account, see Colfer 2002, 25–45). The landing of two small groups in 1169–70 at Bannow and Baginbun on the south-west coast of Wexford initiated a process that had a profound impact on the subsequent evolution of all aspects of Irish life (see Figure 1.1).

The role of the Anglo-Normans mutated aggressively from mercenary to invader and within a relatively short time-span the militaristic expertise of the newcomers enabled them to occupy territory in the east and south of Ireland. Colonisation quickly followed, organised according to the feudal system of land occupation implemented by the Normans in France and in England. This involved the establishment of a hierarchical society based on the European model of sophisticated record keeping. As in England a century before, the European concept of castle building was introduced, as centres of military control and civil administration and also as signature statements of status and domination (Figure 1.2). The locations of feudal manors, based on pre-existing Gaelic land divisions, dictated the siting of early castles. These manors were granted in perpetuity and the manorial framework determined the distribution of the small castles now known as tower houses in the fifteenth and sixteenth centuries.

1.1 An aerial perspective of Bannow Island, with sandbanks and mudflats exposed at low tide, captures the treacherous nature of the estuary. In later centuries, when the channel was moved to the west by shifting sands, the island where the Anglo-Normans first landed was connected to the mainland by a sand dune. The coastal site of Bannow town can be seen to the right (A), identified by the ruins of the medieval parish church of St Mary's

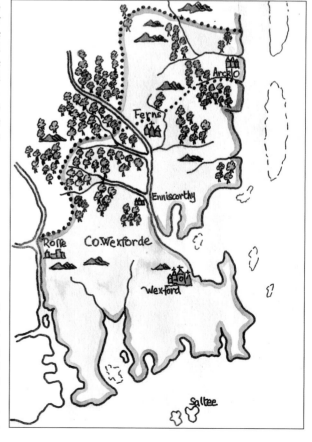

1.2 Co. Wexford's landscape influenced the establishment and success of the Anglo-Norman colony. The mountainous, heavily wooded north and west presented a daunting challenge to would-be settlers, as well as providing a safe refuge for the Irish. Baptista Boazio's late sixteenth-century map (re-drawn) distinguishes between the northern wooded uplands and the lowlands of the south

THE ARRIVAL OF THE ANGLO-NORMANS

Following a meeting with Henry II, king of England and part of France, who granted him permission to hire mercenaries within his kingdom (Orpen 1892, lines 77–100; for a background, see Colfer 2002, 23–5), Mac Murchada directed his recruiting campaign towards the knights of the Pembroke region in south Wales. He promised money and land in return for military service, but to Richard Fitz Gilbert de Clare, earl of Pembroke, better known as Strongbow, he offered his daughter, Aoife, in marriage and, contrary to Irish custom, succession to the kingdom of Leinster after his death (Orpen 1892, lines 325–55; Scott and Martin 1978, 29). In 1167, Mac Murchada returned with a small band and succeeded in re-establishing himself in Uí Chennselaig. In May 1169, a six-hundred-strong advance party, of mixed origin, including Anglo-Norman, French, English, Welsh and Flemish, landed at Bannow Island on the south Wexford coast (Figure 1.1), led by Robert Fitz Stephen and Maurice de Prendergast. They were joined by Mac Murchada with a force of five hundred men. Their combined army marched on the Viking town of Wexford, which was surrendered by its Hiberno-Norse inhabitants after a short siege (Orpen 1892, lines 441–60; Scott and Martin 1978, 31).

Mac Murchada immediately granted the town and all its lands, equivalent to the barony of Forth, to Robert Fitz Stephen and Maurice Fitz Gerald, and the baronies of Bargy and Shelburne (two cantreds on the sea between Wexford and Waterford) to Strongbow's uncle, Hervey de Montmorency, the first land grants issued to Anglo-Norman knights in Ireland. The colony subsequently established in the southern baronies of Forth and Bargy survived undisturbed for more than four centuries, making south Wexford one of the most anglicised parts of Ireland. Leaving Fitz Stephen at Wexford, Mac Murchada marched on Dublin. Possibly fearing a revolt by the Hiberno-Norse of Wexford, Fitz Stephen constructed a fort on a steep rock on the right bank of the River Slaney, 3km up-river from Wexford at a place called *Carrig* (Bennett 1985; Orpen 1892, lines 1395–7; Scott and Martin 1978, 31; ch. 4, below). The remains of this first-recorded fortification built by the Anglo-Normans in Ireland, classified as a ringwork castle, are now included in the INHP at Ferrycarrig.

In May 1170, another small force, led by Raymond le Gros, landed at Dún Domhnaill, now called Baginbun, a headland on the south Wexford coast, already the site of an Iron Age promontory fort (Moore 1996, 26 (no. 226), 94 (no. 962)). They fortified the headland by constructing a second defensive earthwork, described both as 'a somewhat flimsy fortification of branches and sods' and as a castle with gates. When the Anglo-Normans were besieged by an army of Norse and Irish from the city of Waterford, they sallied from the gate of their fort and completely routed their attackers (Scott and Martin 1978, 57–9; for a discussion of the battle of Baginbun, see also Gillingham 1993). Raymond le Gros occupied the fort at Baginbun for several months, awaiting the arrival of the main force led by Strongbow, which eventually landed at Passage in Waterford Harbour. The combined forces soon took the city of Waterford. Mac Murchada brought his daughter, Aoife, to Waterford where she was married to Strongbow, establishing his claim to the kingdom of Leinster (Orpen 1892, lines 1526–31; Scott and Martin 1978, 57, 59, 67). The combined forces then marched on Dublin, which was taken by storm. The three Viking port towns were now in the hands of the Anglo-Normans, effectively giving them control of the seas.

In May 1171, Mac Murchada died and the situation changed dramatically for his former mercenaries (Orpen 1892, lines 1556–731; Scott and Martin 1978, 67, 75). Henry II, alarmed at the prospect of an insubordinate Norman kingdom emerging on the neighbouring island, embargoed all shipping to Ireland and ordered his subjects to return (Scott and Martin 1978, 71; Sweetman 1875–86, vol. i, p. 2, no. 10). In late 1171, the king intervened personally and landed at Crook in Waterford Harbour, with a large retinue of knights (Scott and Martin 1978, 93). At Waterford, Henry made a formal grant of Leinster to Strongbow, reserving to himself all seaports and fortresses. After wintering in Dublin, Henry travelled to Wexford where he spent seven weeks waiting for favourable weather to make the crossing to Wales (Sweetman 1875–86, vol. i, p. 6, no. 34). In 1172, Henry signed a charter (Orpen 1968, vol. i, 274), perhaps while he was still in Wexford, granting extensive estates in Ireland to the Knights Templar, including the manor of Kilcloggan on the Hook Peninsula, consisting of the combined medieval parishes of Hook and Templetown, which still bears their name. The Military Orders provided security at strategic locations throughout Europe and the Templars were installed on the eastern (and western) shore of Waterford Harbour for the same purpose (Colfer 2002, 194–200).

The Knights Hospitaller were introduced into Co. Wexford by Strongbow *c.*1175 when he granted them lands at Ferns and the church of St Michael in Wexford town. About 1210, William Marshal added to their possessions in Wexford town, notably the church of St John, where they established the Hospital of St John, just outside the town wall near a gate that became known as John's Gate. Marshal also granted other unidentified lands to the Hospitallers, described as 'that part of Baliocynan which remained when the land was divided between Brother Maurice, prior of the Hospitallers, and Geoffrey, son of Robert' (Anon. 1891, 11–13). In 1212, several churches in the diocese of Ferns were confirmed to the Hospitallers including St John's of 'Balischauc' (McNeill 1932, 138–41); this is the first mention of Ballyschauc, which was the principal thirteenth-century Hospitaller manor in the county (possibly the Baliocynan of Marshal's grant). Mistakenly identified as Ballyhack on the Cistercian estate of Dunbrody for several centuries, Balischauc has recently been recognised as the medieval parish now known as Ballyhoge. The strategic location of the Hospitallers at Ballyhoge, on the west bank of the Slaney below Enniscorthy, secured the vital river corridor (for the identification of Ballyhoge, see Colfer 2002, 200–3).

Strongbow died in 1176, leaving a baby daughter, Isabella, as heir, and Leinster was taken into the king's wardship. In 1185, the arrival of Prince John, as lord of Ireland, with a large retinue, signalled a change in emphasis from military domination to colonisation of land. Arriving in Ireland initially as mercenaries, the ambitious Anglo-Norman knights, capitalising on the opportunity to acquire new lands, quickly seized the initiative and occupied eastern and southern Ireland. Military control was followed by the creation of a hierarchical landholding system known as feudalism and the introduction of settlers from England and Wales (for an early account of feudalism in the county, see Colfer 2002, 35–45).

STRONGBOW'S LAND GRANTS

Following Strongbow's surrender of Leinster to the king and its re-grant by the service of one hundred knights, his main concern was the orderly occupation of the land in accordance with the laws of feudalism. An analysis of these land grants is essential to an understanding of castle building, for instance, as the manorial layout determined the location and distribution of all types of earthwork fortifications and stone castles for the following four-and-a-half centuries (Figure 1.3). Before allocating land to his principal tenants, the feudal lord reserved demesne manors for his own use, burgage lands for the foundation of towns, and grants intended for the church. Lacking an intimate knowledge of the landscape, the Anglo-Normans, of necessity, utilised

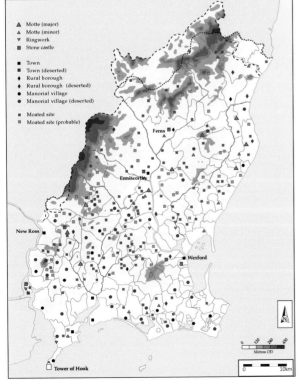

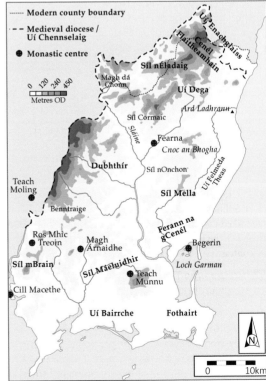

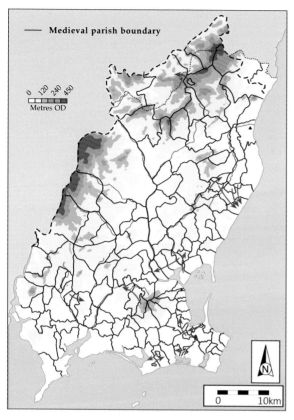

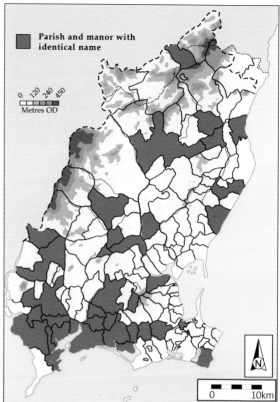

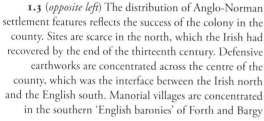

1.3 (*opposite left*) The distribution of Anglo-Norman settlement features reflects the success of the colony in the county. Sites are scarce in the north, which the Irish had recovered by the end of the thirteenth century. Defensive earthworks are concentrated across the centre of the county, which was the interface between the Irish north and the English south. Manorial villages are concentrated in the southern 'English baronies' of Forth and Bargy

1.4 (*opposite right*) Ten main divisions, or trícha cét, were held by dynastic groups in the Mac Murchada kingdom of the Uí Chennselaig. Those were used by Strongbow as convenient units on which to base early land grants

1.5 (*top left*) The medieval parochial system (now referred to as civil parishes) evolved in tandem with the feudal landholding pattern imposed by the Anglo-Normans and marked the colony's progress. The difference in size reflects the sprawling, thinly populated grants in the north, contrasting with small, heavily settled manors in the south

1.6 (*top right*) The sharing of a common name illustrates the affinity between manor and parish, particularly in the south-west of the county

1.7 (*right*) The Irish land divisions became the basis for Anglo-Norman grants. The original names were frequently retained but in a mutilated form, as clerks attempted to integrate them into Latin charters

existing Gaelic territorial divisions in the creation of a feudal landholding system (for an account of Gaelic districts mentioned in Strongbow's grants, see Orpen 1968, vol. i, 387–94; see Figure 1.4). In 1167, there were ten territorial divisions known as *trícha cét* (thirty hundreds) in the kingdom of Uí Chennselaig (O'Donovan 1848–51, vol. ii, 1167). The *trícha cét* was equated by the Anglo-Normans with the Welsh cantreds (Scott and Martin 1978, 185) and used as a convenient unit on which to base primary grants. As well as defining the principal manors, the cantreds frequently coincided with internal diocesan divisions, the rural deaneries (Empey 1985, 73; Nicholls 1984, 556–8). The relationship between civil and ecclesiastical boundaries also applied at a lower level, where the sub-manors of large fiefs underpinned the parochial structure (Otway-Ruthven 1964, 111–22) (Figures 1.5, 1.6). Parishes were generally created in areas of Anglo-Norman settlement by the tithe-paying tenantry on the manors, following the introduction of a parochial tithing system at the Council of Cashel in 1172 (Otway-Ruthven 1964, 111–22; Scott and Martin 1978, 99). In establishing the locations and boundaries of manors, and the extents of earlier Gaelic territorial units, it is imperative to examine the medieval ecclesiastical structure of diocese, rural deanery and parish rather than later county and barony boundaries (Figure 1.7).

Demesne manors

Strongbow's first concern was the setting aside of lands that would be organised as demesne manors for his personal use. Following a campaign in Normandy in 1173, he was given a royal grant of the town of Wexford (Orpen 1892, lines 2902–3), which he then made the principal town and seignorial manor of the lordship (Orpen 1968, vol. i, 373). He visited Ferns on several occasions; he spent eight days there in early 1172 (Orpen 1892, lines 2157–9) and returned shortly afterwards to give his daughter Basilia in marriage to Robert de Quency (Orpen 1892, lines 2741–6). About 1175, Strongbow granted ten carucates and one burgage between the town of Ferns and 'the great water' to the south (presumably the River Bann) to the Knights Hospitaller (Anon. 1891, 11–12). These associations with Ferns suggest that he had decided to retain the Meic Murchada power base and monastic centre for himself. Ferns would become one of the principal demesne manors of his successor.

The manor of Ross, located on the River Barrow and associated with the monastic centre of Ros Mhic Treoin, where the surviving motte at Old Ross represents the early earthwork castle (Moore 1996, no. 955; see Figure 2.32), is also linked with Strongbow (Orpen 1968, vol. i, 394). The extent of the manor was outlined in a charter of Richard Marshal *c*.1232, showing that it corresponded substantially to the large parish of Ross (Orpen 1934, 54–63). The demesne manor of Taghmon, based on an early medieval monastic centre, is described in the same charter, but there is no indication that it was retained by Strongbow. The demesne manors were all based on existing settlement centres and they were presumably selected because of the good-quality soil on which they were located (Gardiner and Ryan 1964).

Primary land grants

Strongbow created primary manors by granting large fiefs to knights in his retinue. The amount of land held by the service of one knight varied considerably, depending on land quality and location. The knight's fee in the frontier region in the north of the county was up to four times the size of those in the relatively secure southern region. Not all tenants held land by knight's service; some free tenants paid a fixed rent and settlers were attracted to towns by the offer of burgage status (Otway-Ruthven 1965, 77–9). Following the granting of primary manors as fiefs to faithful vassals and relatives, the process of subinfeudation was repeated to create secondary manors (Otway-Ruthven 1965, 76). This system of landholding provided a military structure, as a tenant who held land by knight's service was obliged to serve in his lord's army for not more than forty days per fee in any year. The principal objective of granting land by military tenure was to facilitate a permanent garrison, a vital consideration in stabilising a durable colony in a frontier situation. The construction of castles, initially of earth and timber, was essential to this process.

These civil and ecclesiastical boundaries make it possible to establish the approximate extent of feudal land grants (for a full description of Strongbow's land grants, see Colfer 2002, 39–45). Security was a priority in the allocation of Strongbow's early grants. He gave the Duffry (from the Irish words *dubh* and *tír*: 'black country') to his son-in-law, Robert de Quency, by the service of five knights, also making him constable of Leinster (Davies 1990, 11). The Duffry, a heavily wooded district between the Slaney and the Blackstairs Mountains, was an obvious refuge for disaffected Irish and required effective military control. The Duffry had an added significance as it provided access to the Scullogue Gap, a strategic routeway through the Blackstairs Mountains (Orpen 1968, vol. i, 231).

The other routeways through the mountains were also controlled by early land grants. Sometime before 1176, William de Angulo received a large grant, by the service of eight knights, which included modern Moyacomb (*Magh dá Chonn*: 'the plain of the two sources'; a reference to the River Slaney and its tributary, the River Derry) and extended to the waters of Mescordin (?Enniscorthy, the Slaney) (Curtis 1932, vol. i, no. 2), which would have effectively guarded the Slaney Gap between the Blackstairs and the Wicklow Mountains, as well as the valley of the River Derry. It is also possible that this grant was never implemented (Flanagan 1981, 11; Orpen 1892, lines 3034–5, 3060–9).

When de Quency was killed by the Irish of Offaly in 1172, his successor as constable, Raymond le Gros, was given Forth and Idrone (in Carlow), as well as Glascarrig on the east coast of Uí Chennselaig (Orpen 1892, lines 3034–5, 3060–9). His motte-and-bailey castle at St Mullins controlled the Pollmounty Gap and the route along the Barrow Valley to Dublin. His motte-and-bailey also survive at Glascarrig, which was of significance as one of the few landing places on Wexford's east coast.

1.8 Having received a grant of Bargy and most of Shelburne from Diarmait Mac Murchada, later confirmed by Strongbow in 1172, Hervey de Montmorency granted a large estate to the abbey of Buildwas in Shropshire for the establishment of Dunbrody Abbey, the first Anglo-Norman Cistercian foundation in Ireland. Buildwas declined, offering it instead to St Mary's Abbey in Dublin. The offer was accepted in 1182 and eventually, in 1201, the new abbey was consecrated. The ruins, including a fifteenth-century crossing tower, form one of the most impressive Cistercian monuments in Ireland

The confirmation by Strongbow of Diarmait's grant to Hervey de Montmorency (Orpen 1892, lines 3070–1) had a strategic dimension. The two cantreds on the south coast commanded the land approaches to Bannow Bay and Waterford Harbour, initial Anglo-Norman landing places and vital routeways to England. The determination shown by de Montmorency to endow an ecclesiastical foundation on his fief illustrated the priority given within feudal society to the establishment of religious houses. It also represented a strong expression of ownership and a commitment to a permanent presence in Ireland. Having failed in his attempt to attract monks to Bannow (Ward 1981, 445), in 1172 he offered a large estate in the manor of the Island in Shelburne to the monastery of Buildwas in Shropshire, for the foundation of the first Anglo-Norman Cistercian house in Ireland (Gilbert 1884, 151–4; Hore 1900–11, vol. iii, 34–46). Following a harsh report on the location and the natives, Buildwas declined the grant, offering it instead to St Mary's Cistercian abbey in Dublin. The offer was accepted in 1182 and the new monastery, called the Port of St Mary of Dunbrody, was consecrated in 1201 by Herlewyn, bishop of Leighlin, a nephew of the founder. The monastic estate of thirteen thousand statute acres (40 carucates; 5,260 hectares) corresponded to the medieval parish of Dunbrody and part of Killesk. Combined with the Templar manor to the south, the Cistercian estate of Dunbrody protected the eastern shore of Waterford Harbour (for a fuller account, see Colfer 2002, 184–94) (Figure 1.8).

Strongbow ensured the security of Wexford Harbour by granting Fernegenel (the Irish *Ferann na gCenél*), on its northern shore, to Maurice de Prendergast by the service of ten knights (Orpen 1892, line 3072). Fernegenel was an extensive fee and included the district of Síl Mella to the north, as well as land in Kynelaon (identified as the Gaelic district of Cenél Flaitheamhain in the cantred/deanery of Oday in the north of the county) (Ó Dubhagáin and Ó hUidrín 1862, 91). The lands of Kynelaon can be identified from land grants that were made there. Sometime before 1229, Philip de Prendergast granted lands to Walter de Barry in Crosspatrick and Kynelaon by the service of one knight (Brooks 1936b, no. 24; Curtis 1932–43, vol. i, no. 111). Walter and Raymond Barry were lords of Ardamine in 1250, presumably in the Kynelaon of the earlier charter (Brooks 1936a, nos 360–1). The lands granted to Raymond le Gros by Strongbow passed to his nephews before the end of the twelfth century; the Carews held St Mullins by 1195 (Gilbert 1884, 112) and the Cauntetons succeeded to Glascarrig (Brooks 1950, 31). The large Prendergast fief was subdivided. The southern part, the district of Fernegenel, passed into the possession of Robert Fitz Godebert by the service of five knights (Brooks 1950, 146; Orpen 1892, line 3082). The Roche fee was subdivided in the early thirteenth century when Gerald de Rupe subinfeudated the south-eastern part of Fernegenel to his kinsmen the Synnotts (Tresham 1828, 327).

To the north of Fernegenel, Gilbert de Boisrohard, who witnessed several of Strongbow's charters, was granted 'Offelimy on the sea' (Orpen 1892, line 3114), corresponding to the Meic Murchada district of Uí Felmeda on the east coast, still known as the Murroes. At a later date, the coastal routeway to Dublin was protected by the granting (directly from the king) of a manor to Maurice FitzGerald (son of Maurice) by the service of five knights' fees in the district of Uí Enachglaiss south of Arklow. This manor is represented by the parishes of Inch and Kilgorman in the north of Co. Wexford but in the diocese of Dublin.

These grants were the only ones made by Strongbow for which there is documentary evidence. He presumably also made grants to knights who had been in Ireland in the early days of the conquest. In Shelmalier, the family of de Heddon acquired the fee of Magh Arnaidhe (later Adamstown) by the service of two knights (Brooks 1950, 96–9) while the de Londons were granted the manor of Roscarlon (Rosegarland) at the head of Bannow Bay by three knights' fees (Brooks 1950, 103). William de Denne received the substantial manor (or barony) of Kayer situated on the west bank of the Slaney below Enniscorthy by the service of three knights (Brooks 1950, 43–6). Other followers presumably received land grants from him also; from charter evidence, the Brownes, Codds and Russells came with Strongbow, but details of their fiefs emerge only at a later date.

The *Song of Dermot and the earl* records that, in an effort to appease the Irish, Strongbow granted the kingdom of Uí Chennselaig to Diarmait's nephew, Muirchertach Mac Murchada, and the 'pleas of Leinster' to his son Domhnall Caomhánach (Orpen 1892, lines 2185–90). The significance of these grants is not clear; the *Song* states that 'these two were kings of the Irish of the country' and that Strongbow's intention was to 'appease the Irish' (Orpen 1892, lines 2189–90, 2199–200). The grants must have been politically motivated, with the intention of keeping the Irish at peace. The strategy was successful as the colony in the liberty of Wexford was allowed to flourish without resistance for almost a century. The newcomers did not allow the rights of the Irish to interfere with the exploitation of their newly acquired fiefs. United by ties of race and kinship, they regarded themselves as frontier warriors and superior to those who came after them. In turn, these freebooters were regarded with ill-disguised suspicion by officialdom. This is illustrated by the words attributed to Maurice Fitz Gerald in the *Expugnatio*: 'Just as we are English to the Irish, so we are Irish to the English' (Scott and Martin 1978, 80).

MARSHAL'S LAND GRANTS

Before his death in 1176, Strongbow had allocated much of the land of Uí Chennselaig to his henchmen. William Marshal succeeded as lord of Leinster by his marriage to Strongbow's daughter Isabella. In danger of shipwreck on the occasion of his first crossing to Ireland in 1200 (Crouch 1990, 79), Marshal vowed to endow a religious foundation wherever his ship reached safe harbour. He evidently arrived at Bannow Bay as it was there that he gave land for the monastery at the head of a small inlet. It was colonised with Cistercian monks from Tintern Abbey in Marshal's manor of Chepstow and named Tintern Minor or *de Voto* ('of the vow'). Marshal's charter can be dated to 1207–13 from the names of the witnesses (Orpen 1968, vol. ii, 207). The land granted to the Cistercians was part of Hervey de Montmorency's fief, but it reverted to Marshal after de Montmorency's death in 1205. The monastic estate, equivalent to the civil parishes of Tintern and Owenduff, consisted of fifteen thousand statute acres (6,070 hectares; for a full account, see Colfer 2002, 185–94) (Figure 1.9).

To facilitate the organisation of his lordship, the liberty of Leinster was divided into the four shires or counties of Wexford, Kilkenny, Carlow and Kildare (Otway-Ruthven 1980, 186). The medieval county of Wexford included part of modern Co. Wicklow, being equivalent to the diocese of Ferns. The progress of settlement in medieval Wexford was influenced considerably by changes in ownership of several early grants. The town of Wexford with the cantred of Forth, initially given to Fitz Stephen and Fitz Gerald, reverted to Strongbow and it was subsequently subdivided, presumably by Marshal.

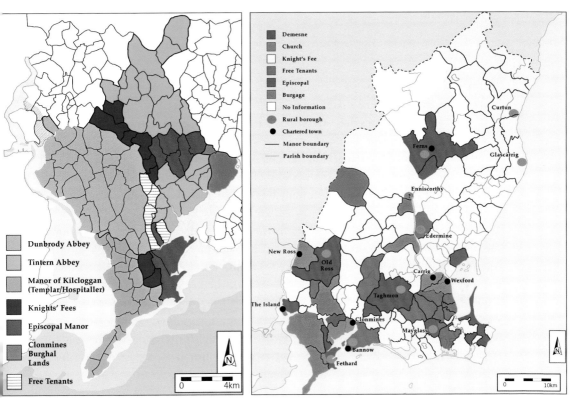

1.9 (*above left*) Cistercian abbeys at Dunbrody and Tintern, a Knights Templar preceptory at Kilcloggan and two episcopal manors at Fethard and Kinnagh ensured that the territory in south-west Wexford, bordering Waterford Harbour, remained mostly in the hands of the church
1.10 (*above right*) The early thirteenth-century Anglo-Norman settlement created contrasting landholding patterns that resonate in the landscape to the present. Apart from the demesne manor of Ferns, the north of the county was parcelled out in sprawling knights' fees, which ultimately proved to be untenable, while the south was divided into a complex of smallholdings of disparate types, which formed the template for a permanent colony

Densely colonised and divided into small holdings, some held by knight's service and others by socage tenure (land held by the payment of money rent or other non-military services), the settlement pattern in Forth was noticeably different to the rest of the county (Figure 1.10). The principal families holding by knight's fee were the Staffords of Ballymacane, the Synnotts of Ballybrenan, the Codds of Carne, the Lamports of Ballyhire and the Frenches of Ballytory (Brooks 1950, 119–27). Families holding as free tenants included the St Johns of Ballymore, the Butlers of Butlerstown, the Waddings of Ballycogley, the Rossiters of Rathmacknee and the Esmonds of Johnstown (Colfer 2002, 94–6). The parishes of Rosslare and Ballymore in the south of the barony were retained as demesne manors. The descendants of the Ostmen (Norse) of Wexford town continued to hold land around Rosslare and maintained their distinct identity for over a century (Hore 1925, 20).

Hervey de Montmorency's fief, represented by the modern baronies of Bargy and Shelburne, reverted to the lord of Leinster following Hervey's death in 1205. Much of

Shelburne had been alienated to the Cistercians at Dunbrody and Tintern and to the Knights Templar at Kilcloggan. De Montmorency established his headquarters on an island (no longer an island due to land reclamation) in the River Barrow now known as Greatisland. The island was subsequently known as Hervey's Island and the manor of the island was later administered with the demesne manor of Ross (Orpen 1968, vol. ii, 393; Sharp and Stamp 1913, 307). Several small sub-manors were held by knight's service: these included the Keating manor of Slievecoiltia, the de Tullos manor of Tullostown, the Russell (later Sutton) manor of Ballykeerogemore and the de Ponte Chardun manor of Killesk, which later became a well-known FitzGerald fee (Colfer 2002, 98–102).

A previously unnoticed charter of de Montmorency, dated to 1177, shows that he had failed to find a tenant for the cantred of Bargy before his retirement to Christ Church, Canterbury, *c*.1180. The charter details the grant of a large fief by de Montmorency to Osbert Fitz Robert, which must have extended over most of Bargy as it was valued at fifteen knights' fees. It was offered to Fitz Robert for the service of only three knights, however; obviously an indication of the difficulty experienced by de Montmorency, and presumably others, in persuading suitable personnel to occupy manors in Ireland. In this case, even the reduced offer failed, as there is no further mention of Fitz Robert as a landholder in Bargy (Flanagan 2006, 232–42).

Marshal also struggled in attracting tenants after the reversion of de Montmorency's manors to him *c*.1205. As well as installing some new tenants in the cantred of Bargy, Marshal granted much of the land to holders of existing fiefs and in so doing created 'split' manors (Colfer 2002, 96–7). The manor of Ballymagir was added to the de Heddon manor of Magh Arnaidhe (later Adamstown) (Brooks 1950, 96). The family of Devereux, Marshal's kinsmen from his manor of Strigoil (Crouch 1990, 80, 138), acquired these manors by marriage *c*.1250 (Brooks 1950, 96). The Keatings, witnesses to the charters of Dunbrody and Tintern, were granted the manor of Kilcowan in Bargy, establishing their headquarters in the townland of Hooks. Other branches of the family held the manors of Slievecoiltia and Kilcowanmore (Brooks 1950, 10, 37, 115).

The Boscher (Busher) manor of Ballyanne in Bantry was also increased by the addition of the detached manor of Ballyconnick. The de Londons of Rosegarland acquired the manor of Duncormick, where they built a motte castle beside a small estuary, the mound of which survives. A recent partial excavation beside the motte revealed the ditch of the bailey enclosure. Of particular interest is the discovery of a King John coin, indicating that the site was occupied in the first decade of the thirteenth century, coinciding with Marshal's allocation of the lands in Bargy (Dehaene 2009, 59–65).

The Ambrose manor of Ambrosetown, the FitzHenry manor of Kilcavan, the Brownes of Mulrankin, the Cheevers of Ballyhealy, the Hores of Tomhaggard and the Whittys of Ballyteige completed the manorial structure of Bargy, where most of the

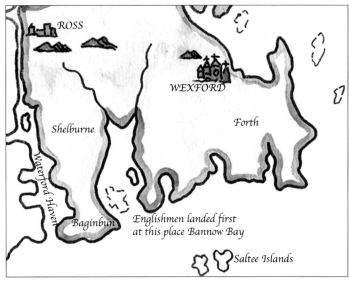

1.11 A note on Boazio's map of 1599 (re-drawn) records that the 'Englishmen landed first at this place Bannogh Baie', an indication of an enduring folk memory and the significance of the location among the descendants of the first arrivals, four centuries after the event. The inclusion of Baginbun indicates its importance as a landing place

land was held by knight's service (Brooks 1950, 81). The creation of so many small manors in the three southern baronies created the landscape matrix and the social milieu that facilitated the building of a remarkable number of tower houses in later centuries.

The achievements and reputation of their European Norman forebears gave the newcomers tremendous confidence in their own ability as warriors and as conquerors of new lands. The initial landing places were quickly absorbed into the mythology of the first colonists and their descendants. The status of the landing places and the 'first comers' resembled the significance attached to the Pilgrim Fathers' arrival in New England in the early seventeenth century. In an act of commemoration, Bannow, although far from being ideally located, became the site of one of the first Anglo-Norman chartered boroughs and ports, established by Hervey de Montmorency, a member of the first group. The memory of the first landing emerges on Baptista Boazio's map of 1599, which refers to Bannow as where 'Englishmen first landed' (Andrews 1997, 60; see Figures 1.1, 1.2, 1.11).

The landing at Baginbun, and the defeat of the army from Waterford, was also regarded as significant. Four centuries after the event, the rhyme 'at the creek of Bagganbun, Ireland was lost and won' was recorded by an English historian (Hanmer 1571, 272). This connection with their ancestors demonstrates the colonists' memory of their origins and the value that they placed on attributes inherited from their European forebears, renowned for their military prowess (Davis 1997, 31). These qualities underpinned a distinctive colony in the southern baronies of Forth and Bargy, symbolised by the building of numerous small castles, known as tower houses, during the endemic civil strife of the fifteenth and sixteenth centuries.

BIBLIOGRAPHY

Andrews, J. 1997. *Shapes of Ireland: maps and their makers, 1564–1839*. Dublin.

Anon. 1891. *Calendar of ancient deeds and muniments preserved in the Pembroke Estate Office*. Dublin.

Bennett, I. 1985. 'Preliminary archaeological excavations at Ferrycarrig ringwork, Newtown td, Co. Wexford'. *Journal of the Wexford Historical Society*, 10, 25–43.

Brooks, E. (ed.). 1936a. *Register of the hospital of St John the Baptist Dublin*. Dublin.

Brooks, E. (ed.). 1936b. 'Unpublished charters relating to Ireland, 1177–82, from the archives of the city of Exeter'. *Proceedings of the Royal Irish Academy*, 43C11, 313–66.

Brooks, E. 1950. *Knights' fees in counties Wexford, Carlow and Kilkenny*. Dublin.

Colfer, B. 2002. *Arrogant trespass: Anglo-Norman Wexford, 1169–1400*. Wexford.

Colfer, B. 2004. *The Hook Peninsula, County Wexford*. Cork.

Colfer, B. 2008. *Wexford: a town and its landscape*. Cork.

Colfer, B. 2013. *Wexford castles: landscape, context and settlement*. Cork.

Crouch, D. 1990. *William Marshal: court, career and chivalry in the Angevin Empire, 1147–1219*. London.

Curtis, E. (ed.). 1932–43. *The calendar of Ormond deeds, 1172–1350*. 6 vols. Dublin.

Davies, R. 1990. *Domination and conquest: the experience of Ireland, Scotland and Wales, 1100–1300*. Cambridge.

Davis, R. 1997. *The Normans and their myth*. London.

Dehaene, G. 2009. 'Medieval rural settlement beside Duncormick motte, Co. Wexford'. In Corlett, C. and Potterton, M. (eds), *Rural settlement in medieval Ireland in the light of recent archaeological excavations*, 59–65. Dublin.

Empey, C. 1985. 'The Norman period: 1185–1500'. In Nolan, W. (ed.), *Tipperary, history and society: interdisciplinary essays on the history of an Irish county*, 71–91. Dublin.

Flanagan, M. 1981. 'Mac Dalbaig, a Leinster chieftain'. *Journal of the Royal Society of Antiquaries of Ireland*, 111, 5–13.

Flanagan, M. 2006. 'An early Anglo-Norman charter of Hervey de Montmorency'. In Meek, M. (ed.), *The modern traveller to our past: Festschrift in honour of Ann Hamlin*, 232–42. Dublin.

Gardiner, M. and Ryan, P. 1964. *Soils of County Wexford*. Dublin.

Gilbert, J. (ed.). 1884. *Chartularies of St Mary's Abbey, Dublin*. 2 vols. London.

Gillingham, J. 1992. 'The beginnings of English imperialism'. *Journal of Historical Sociology*, 392–409.

Gillingham, J. 1993. 'Conquering the barbarians: war and chivalry in twelfth-century Britain'. *Haskins Society Journal*, 4, 67–84.

Hanmer, M. 1571. *The chronicle of Ireland*. Dublin.

Hore, P. 1900–11. *History of the town and county of Wexford*. 6 vols. London.

Hore, P. 1925. 'The barony of Forth'. *The Past*, 3, 9–40.

McNeill, C. (ed.). 1932. *Register of Kilmainham*. Dublin.

Moore, M. 1996. *Archaeological inventory of County Wexford*. Dublin.

Murphy, C. 2016. 'Dr Billy Colfer: a bibliography'. In Doyle, I. and Browne, B. (eds), *Medieval Wexford: essays in memory of Billy Colfer*, 32–4. Dublin.

Nicholls, K. 1984. 'Land of the Leinsterman'. *Peritia*, 3, 535–58.

Ó Dubhagáin, S. and Ó hUidrín, G. 1862. *Topographical poems*, ed. J. O'Donovan. Dublin.

O'Donovan, J. (ed.). 1848–51. *Annals of the kingdom of Ireland by the Four Masters*. Dublin.

Orpen, G. (ed.). 1892. *The song of Dermot and the earl*. Oxford.

Orpen, G. (ed.). 1934. 'Charters of Earl Richard Marshal of the forests of Ross and Taghmon'. *Journal of the Royal Society of Antiquaries of Ireland*, 64, 54–63.

Orpen, G. 1968. *Ireland under the Normans*. 4 vols. Reprint. Oxford.

Otway-Ruthven, J. 1964. 'Parochial development in the rural deanery of Skreen'. *Journal of the Royal Society of Antiquaries of Ireland*, 94, 111–22.

Otway-Ruthven, J. 1965. 'The character of Norman settlement in Ireland'. In McCracken, J. (ed.), *Historical Studies*, 5, 75–84.

Otway-Ruthven, J. 1980. *A history of medieval Ireland*. Reprint. London.

Scott, A. and Martin, F.X. (eds). 1978. *Expugnatio Hibernica by Giraldus Cambrensis*. Dublin.

Sharp, J. and Stamp, A. 1913. 'Inquisitions post mortem, Edward I'. *Calendar of Inquisitions post mortem, vol. 4: Edward I* (London). *Online*: www.british-history.ac.uk/inquis-post-mortem/vol4 (accessed 17 March 2019).

Sweetman, H. (ed.). 1875–86. *Calendar of documents relating to Ireland, 1171–1307*. 5 vols. London.

Tresham, E. 1828. *Rotulorum patentium et clausorum cancellariae Hiberniae calendarium, vol. i, pars i: Hen. II–Hen VII*. Dublin.

Ward, J. 1981. 'Fashions in monastic endowment: the foundations of the Clare family'. *Journal of Ecclesiastical History*, 32, 427–51.

CHAPTER TWO

A second Pale? The growth and decline of Anglo-Norman Wexford, c.1200–1400

MICHAEL POTTERTON

INTRODUCTION

It is clear that the half-century or so after the arrival of the Anglo-Normans in Ireland was a period of intensive settlement, expansion and consolidation (Orpen 1968, vol. iii, 291; Lydon 1987b; Cunningham 1987; Hartland 2018; ch. 1). Strongbow's authority and diplomatic skills followed by William Marshal's experience and tactical astuteness contributed to this period of relative calm and stability in Leinster especially. Marshal was an effective administrator who oversaw the comprehensive subinfeudation of the south of the county (ch. 1), building castles and driving urban growth. The status quo continued under Marshal's eldest son, William II (1219–31). There can be little surprise then, that Co. Wexford has a greater concentration of Anglo-Norman settlement features than almost every other county in the country. A large percentage of these churches, castles, boroughs and manor centres were established on sites known to have existed as settlements before 1169. The repurposing of Gaelic sites certainly had its advantages, but in due course it would also contribute to the decline of the Anglo-Norman colony; it was only a matter of time before the native Irish would rise again to reclaim their homelands.

GROWTH

The manor

As elsewhere, the bedrock of Anglo-Norman settlement in Ireland was the manor (Bailey 2002; Murphy 2015; Graham 1985). At the core of the average manor was a defended residence with associated buildings, gardens, orchards, a chapel and a bake-house or bread oven; the farm buildings would have included a granary, a dove-cot, a haggard, a cattle shed, a stable and a dairy. There would have been a mill, a market place, a fishery and/or a fishpond and a rabbit warren. Many of these nucleated settlements developed as manorial villages, and those that were granted a charter of incorporation became boroughs (Murphy and Potterton 2010, 169–92). Some evolved into fully fledged towns, but the majority were rural boroughs; that is to say, they were 'incorporated' but their primary functions remained agrarian. Agricultural regimes balanced livestock-rearing and the primary land-uses of arable, meadow, pasture and woodland. The settlers introduced the three-field rotation system to Ireland, leaving a third of the manor fallow at any given time.

The seignorial lord held lands directly from the king and essentially sub-let manors to his principal tenants, retaining certain *demesne* ('belonging to a lord') lands for his own use. These tenants, in turn, granted secondary manors to their own tenants, effectively creating a feudal pyramid scheme in which each layer was bound to those above and below it by ties of loyalty and responsibility. One of the most remarkable features of the manorial system is the quantity of documentary material that it generated. Unfortunately, the majority of the rentals, inventories, valuations and financial accounts for medieval Ireland were lost in the Public Records Office fire of June 1922, but because so many of the Wexford tenants-in-chief also held lands in England, copies of some Wexford-related documents survive in London. And so, records exist for ten manors and boroughs in the county (Murphy 2009, 3–4, fig. 2). Documentary evidence for manorial buildings survives for five places in the south of Wexford, but nowhere else in the county (Murphy 2015, 74, fig. 4.1; 2009).

By the mid-thirteenth century much of Wexford had been settled and manorialised, the south of the county particularly. While many of the people living on the manors were settlers from Wales, England, Flanders, Normandy and elsewhere, it is clear that Irish tenants formed an important component of the manorial population (Colfer 2002a, 122–5; 2002b). This is inferred by place-name evidence as well as the names of tenants listed at the Dissolution (for example, 50 per cent of the names on the Tintern estates were Irish; 16 per cent at Dunbrody; 12 per cent at Kilcloggan; Colfer 2004, 55, 60, 61).

Some fifty manorial villages developed in Wexford, mostly in the south of the county (Colfer 1987, 81–3; 2002a, 131–5, 243, 267–8; 2004, 35; 2013, 34; Roche 1987). Most were deserted by the end of the Middle Ages, although a dozen or so survive as small nucleated settlements to the present day, mostly along the south coast (for example, Ballyhack, Churchtown, Ramsgrange and Slade on the Hook Peninsula: see Colfer 2004, 42). Other former manorial villages can be identified across the county at locations where a castle – often in the form of a motte and/or a later tower house – sits next to an ecclesiastical site (frequently a parish church) near a river or a stream (sometimes with evidence for milling activity in the Middle Ages) or fishing port.

The documentary evidence for Old Ross is among the most comprehensive of any manor in Ireland (Mills 1892; Lyons 1981; 1982; Colfer 2002a, 75; Murphy 2007). To get a snapshot of activity on a Wexford manor in the late thirteenth century, one can peruse the accounts for Old Ross in the 1280s. At that time there were almost 2,500 sheep on the manor and, while oats dominated the arable landscape, wheat, rye and barley were also grown. Several cattle and sheep had died of murrain (but the hides, fleeces and meat were sold), sheep were washed and sheared, horses were shod, cheese and butter were made (from ewes' milk, probably: see Murphy 2009, 6; 2015, 98), leeks and apples were sold, dung was removed from the new hall, houses and doors were repaired, the sheepfold was thatched, sand was carted from the seaside to improve the land, wheat, rye and oats were threshed and aired, horses were delivered to Dublin by a boy, fields were weeded, grain was reaped, bound, gathered and stacked in the grange, thatch was mowed, ploughs were repaired and land was burned off in preparation for sowing. Among the occupations mentioned are carpenter, cowherd, clerk, dairymaid, doorkeeper, harrower, mason, ploughman, reeve, shepherd, smith and watchman. Sundry purchases included boards, chalk, cord, fodder, iron, linen cloths, locks, nails and soap.

The reference to 'le Conegar' at Old Ross in March 1307 is clear evidence of the presence there of a special area for breeding and keeping rabbits (Sharp and Stamp 1913; P. Murphy 2016, 304). Rabbits were introduced to Ireland by the Anglo-Normans and new evidence is coming to light for their presence in Wexford. Paul Murphy has recently made a very convincing case for the practice of rabbit farming on Bannow Island during the time it formed part of the lands of Tintern (P. Murphy 2016). Nearby, at Tintern Abbey itself, rabbit bones were discovered during archaeological excavations by Ann Lynch (McCormick 2010), suggesting that rabbit farming was practised there too. A rabbit warren at Wexford is referred to in 1355, while another near Rosbercon is mentioned in 1418 (Hore 1900–11, vol. v, 113; Shine 2018, 157–8).

New settlers continued to arrive in Wexford from overseas throughout the thirteenth and into the fourteenth century. Billy Colfer's analysis of the probable origins of the surnames of Wexford's colonists suggests that those who arrived before *c.*1250 were mostly from Wales and western England, whereas those who arrived in the subsequent three-quarters of a century or so were more likely to be from other parts of England (Colfer 2002a, 125–30, esp. fig. 48). Some of the later arrivals settled in the boroughs, while others – especially those who were attracted by the opportunities of a 'new frontier' and not put off by the challenges of living in a hostile environment – chose to live on the periphery of existing manors, often on marginal land that had not been snatched up in the late twelfth century. The partition of Leinster in 1247 probably provided incentives for newcomers to arrive and perhaps acted as a stimulus to the construction of some of the moated sites across the region. Moated sites were the typical defended farmstead of the second wave of settlers and they emerge in Ireland in the second half of the thirteenth century (Glasscock 1970, 162–77; Barry 1977a; 1987, 84–93; 1988; 2003; Aberg 1978; O'Conor 1998, 58–69; O'Keeffe 2000, 73–80; Murphy and Potterton 2010, 202–7; Gardiner and O'Conor 2017, 136–41; Ó Súilleabháin et al. 2017, 156–61; ch. 3). There is some evidence that the second wave of settlers were looked down upon by the initial colonists (ch. 1, p. 12).

2.1 This reconstruction drawing by Simon Dick of the moated site at Coolamurry is based on the results of excavations directed by Grace Fegan for Valerie J. Keeley. It demonstrates the scale of the water-filled moat and the entranceway (image courtesy of V.J. Keeley. Reproduced courtesy of Transport Infrastructure Ireland (formerly the National Roads Authority))

Wexford has the densest concentration of moated sites of anywhere in Ireland; for comparison, see the Dublin region, which was also densely settled by the Anglo-Normans (Murphy and Potterton 2010, 201, fig. 6.15). Some 135 definite examples and forty-eight possible sites are known from Co. Wexford (Barry 1977a; 1977b; 2016; Colfer 1987, 78–81; 2013, 59; Culleton et al. 1994, 58–67; Moore 1996, 95–109; Mullins 2003; Eogan and Kelly 2016, 214–18; FitzPatrick and Ó Drisceoil 2016, 400–3). Quite remarkably, according to some counts, there are almost as many identifiable moated sites in Wexford as there are recorded ringforts (Moore 1996, passim). The scarcity of moated sites in the south of the county is a reflection of the density of the initial settlement there and the absence of opportunities for settlers of the second wave.

Archaeological excavation at Coolamurry (Figure 2.1) revealed a previously unrecorded moated site of thirteenth-/fourteenth-century date (Fegan 2009; Gardiner and O'Conor 2017, passim). There was locally made pottery including Leinster Cooking Ware and Wexford-type ware, as well as a copper-alloy dividers that may have been from the toolkit of a stone-mason or stone-cutter – perhaps a 'dual-income farmer' (Gardiner and O'Conor 2017, 139). The complex entranceway at Coolamurry hints at some affluence and a need to defend it – things appear to have been going well in the mid-thirteenth century. Excavations at the Camaross moated site revealed evidence for intensive agriculture in the form of two or three cereal-drying kilns (Tierney 2009, 189; Gardiner and O'Conor 2017, 137–9, 152; Eogan and Kelly 2016, 214). The occupants appear to have been producing surplus grain, perhaps to sell at a nearby market. There were also gaming pieces, a spindle whorl, a possible aquamanile and an iron blade. The only rural pottery kiln known from medieval Wexford was found at Camaross, and the pottery assemblage there included Leinster Cooking Ware, Wexford-type ware and local copies of Ham Green and Redcliffe wares (Tierney 2009, 194–5; see below).

The borough

The thirteenth century was generally a boom-period for urban foundation and expansion in Ireland, and this seems to have been the experience in Wexford too (Bradley and King 1990; Colfer 1987, 82–6; 2002a, 135–67, 269–72; ch. 3). The new arrivals expanded the existing urban centres at Ferns and Wexford, and established new towns at Enniscorthy and New Ross. They founded boroughs at Bannow, Carrick, Clonmines (Figure 2.2), Courtown, Edermine, Fethard-on-Sea, Gorey, Greatisland, Mayglass, Old Ross and Taghmon. All told, there were about fifteen urban settlements in medieval Wexford, more than two thirds of which were in the south of the county (Bradley and King 1990, fig. 1; Colfer 2002a, 135–68; Murphy 2009, 2, fig. 1). More than half of medieval Wexford's urban centres continue to function today – four as towns and four as villages – almost every one of them on the site of a pre-1169 church or settlement (Colfer 2002a, 150–1; Culleton 1999, 203–15). Being situated at a tried-and-tested location was an advantage for any new settlement; being defended by a circuit of walls and gates was another. New Ross (Figure 2.3) and Wexford town were certainly walled (ch. 3), and there are some indicators that Clonmines and Fethard were too (Thomas 1992, vol. ii, 55; Moore 1996, no. 1447).

Ferns is one of the oldest urban settlements in Wexford. According to tradition, it was home to a church founded in the early 600s by St Maedhog/Mogue and in 1111 it was selected as one of the five cathedral sees of Leinster (Hore 1910, Gwynn and Hadcock 1970, 78–9; Doyle 2016, 51–5; Moore 1996, no. 1440). It was also the ancient capital of the Uí Chennselaig and in the twelfth century, before the coming of the Anglo-Normans, it possessed a strongly fortified castle and a royal residence (O'Donovan 1848–51, *s.a.* 1166; Colfer 2013, 60–9; see also O'Keeffe 2015, 196, fig. 89). There was an Augustinian priory (Moore 1996, no. 1444) established by Diarmait Mac Murchada. After 1170, it became a principal seignorial manor of the Marshals, and this clearly caused disputes with the bishop (Orpen 1968, vol. iii, 29–31), who was granted the right to hold a weekly market and an annual fair there in

2.2 Situated on the bank of the River Spur, some of the stone buildings that once formed part of the medieval borough of Clonmines stand now in splendid isolation. Traces of streets, defences and other features can also be seen, depending on light and vegetation (© National Monuments Service Photographic Unit)

2.3 Maiden Gate at New Ross incorporates some fifteenth-century features as well as part of the wall built *c.*1300. The gateway facilitated the screening of people coming and going to and from the town as well as the collection of taxes

2.4 The first cathedral at Ferns was built soon after the elevation of Ferns to the status of episcopal see in the early twelfth century. It was largely rebuilt during the episcopacy of John St John in the thirteenth century

1226 (Sweetman 1875–86, vol. i, no. 1429). Ferns appears to have been made up of two distinct manors, the bishop's part and that belonging to the Marshals (the latter was granted by Richard Marshal to his sister-in-law Eleanor, countess of Pembroke, as part of her dower in 1232 (Sweetman 1875–86, vol. i, p. 289, no. 1950)). Ferns Cathedral (Figure 2.4) appears to have been rebuilt under the episcopacy of John St John (1223–53) (O'Keeffe and Carey Bates 2016, 84–92; Gwynn and Hadcock 1970, 78–80; Hore 1900–11, vol. vi, 185; Moore 1996, no. 1445). The success of Ferns is indicated by the fact that by about 1280 the population had reached some two hundred burgesses (Hore 1900–11, vol. vi, 190–1; Bradley and King 1990, 49).

One of Ireland's five Viking towns, Wexford is situated where the River Slaney flows into the Irish Sea (Hadden 1969; Colfer 1991; 2002a, 158–67; 2008; Thomas 1992, vol. ii, 210–14; Moore 1996, no. 1471; McLoughlin forthcoming; ch. 3). Its location – opposite Pembroke across the Irish Sea (Wexford is about equidistant from Dublin and Pembroke) – suited the new settlers and they expanded it as an administrative and trading hub. Ownership of the town descended from Strongbow to the Marshals to the de Munchensys to the de Valences. When Joanna de Valence died in 1307 an inquisition found that there were 365½ burgages in the town (Hore 1900–11, vol. v,

2.5 The town of New Ross was established on the banks of the River Barrow by William Marshal in the early thirteenth century. The river and the rich agricultural hinterland were key assets as the town grew rapidly in size and wealth (image courtesy of Cóilín Ó Drisceoil (Kilkenny Archaeology))

102). A Franciscan friary was founded there in 1230 (Moore 1996, no. 1493), or possibly a bit later by the Bigods (Colfer 2002a, 210), while evidence for daily life has been revealed by the excavation of a number of thirteenth-century houses (Bourke 1995; Moore 1996, no. 1473; McLoughlin and Stafford 2016). The town's walled circuit was completed (by Stephen Devereux) by about 1300 (Moore 1996, no. 1471; Colfer 2008, 66). Income was derived from mills and the ferry (Hore 1900–11, vol. v, 102), and a guild merchant was established in 1317 (Hore 1900–11, vol. v, 103).

Enniscorthy on the Slaney was the principal manor of the Duffry (Bradley and King 1990, 34; Colfer 2010b; Moore 1996, no. 1436), which passed through marriage from the de Quencys to the Prendergasts, who evidently preferred it to their caput centred on the motte at Motabeg (Colfer 2013, 42, 46). In 1226 Bishop St John was granted the right to hold a market at Enniscorthy once a week and a fair once a year (Sweetman 1875–86, vol. i, no. 1429). The following year the bishop swapped his holdings at Enniscorthy with the Prendergasts in return for lands elsewhere in the diocese (Gwynn and Hadcock 1970, 175; Hore 1900–11, vol. vi, 343; Moore 1996, no. 1436), thus merging the two manors at Enniscorthy into a single entity, spanning the Slaney. Gerald de Prendergast founded a monastery of the order of St Victor, who followed the rule of St Augustine, c.1230 (Moore 1996, no. 1324; Colfer 2002a, 147).

When the port of Waterford was taken into the king's hand William Marshal established his own port at New Ross (Figure 2.5), which became the manorial caput

2.6 The grant of pontage to the citizens of New Ross and Rosbercon, 20 November 1313. Plans were drawn up for a new bridge between New Ross and Rosbercon and, to fund the project, taxes were to be levied on a wide range of goods traded locally (C66/140, m4: patent roll 7 Edward II, courtesy of the National Archives of the United Kingdom)

and a thriving urban centre (Thomas 1992, vol. ii, 175–9; Moore 1996, no. 1453; Colfer 2002a, 171–82; Doran 2012; Ó Drisceoil 2017; Stafford forthcoming; ch. 3). The town was surrounded by a rich agricultural hinterland and it attracted large numbers of settlers. The rents recorded for the town in the thirteenth century suggest a population of about five hundred burgesses (Bradley and King 1990, 101; Empey 2017, 64). Its location on the tidal estuary of the Barrow some 40km from the open sea enabled ships to gain access to the heart of the Marshal lordship without having to sail via Waterford, which was in royal hands. New Ross developed as part of an international trade network, exporting hides, boards, wool, wheat, oats, barley, beans, wine, meat and fish and importing wine, salt and iron among other things (Dryburgh and Smith 2005, 279–81, 283–4, 291, 294–5; Hore 1900–11, vol. i, 134, 162, 165). The port grew rapidly, outpacing Wexford and even crown-backed Waterford. In 1215, King John permitted ships to ply their trade directly with New Ross only if it did not compromise trade in Waterford (Hore 1900–11, vol. i, 133; Orpen 1968, vol. i, 9). This permission was revoked – probably as a reaction to the success of New Ross – then partly reinstated and became a hotly contested point for much of the thirteenth century (Hore 1900–11, vol. i, 66, 134, 137–40, 141, 205–11; Orpen 1968, vol. i, 10; McEneaney 1979).

An Augustinian priory was founded at New Ross in the late thirteenth/early fourteenth century (Moore 1996, no. 1460), while across the river at Rosbercon a

2.7 The large medieval parish church at Bannow, from the south-east. Inside the church is an effigial slab and several features carved from Dundry stone, including a fine baptismal font. The church was fortified in the fourteenth century (image courtesy of Christiaan Corlett)

Dominican friary was possibly founded in 1267 by the Graces or the Walshes (Moore 1996, no. 1463; Gwynn and Hadcock 1970, 229; Colfer 2002a, 210; Shine 2018). Taxes were levied in 1313 in aid of the construction of a new bridge joining New Ross (Figure 2.6) and Rosbercon (Dryburgh and Smith 2005, 49–51). This *pontage* – or 'bridge tax' – was payable on a remarkable array of goods, providing a fascinating insight into the weekly market at New Ross: wine, cheese, butter, salt, honey, corn, onions, garlic, livestock, fish, meat, wool, hides, skins, fells, fleeces, yarn, linen, canvas, cloth, hemp, boards, timber, brushwood, oil, stone, lead, tin, iron, steel, nails, horse-shoes, coal, potash and millstones. In due course New Ross overshadowed Rosbercon and, having previously been a borough in its own right, the latter became a suburb of the former.

Bannow (Figure 2.7) is one of the few Anglo-Norman church sites in Wexford for which there is no evidence for a pre-twelfth-century church (Bradley and King 1990, 1–12; Colfer 2010a). It is also the place at which the first Anglo-Normans arrived in Ireland in 1169 and so perhaps the immediate need to establish an encampment (that later became a borough) superseded the desire to build upon an existing settlement. The borough was initially held by Hervey de Montmorency who granted it to the prior and chapter of Christ Church, Canterbury, who, in turn, granted it to Tintern

2.8 The medieval seal of
Clonmines incorporated a
towered stone fortification with
battlements. The timber panels
in the foreground may represent
quay walls or riverside
revetments (drawing by Billy
Colfer after seal impression in
the British Library)

Abbey (Hore 1900–11, vol. ii, p. 27; Moore 1996, no. 1423; Magahy 2016). It had a
shallow harbour as well as a hall and a thatched grange (Sharp and Stamp 1910).
Thirteenth-century pottery has been found in the fields around Bannow (Colfer 1988,
11), which was worth £31 in 1247 (Orpen 1968, vol. iii, 86). John Bradley and
Heather King calculated that the early fourteenth-century population of Bannow was
almost 160 burgesses (Bradley and King 1990, 2).

   Situated on the River Scar at the head of Bannow Bay, Clonmines (Figure 2.8) was
also held initially by Hervey de Montmorency but it came into the hands of the
Marshals in the early thirteenth century (Furlong 1968; Bradley and King 1990, 13;
Thomas 1992, vol. ii, 54–5; Byrne 1995; Moore 1996, no. 1428; Colfer 2002a, 142–
5, 155–7; 2010a). Roughly midway between Wexford (20km) and Waterford (25km),
the borough of Clonmines was probably established by William Marshal, possibly as
a back-up port for when New Ross was inaccessible due to bad weather in the winter
months (Colfer 2002a, 144–5; 2004, 36–7). It could also have been used as an
alternative when the port at New Ross was out of commission due to royal
prohibition. One of the attractions of the area was the presence of silver mines (hence
the name element 'mines') (Connolly 1998, 519–20). Some of the borough's stone
buildings survive, and its outline can be made out in field boundaries and low
earthworks. Among the ruins are the vestiges of an Augustinian priory, founded in the
early fourteenth century (possibly by the Meic Murchada/Kavanaghs: Eames and
Fanning 1988, 74; Colfer 2002a, 210) and enlarged in 1385 (Gwynn and Hadcock
1970, 233, 297; Moore 1996, no. 1432; Colfer 2004, 76). There is some evidence of
the medieval street pattern on the ground (Glasscock 1971, 293). The borough was

certainly enclosed, possibly by a walled circuit (Thomas 1992, vol. ii, 54–5). If so, then Clonmines is one of the very few examples of a failed walled town in medieval Ireland (Rindoon, Co. Roscommon, being the other: Thomas 1992, vol. ii, 185–6; Shanahan and O'Conor forthcoming).

Like most Wexford boroughs, Fethard-on-Sea was established on the site of a pre-Anglo-Norman church, in this case dedicated to St Aidan/Mogue (Bradley and King 1990, 73; Colfer 2002a, 211; 2004, 51; 2013, 46; Moore 1996, nos 1447, 1449). Fethard was an episcopal manor of the diocese of Ferns, and the borough may have been founded by Bishop St John (Hore 1900–11, vol. iv, 308–10), although the heirs of Strongbow also maintained an interest in Fethard (Bradley and King 1990, 73). Fethard functioned as a private port for the episcopal manors (Colfer 2004, 36) and it may have been the bishops' principal borough in Wexford, with a population of about 120 burgesses (Colfer 2004, 51). Some of the medieval burgage plots are still discernible in the modern streetscape.

Greatisland was part of Diarmait Mac Murchada's grant to Hervey de Montmorency in 1169 (chs 1, 3). When the childless de Montmorency became a monk at Canterbury, Greatisland reverted to Strongbow's heirs, the Bigod earls of Norfolk. The borough was strategically sited on what was then an island at the convergence of the Barrow and the Suir at the entrance to Waterford Harbour – an advantageous position for a trading centre. A ferry here facilitated travel between Wexford and Waterford and provided revenue for the Bigods, as did the local weirs and mills (Murphy 2007, 87). By the 1230s a masonry castle had been built on the island (Sweetman 1875–86, vol. i, pp 278–9, no. 1872) and there appear to have been about one hundred burgesses in the 1280s, a number of whom may have been involved in the manufacture of millstones because some were purchased there in 1285 (Hore 1900–11, vol. iii, 200, 201). Beer was brewed and there was a common oven (Hore 1900–11, vol. iii, 205). The exact location of the town is not known, but it may have been situated within the monastic enclosure still visible there (Flynn and Grennan 2016, 62–72; see also Ní Dhonnchadha 2002; Gwynn and Hadcock 1970, 386).

The medieval borough of Taghmon was established at the site of a pre-Anglo-Norman church founded in the early seventh century by St Fintan Munna (*Teach Munna*, Taghmon, the church of Munna) (Moore 1996, no. 1465). Situated at a strategic location in the foothills of Forth Mountain, Taghmon is one of the handful of Anglo-Norman urban settlements in Co. Wexford still occupied in the twenty-first century. It was the caput of a seignorial manor held by the de Valences and by 1324 it had forty-eight burgesses and the same number of burgages (Hore 1900–11, vol. v, 412; Moore 1996, no. 1465; Sharp and Stamp 1910).

The borough of Courtown, held by Christiania de Marisco from Aymer de Valence, was established on a pre-Anglo-Norman church site (*Killellin*) (Bradley and King 1990, 24), as was Old Ross (Culleton and Colfer 1975; Colfer 2002a, 140–2; 2013,

2.9 These two gargoyles from Co. Wexford are now among the collections of the Royal Society of Antiquaries of Ireland on Merrion Square in Dublin. They were found near the motte at Old Ross and must once have formed part of a stone building nearby (courtesy of the Royal Society of Antiquaries of Ireland)

48; Marshall and McMorran 2016). Old Ross passed to the crown in 1306, and in that year King Edward I granted it to Thomas de Brotherton along with the marshalship of England. At Old Ross (Figures 2.9, 2.32) there were two halls, a chapel, a sheepfold, a water-mill and an oak wood of twenty acres (Sharp and Stamp 1913). Edermine on the River Slaney was held by the Marshals and in 1232 Richard granted it to his sister-in-law Eleanor, countess of Pembroke and sister of the king, as part of her dower (Sweetman 1875–86, vol. i, no. 1950; Colfer 2002a, 147). Mayglass was an episcopal manor of the bishop of Ferns (Hore 1900–11, vol. vi, 190), and a borough was founded there on the site of a possible pre-Anglo-Norman church, perhaps by Bishop St John (Bradley and King 1990, 94). It appears to have been a very small settlement with only ten burgesses. Very little is known about the (probable) medieval borough at Gorey and, to date, not much more is known about Carrick. In the early fourteenth century the borough of Carrick had a population of more than 110 burgesses, as well as two mills, a court and a ferry (Hore 1900–11, vol. v, pp 33, 102; Sharp and Stamp 1908; 1910; ch. 4).

The church

The church played a very significant role in the settlement and security of Wexford – both rural and urban – throughout the Middle Ages. The Cistercians at Dunbrody and Tintern held almost thirty thousand acres (12,140 hectares) between them and, together with the military orders (who were well-experienced in frontier lordship), they were instrumental in the relative stability of south-west Wexford and the Waterford Harbour region generally (Colfer 2002a, 185, 216, fig. 91, 221–2; ch. 1). The Cistercian monks of Graiguenamanagh in Kilkenny also held large estates in

2.10 The late thirteenth-century crossing tower at Tintern Abbey is one of the finest in the country. It reaches 27m in height, including a crenellated parapet added in the fifteenth century (National Monuments Service Photographic Unit)

2.11 Rathumney was a grange of Tintern Abbey and the thirteenth-century hall-and-chamber there was surely part of a complex of buildings associated with this monastic out-farm. Such a structure is unusual in Ireland and is clearly influenced by English architecture (© National Monuments Service Photographic Unit)

Co. Wexford (White 1943, 195). Sheep-farming was an important part of the economy of the Cistercian estates, and this is reflected in local toponyms (for example, Rathnageeragh, Ramsgrange, Lambstown) as well as the documentary and archaeological records (Colfer 2004, 54–5; Murphy 2009; McCormick 2010).

When de Montmorency became a monk at Christ Church, Canterbury, he granted some of his lands in south Wexford to Christ Church, at least some of which they retained beyond *c.*1230 but rented back to the community at Tintern after 1245 (Hore 1900–11, vol. ii, 27; Colfer 2004, 47, 50)(Figure 2.37). Other sections of de Montmorency's lands came into the hands of the bishop of Ferns. The monastic estates of Dunbrody also grew in the thirteenth century (Colfer 2002a, 185–94; 2004, 42–4). The income generated by this expansion may have helped to fund the construction of the large but simple Gothic church built there in the 'Early English' style in the first half of the century (Stout 2016; Stalley 1987, 244, passim; Colfer 2007). It is the second longest Cistercian church in Ireland (after Graiguenamanagh) and sits among a rare array of surviving thirteenth-century buildings and features.

The results of her excavations at Tintern led Lynch to conclude that for the community there 'the thirteenth century seems to have been a period of relative stability and prosperity, with agriculture and trade well established' (2010, 195). This prosperity is reflected in the architecture, and it is clear that the original buildings were replaced at the end of the thirteenth century (Stalley 1987, 111–12; Lynch 1990; 2010; Colfer 2007; Moore 1996, no. 1325). The crossing tower (Figure 2.10) is particularly important as one of the earliest surviving examples of its kind in Ireland (Lynch 2010, 18–24, 48–9).

Tintern operated a number of granges or monastic out-farms, including one at Rathumney, which may have been the headquarters of this detached part of their estates (Colfer 2002a, 190; Lynch 2010, 191–2). The surviving thirteenth-century hall-and-chamber at Rathumney (Figure 2.11) is exceptionally rare in an Irish context (Colfer 2002a, 135, 186, 190; 2013, 53–7, 152–8; Moore 1996, no. 1495; Sweetman 1999, 96–9). This residential building has been dated (tentatively) by Tadhg O'Keeffe to *c.*1280–1300 (2015, 235, 237, fig. 111), who remarks that it is reminiscent of English manorial architecture and is 'a rare survival of a high-status freehold residence'.

The Knights Templar at Kilcloggan managed an efficient manor focused on agriculture, notably arable production and sheep-farming, but also dairying and pig-rearing (Hore 1900–11, vol. iv, 275–7; Colfer 2004, 56; M. Murphy 2016; Mac Niocaill 1961). After Clonoulty, Co. Tipperary, it was the second most valuable Templar property in the country (M. Murphy 2016, 171). They had poultry, more than ten beehives, a brewery, a windmill and several well-furnished churches. The field patterns (and possible house sites) visible on old aerial photographs, in addition to finds of thirteenth-century pottery sherds, indicate the presence of a busy farming community associated with Templetown Church at this time (Colfer 2002a, 200, fig. 86, 206; 2004, 59). In the years following the suppression of the Templar order in 1307, much of their property was transferred to the Hospitallers (Mac Niocaill 1961; Nicholson 2016, 9–11; Hore 1900–11, vol. v, 102). This was the case in south Wexford, where the Templars' estates at Kilcloggan eventually passed to the Hospitallers in 1326 (Colfer 2004, 50).

Apart from the Cistercians and the military orders, the only religious house in a rural setting in medieval Wexford was St Mary's Carmelite priory at Horetown, which was founded by the Furlong family in the fourteenth century (Gwynn and Hadcock 1970, 286, 289; Moore 1996, no. 1321).

In addition to the rural foundations, other orders established religious houses in or just outside urban centres. Franciscan friaries were founded at New Ross and Wexford in the mid-thirteenth century (Gwynn and Hadcock 1970, 241, 257, 261; Colfer 2002a, 210). The Augustinians were established in Clonmines, Ferns, Enniscorthy, New Ross and Wexford (Gwynn and Hadcock 1970, 154, 156, 175, 197–8, 295, 297, 301, 305; Colfer 2002a, 210; Moore 1996, no. 1481), while the only priory in Ireland of the Benedictine order of Tiron was at Glascarrig (Gwynn and Hadcock 1970, 112). At Taghmon, a convent of nuns of pre-Anglo-Norman origin appears to have been a cell of the Arrouaisian house at Hogges Green in Dublin (Gwynn and Hadcock 1970, 324). The Marshals founded a house of Fratres Cruciferi in New Ross in the thirteenth century (Gwynn and Hadcock 1970, 215; Ó Drisceoil 2017, 305–7; Colfer 2002a, 172, 209), while there was also a hospital in that town (Gwynn and Hadcock 1970, 355). A large hospice in Wexford town catered for knights travelling to and from England (Gwynn and Hadcock 1970, 339).

The bishop of Ferns, who owned about 12,500 statute acres, was one of the principal landholders in medieval Wexford (Colfer 2002a, 212–15). He held the most profitable demesne in the county in the thirteenth century (Colfer 2013, 60–1) and, with the exception of Dublin, Ferns was the wealthiest diocese in the whole of the country in 1303–6 (Whelan 2018, 28). Nonetheless, the fact that the manor of Ferns was coterminous with one large parish suggests that little development took place there or that it was abandoned at an early stage. Conversely, the patchwork of much smaller parishes and manors in the south of the county is reflective of intensive occupation, agriculture and development.

The castle

The majority of the early castles built by the settlers in Wexford were mottes or ringworks constructed of earth and timber (ch. 1; ch. 3). While the fortifications operated individually, defending a local area, they were also part of a wider security network functioning on several levels. The large Hospitaller manor of Ballyhoge, for instance, was defended by a series of thirteenth-century earthworks and stone castles (Colfer 2002a, 203). As with urban settlements, many early earth-and-timber

2.12 The Anglo-Normans under Raymond le Gros disembarked on the sheltered beach at Baginbun in the early summer of 1170 and quickly fortified the headland. It is likely that a promontory fort had existed there for many centuries before le Gros arrived (image courtesy of Michael Harpur and eOceanic)

2.13 Ferns Castle is one of a handful of 'towered keeps' in Ireland. The design appears to have originated in France and excavations at Ferns Castle revealed clear evidence for trade with southern France and south-west England

2.14 Nothing survives above ground of Wexford Castle, but its original form as a towered keep (like Ferns Castle) is indicated by this sketch – to the west of the walled town – on one of the Down Survey maps of 1665 (NLI MS 725; image courtesy of the National Library of Ireland)

fortifications were erected at or beside sites previously occupied by Gaelic communities – for example, Baginbun (Figure 2.12), Dunanore, Duncormick, Kilmokea, Loggan and Newcastle/Dungorey (Colfer 2013, 40–2, 47). Of the twenty-nine recorded defensive earthworks in Wexford, nineteen are adjacent to a church, a dozen of which were parish centres. Nine of these contain the place-name element *cill* ('church'), suggesting the former presence of a pre-Anglo-Norman church (Colfer 2013, 48; Breen 2007, 70, fig. 4).

Six stone castles are known to have been built in Co. Wexford in the early thirteenth century – Carrick, Enniscorthy, Ferns (Figure 2.13), Greatisland, Old Ross and Wexford (Colfer 2002a, 64–70; 2013, 51). Most of these appear to have superseded earlier earthwork castles, most were associated with boroughs, and most were on seignorial manors. O'Keeffe classifies the site at Carrick as a promontory fortification, like Baginbun and Glanworth (O'Keeffe 2015, 194n39). On the death of William Marshal II in April 1231 the castles of Wexford, Ross, Carrick and Greatisland were taken into the king's hand (Sweetman 1875–86, vol. i, pp 278–9, no. 1872). Wexford Castle (Figure 2.14), a 'stone castle with towers roofed with shingles (*cindulis*)' (Sharp and Stamp 1910), was the seat of government for the entire liberty and appears to have been one of a handful of 'towered keeps' (along with Ferns,

Carlow, Lea, Terryglass and perhaps Tullow: Toy 1939, 126; Leask 1951, 47–51; Moore 1996, nos 1442, 1472; Colfer 2008, 75–9; 2013, 62–4; O'Keeffe 1985; 2015, 232–4). Towered keeps appear to have originated in France and, as such, the Irish examples reflect William Marshal's French connections and his role in introducing such innovations to Ireland. Wexford Castle was built outside the town's defences, which, as the administrative hub of the entire liberty, made it less vulnerable to attack from the townspeople. The castle was mostly demolished in the 1720s and the stones were used to rebuild Killinick Church (Colfer 1988, 11; 2008, 75, 79). It is likely, though, that the footprint of the castle survives beneath the eighteenth-century barracks that took its place.

Commerce, overseas contacts and the generation of wealth

The towns and boroughs were a focal point for craft and commerce, and the documentary sources provide a useful overview of the occupations and activities one might encounter there. Among the members of the Dublin Guild Merchant in the thirteenth century were mercers, palmers, a chaplain and a cleric from Wexford (Connolly and Martin 1992, 20, 58, 60, 69, 70, 72, 94, 115). There was also a tanner from Ferns, a mercer from Enniscorthy and a sergeant (*serviens*) from Taghmon (Connolly and Martin 1992, 51, 62, 79). From New Ross there was a palmer, a cook, a forester, a merchant and several tailors (Connolly and Martin 1992, 68, 83, 90, 92, 96, 107). The inclusion in 1254–5 of Elyas de Ros *mercenarius* is intriguing, given the contention by Eljas Oksanen that 'the medieval Latin word *mercenarius* was certainly not a title to be bandied about in polite society, but a term of abuse, signifying an untrustworthy hireling' (Connolly and Martin 1998, 94; Oksanen 2012, 225). The mid-thirteenth-century poem on the walling of New Ross mentions blacksmiths, butchers, carpenters, cloth-workers, cordwainers, drapers, fishermen, fullers, hucksters, mariners, masons, mercers, saddlers, tailors, tanners, tent-makers and vintners (Seymour 1929, 23–8; Shields 1976; Busby 2017, 107–27), while elsewhere can be found references to more tailors as well as gaunters, goldsmiths, spicers, nappers and wimplers at New Ross (Hore 1900–11, vol. i, 143; vol. v, 94, 114–15; Mills 1892, 55) and a mercer in Wexford in 1324 (Hore 1900–11, vol. v, 105). Brewing was another important occupation. Indeed, according to an early thirteenth-century Franciscan *Liber exemplorum*, a Wexford man was miraculously saved from hell because his sister used to dedicate two gallons from each brewing to the Virgin Mary (Jones 2011, §46; Downham 2018, 303).

The concentration of urban centres along navigable river systems and the coast reflects the key role of commerce and trade for the settlers. Indeed, Wexford had as many as seven ports with international trading connections in the thirteenth and fourteenth centuries (Colfer 2002a, 234; 2013, 77). Wexford's overseas trade included wheat, wine and fish (especially herrings), linen and woollen cloth (Scott and Martin

2.15 Among the artefacts recovered during archaeological excavations at Tintern Abbey was this late thirteenth-century silver penny of Alexander III of Scotland. Its worn condition suggests that it had been in circulation for some time – perhaps fifty years (© National Monuments Service Photographic Unit)

1978, 35; Sweetman 1875–86, vol. i, p. 6, no. 34; Hore 1900–11, vol. v, 111). In 1293 there are records of hogsheads of wine arriving into Wexford from St Emilion on the Dordogne (Hore 1900–11, vol. v, 96). A French trading token (a jetton) of early fourteenth-century date was found at Tintern (Lynch 2010, 92), where a silver penny of Alexander III of Scotland (Figure 2.15), dating to *c.*1280, was also found on the floor of the collation bay, and thirteenth-/fourteenth-century grisaille window glass was brought in from either England or the Continent (Lynch 2010, 171–2, 144–6). Salmon was shipped from Wexford to England in 1388–9 (Hore 1900–11, vol. v, 123–4). Spanish sheep-leather (*bazanni de Ispannia*) was being sold at New Ross in 1313 (Dryburgh and Smith 2005, 49–51), while wine was exported from that town to England in the 1380s (Hore 1900–11, vol. v, 123–4). In April 1292, a ship called *Le Aliz* of Harwich, carrying wine and other merchandise, was seized by the authorities at New Ross for contravening a royal order that no ships should bypass the port of Waterford in favour of New Ross (Sweetman 1875–86, vol. iii, p. 481, no. 1087).

A number of Italian traders and financiers are known to have been at work in Wexford in the Middle Ages. Merchants of Lucca were appointed collectors in Wexford and New Ross in the thirteenth century (O'Sullivan 1962, 65, 71), and that is probably what brought Percival de Lucca there in 1277–8 (Hore 1900–11, vol. v, 91). New Ross attracted a range of Italian merchants, including several Florentine wool-traders and money-lenders in 1217 (O'Sullivan 1962, 102, 122). Lapis Tynache was a merchant of Florence based in New Ross (O'Sullivan 1962, 115, 118), Andrew Gerardi was a wine merchant in 1307 (O'Sullivan 1962, 120), while Cambinus Donati was there in *c.*1314–15 (O'Sullivan 1962, 121).

2.16 Situated at the highest point in the town, St Mary's Church in New Ross is likely to have been the largest parish church in medieval Ireland. The tall lancet windows (seen here) at the east end are typical of the early thirteenth century

There remains a good variety of tangible evidence for Wexford's international connections in the Middle Ages. Imported oolitic ('egg-stone') yellow limestone from the quarries at Dundry near Bristol has been found at a range of sites across Ireland (Waterman 1970; Knight 2007). There is a concentration of these sites in south Wexford – including Dunbrody, Ferns, New Ross and Tintern, all of which are associated with William Marshal (Waterman 1970, 64, 67; Stalley 1997, 390; Stout 2016, 101–3, 115). Dundry stone makes up *c.*60 per cent of the dressed stone at Tintern Abbey (Lynch 2010, 126–7, 172, 182–8). The collation bay has some fine cut-and-dressed Dundry stone on the corners, the abbots' seat and the lectern base, while it was also used in the abbey church, the cloister arcade and perhaps the domestic buildings and the chapter-house doorway (Lynch 2010, 66–71, 71–3, 76, 91, 126–31). One very fine thirteenth-/fourteenth-century stone with diaper ornament is 'unique in an Irish context and may represent an example of sculpture (or a sculptor) imported from England' (Moss 2010, 127–8). Features carved from Dundry stone have also been identified at Bannow Church (Corlett and Kirwan 2016, 271–2, 289), Churchtown (Waterman 1970, 64, 69), Clonmines (Waterman 1970, 64, 73), Ferns Church (Moore 1996, no. 1457), Fethard Castle (Waterman 1970, 64, 73), Hook Lighthouse (Murtagh 2016, 132, 157; Hayden 2000) and Selskar Abbey in Wexford town (Waterman 1970, 64, 70, 73; Moore 1996, no. 1481). The sill stones of the east

2.17–2.19 Just a handful of medieval fonts carved from Dundry stone are known from Ireland, and three of these are in south Co. Wexford, at Bannow (**2.17**), Fethard (**2.18**) and Rathaspick (**2.19**). The similarities between these three Wexford examples suggest that they were carved by the same stoneworker, probably someone familiar with the fossiliferous oolite from the Dundry quarries to the south-west of Bristol. The stone would have been shipped *c.*300km via the Bristol Channel and St George's Channel to Ireland's south-east coast. It is not possible to know if the fonts were carved before or after transport to Ireland, but either way they are a clear reminder of the close ties between Wexford and the Bristol region in the Middle Ages (images courtesy of Christiaan Corlett)

2.17

2.18

2.19

window of St Mary's Church in New Ross (Figure 2.16) can be added to this list (Waterman 1970, 64, 67, 68), while some of the monumental effigies in that church seem to be carved from Bath and Doulting (Somerset) stone (Waterman 1970, 73). Dundry stone fonts are exceptionally rare in an Irish context, and yet there are at least three in Wexford – at Bannow, Fethard (possibly originally from Dunbrody: Waterman 1970, 67) and Rathaspick (Waterman 1970, 64, 67; O'Keeffe 2015, 115; Corlett and Kirwan 2016, 288) (Figures 2.17–2.19). The Bannow example is probably the finest and most elaborate Romanesque font in the country, and all three were probably carved by a native of south-west Britain who had settled in south-east Ireland (Corlett 2012, 19; O'Brien 2015, 42).

Archaeological excavations across the county have yielded a large corpus of medieval pottery. The discovery at Carrick, Ferns Castle, Hook Lighthouse, Old Ross and Wexford town of Ham Green ware from the kilns outside Bristol ties in well with the use of Dundry stone as outlined above (Sweetman 1979, 226; Marshall and McMorran 2016, 256; McLoughlin and Stafford 2016, 354–5, 362; Hayden 2000; ch. 5). Bristol Redcliffe wares have been found at Camaross, Carrick, New Ross and Wexford town (Eogan and Kelly 2016, 218; Noonan 2007; Kiely and Lyttleton 2004; ch. 5).

The discovery of polychrome pottery at Ferns Castle indicates contact with southern France in the late thirteenth century (Sweetman 1979, 225, 240–1), but most of the pottery recovered was made locally and without influence from overseas (Sweetman 1979, 241). A similar pattern has been noted in the motte field at Old Ross, where fieldwalking in 2012 identified thirteenth- and fourteenth-century domestic pottery, mostly of local origin with a few sherds of imported wares (Marshall and McMorran 2016, 255–7). Nonetheless, Saintonge wares, from the wine-rich region of Bordeaux, have turned up at Carrick, Ferns Castle, Wexford town, MacMurrough Castle near New Ross and on several sites in New Ross itself (McLoughlin and Stafford 2016, 354, 361; Sweetman 1979, 225; Cotter 1987, 44; McCutcheon 1998; Moran 2007; Noonan 2007; ch. 5). Almost 2 per cent of the pottery found at Tintern Abbey was from Saintonge (McCutcheon with Papazian 2010).

Leinster Cooking Ware is almost ubiquitous on medieval sites in Wexford, and Wexford-type wares are also commonly found. The latter were probably produced in New Ross, Wexford and a handful of other sites (including Camaross; see below) and tend to be copies of imported wares such as Redcliffe and Saintonge (McCutcheon with Papazian 2010, 152, 155; McCutcheon in Fegan 2009, 106). A Normandy-type jar found at Tintern may also have been a local copy (McCutcheon with Papazian 2010, 156).

The international connections and the general wealth of thirteenth-century Wexford are further reflected by the presence of an assemblage of medieval floor tiles almost unrivalled in Ireland outside Dublin. There are fine examples (both line-impressed and two-colour) from Clonmines Priory, Dunbrody Abbey, Ferns

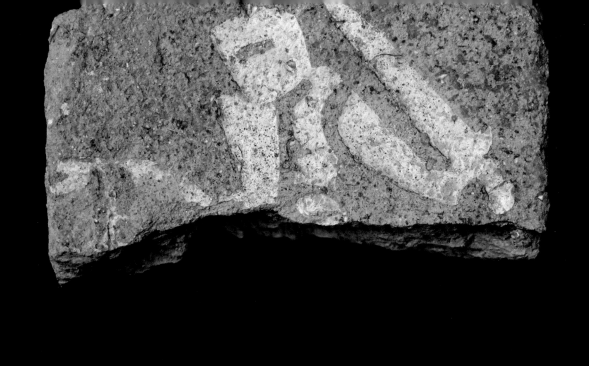

2.21 (*above*) This fragment of floor tile was unearthed during works close to the cathedral at Ferns in 2016. It depicts a sword-brandishing knight on horseback and probably dates to the thirteenth century. This could be a 'tournament' tile, a type previously unknown from Ireland (image courtesy of Christiaan Corlett)

2.20 (*right*) This very unusual design appears on a broken medieval floor tile from St Mary's Church in New Ross. It is likely to date to the fourteenth century and seems to depict a crowned person holding a long-handled stave (or fleur-de-lis?) in each hand (after Eames and Fanning 1988, 105 (T61))

Cathedral, St Mary's Church at New Ross and Tintern Abbey (Eames and Fanning 1988, passim, esp. 74–5; Lynch 2010, 133–4). Typically, the tiles depict lions, eagles, vine scrolls, fleur-de-lis and foliage. A unique example from New Ross is a 'very strange crowned man standing between two staves' (Eames and Fanning 1988, 24 (T61)) (Figure 2.20). Another unparalleled tile is one from Ferns depicting a bird or a stag with an arrow through its neck (Eames and Fanning 1988, 24 (T66)). Two-colour tiles are characteristically thirteenth century in origin and were probably imported from France (Eames and Fanning 1988, 29, 32). Tiles from Clonmines and Dunbrody bear a striking similarity to examples found in Chester, and may have been imported from there (Eames and Fanning 1988, 34–5). The early two-colour variety of tile found at New Ross, perhaps reflects 'contact with southern England in the thirteenth century' (Eames and Fanning 1988, 54). In this context, it is interesting that some of the thirteenth-century ridge tiles from Tintern have close parallels with Cornish examples (Wren 2010, 142). Roof tiles were also excavated at Ferns Castle in the 1970s (Sweetman 1979, 232–3). In 2016 part of an inlaid and glazed medieval floor tile was found by a grave-digger near Fethard Cathedral (Corlett 2018; Byrne 2018) (Figure 2.21). The tile displays the upper portion of a mounted knight and is of a type known from thirteenth-century contexts in southern Britain. Chris Corlett surmises that it is associated with the Marshal family and may have formed part of a tiled floor in a chapel near the cathedral (2018).

Line-impressed tiles are generally a little later than the two-colour varieties, with a floruit in the fourteenth century and a little later (Eames and Fanning 1988, 57). It is not surprising, therefore, in the light of the later local replicas of earlier imported ceramics mentioned above, that the 'interesting group' of sites in south Wexford from which line-impressed tiles are known – Clonmines, Dunbrody and Tintern (with some designs common to all three sites) – 'may reflect a local industry' (Eames and Fanning 1988, 57).

There is a significant corpus of figure sculpture from Co. Wexford, almost all of which dates to the thirteenth century. At Bannow there is a late thirteenth-century double head-slab (Hunt 1974, vol. i, cat. 260, pp 236–7; vol. ii, pl. 98), while the mid-thirteenth-century effigy of a bishop in Ferns Cathedral (Hunt 1974, vol. i, cat. 262, pp 237–8; vol. ii, pl. 65) is likely to commemorate John St John (d. 1243), the first Anglo-Norman bishop of Ferns (Figure 2.22), and the head-slab with ship carving in St Selskar's, Wexford town, probably dates to *c*.1300 (Hunt 1974, vol. i, cat. 275, p. 240; vol. ii, pl. 106)(Figure 3.9). The most remarkable collection, however, is at St Mary's Church in New Ross, which was probably the largest parish church in medieval Ireland, 'designed on a scale as grand as most Irish cathedrals', vigorous, striking and reflecting the town's 'mercantile splendour' (Stalley 1971, 81–3). One thirteenth-century head-slab fragment there recalls 'ISABEL LA FE' ('Isabel the wife of …') (Hunt 1974, vol. i, cat. 264, p. 238; vol. ii, pl. 95) and another bears the letters 'WIL … DOV:' (Hunt 1974, vol. i, cat. 265, p. 238; vol. ii, pl. 101), while the so-called

'Bambino' Stone is one of several others dating to the same century (Hunt 1974, vol. i, cat. 266, p. 238; vol. ii, pl. 39; vol. i, cat. 267, pp 238–9; vol. ii, pl. 40; vol. i, cat. 269, p. 239; vol. ii, pl. 97; vol. i, cat. 270, p. 239). The effigy of 'ROGE/RUS CLERICUS' probably commemorates Roger the Clerk who was provost of New Ross in the 1280s (Hunt 1974, vol. i, cat. 272, p. 239; vol. ii, pl. 44).

According to John Hunt, the head-slab of Alis La Kerdif (almost certainly related to Robert Le Kerdif, provost of New Ross in 1285, and Reginald Kerdif of Ross, 1288–9: Hore 1900–11, vol. v, 95) is 'a good example of this type of funerary memorial – a less expensive form than the whole figure, and which was within the reach of burgesses and citizens of middle-class standing' (Hunt 1974, vol. i, cat. 268, p. 239; vol. ii, pl. 96) (Figure 2.23), Hunt believed, produced by a competent mason of a Norman workshop – probably the same atelier that produced no. 265. Kerdif is depicted with a ring brooch at her neck (Deevy 1998, 139). The other remarkable mid-thirteenth-century female effigy at New Ross was 'originally a very beautiful and well-carved figure … one of the most important remaining in the south-east of Ireland' (Hunt 1974, vol. i, cat. 263, p. 238; vol. ii, pl. 19). It is carved from Dundry stone and was possibly imported already complete. Hunt states that this figure is likely to represent the cenotaph of Isabella of Leinster, daughter of Strongbow and wife of William Marshal. Another Dundry stone effigy (of a layman, c.1300) is 'an impressive sculpture by a competent artist conversant with the West-of-England style, if not himself a member of that school'

2.22 This effigial monument from Ferns Cathedral is likely to represent Bishop John St John, who died in 1243. The bearded man is wearing a chasuble, maniple and mitre and his head is resting on a cushion. Faint traces of polychrome can be seen in the floral design on the slab sides

(Hunt 1974, vol. i, cat. 273, p. 239; vol. ii, pl. 45), while one late thirteenth-/early fourteenth-century effigy fragment is made of stone from Doulting in Somerset (the same stone used for Wells Cathedral) (Hunt 1974, vol. i, cat. 271, p. 239). Significantly, there is almost no figure sculpture of note from the late fourteenth or fifteenth century.

Less impressive, perhaps, than the figure sculpture of Dundry, Bath and Doulting stone, a series of fine thirteenth- and early fourteenth-century grave-slabs from south Wexford is nonetheless a reminder of the wealth and diversity of the population at this time. A thirteenth-century slab at Templetown (Figure 2.24), rediscovered in 1991, depicts a floriated cross with a lamb at its foot (*Agnus Dei*) – part of the iconography of St John the Baptist (Cloney 1997; Caffrey 2016, 155–6, fig. 8.4). A grave cover in the chancel of St Catherine's parish church, Tacumshin, also has an incised floriated cross, with an inscription commemorating John Ingram, possibly a canon at Ferns in 1304 (Moore 1996, no. 1218). Two coffin-shaped grave-slabs at the site of the medieval parish church at Rosbercon are decorated with incised fleurs-de-lis and both were probably carved in the thirteenth or fourteenth century (Shine 2018, 149–50). A third similar one was found nearby (O'Doherty 1982, 380).

2.23 The Kerdiff (or Cardiff) family were prominent in New Ross in the late thirteenth century, and this coffin-shaped funerary slab in the chancel of St Mary's Church commemorates Alis La Kerdif (✠ ICI : GIT : ALIS : LA : KERDIF). Insert: (*left*) ring brooch depicted below her neck

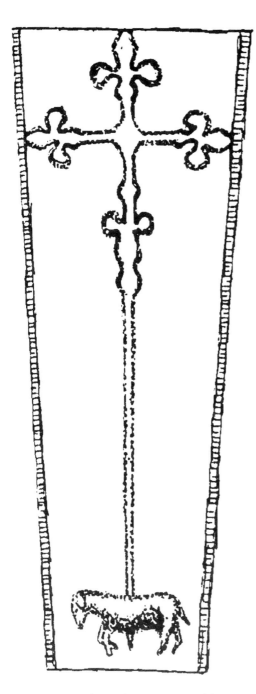

2.24 In 1991 a thirteenth-century grave-slab was rediscovered in the graveyard of the ruinous Templar church at Templetown on the Hook Peninsula. The floriated cross on the coffin-shaped slab appears above a lamb, perhaps the *Agnus Dei* as used on Templar seals (after Colfer 2002, fig. 87A)

2.25 Among the funerary memorials at Fethard Church are several that commemorate medieval bishops. The example pictured here is associated with Bishop Thomas Denne (or Dene), who lived in Fethard in the late fourteenth century and who died *c.*1400

2.26 The arched recesses (one with attached pilasters) in the chancel of the ruinous medieval parish church of Killag (also known as Ballymagir) are now empty, but they would once have accommodated the tombs of wealthy parishioners and clerics

The presence of episcopal funerary effigies at Fethard is a reminder of its significance in the thirteenth and fourteenth centuries (Colfer 2004, 51, 79; Cloney 1989, 92–7). One of the effigies is likely to commemorate Bishop Denne, and its Anglo-Norman French inscription is a reflection of the linguistic diversity of the area at that time (Cloney 1989, 95–6) (Figure 2.25). It is likely that these effigies are but a portion of what once existed in Wexford. The chancel of the parish church at Killag – for long associated with the Devereux family – is lined with now-empty tomb niches that hint at the wealth of the community there in the thirteenth and fourteenth centuries (O'Keeffe 2015, 116; Moore 1996, no. 1254; Corlett 2015) (Figure 2.26).

Anglo-Norman sarcophagi in Ireland are, according to John Bradley, a phenomenon primarily of the south-east (1988). This, he contends, is a reflection of the adoption of 'English fashions' in the thirteenth and fourteenth centuries. Indeed, many of these stone coffins are carved from oolite limestone imported from the

2.27 The distinctive tower at Hook Head – at the most southerly tip of Leinster – was probably
built in the mid-thirteenth century and is one of the oldest working lighthouses in the world.
Farming on the peninsula is dominated by arable and sheep-rearing, much as it was in the Middle
Ages (image courtesy of Michael Harpur and eOceanic)

2.28 Located on the first floor of the south-east tower, the rib-vaulted chapel in the castle at Ferns is the most accomplished of its type in Ireland. There is an aumbry, a piscina, a fine sedilia and a recess for the altar

2.29 This gold ring brooch was found in the Franciscan friary in Enniscorthy in the nineteenth century and is now in the British Museum in London. It is set with two rubies and four emeralds and is inscribed +AMES:AMIE:AVES M PAR CES PRESET (© The Trustees of the British Museum. All rights reserved)

south-west of England. They are the memorials of better-off members of society – abbots and local dignitaries. Six (20 per cent) of the thirty examples recorded by Bradley in Ireland are in south Wexford – two in New Ross and two in Wexford town, as well as one in Fethard and another in Bannow (1988, 79–80, fig. 2, 89–90, fig. 7).

While it is often assumed that Hook Tower (Figure 2.27) was built by William Marshal I, investigations carried out by Ben Murtagh since the 1990s suggest a date of construction in the mid-thirteenth century, perhaps at the instigation of Walter Marshal and probably replacing an earlier beacon (Murtagh 2016, passim; see also Moore 1996, no. 1494; Colfer 1985; 2004, 84–92). The building of such a remarkable lighthouse is indicative of the scale of infrastructural investment made by the Marshals and others in Wexford. High status and wealth are reflected in other architectural projects such as Ferns Castle, which houses the 'most remarkable Anglo-Norman castle chapel in Ireland' (O'Keeffe 2015, 178; O'Keeffe and Coughlan 2003, 138–42; see also Stalley 1971, 26–7) (Figure 2.28). The earliest recorded windmill in Ireland, first mentioned in 1281, was at Kilscanlan, to the south-east of New Ross (Aalen et al. 1997, 225). In the late thirteenth century, the justiciar removed some 'marble pillars' (aisle pillars of Purbeck, perhaps) from Dublin Castle for use in Dunbrody Abbey (Sweetman 1875–86, vol. iii, p. 13, no. 2; O'Keeffe 2015, 221n113). Dunbrody itself was one of the most attractive Cistercian churches in the country, displaying intricate detail and fine craftsmanship, reminders of its lavish endowment (Stalley 1971, 120–4).

The brooch on the head-slab of Alis La Kerdif at New Ross (see above) is a motif that could be used to symbolise the wealth of some of the church patrons in the thirteenth century. Mary Deevy recorded three ring brooches from Co. Wexford (1998, 30, 114, 121–2). Two belong to her Class 6, which are thirteenth or fourteenth century, while the third is Class 3, which was probably made in the twelfth or thirteenth century (Deevy 1998, 17, 22–3). Given that this latter example is from Tintern Abbey, it is more likely to date to the thirteenth century (Lynch 2010, 163–5, pl. 89, fig. 76). The gold ring brooch from the Franciscan friary at Enniscorthy (Figure 2.29) is particularly impressive (Deevy 1996, 10; 1998, 121–2, pl. 18). It is set with rubies and emeralds and has a Lombardic inscription that reads '+AMES:AMIE:AVES M PAR CES PRESET' (by this gift you have the friend you love). Similar wealth is evidenced by the discovery at Ferns Castle of several fragments of silk, 'probably imported from France or England' in the late thirteenth/early fourteenth century (Sweetman 1979, 239, 241).

DECLINE

The Anglo-Norman colonists in Ireland enjoyed rapid advances in the first half of the thirteenth century, peaking in about 1260. After that, a series of natural disasters, absenteeism, increasing demands on limited resources, land disputes, crime and war conspired to reverse the settlers' fortunes and allow the Gaelic Irish to regain lost land, wealth and authority (Lydon 1987a; 1987d; O'Byrne 2007, passim; Colfer 2008, 58–63). Events in England, including the Second Barons' War in the 1260s, had fallout in Ireland, adding considerably to the existing instability. Crown forces under Justiciar Geoffrey de Geneville were heavily defeated at Glenmalure in the 1270s (Gilbert 1884, vol. ii, 318). Infighting among the settlers, general lawlessness and opportunism combined to catalyse the Irish revival, especially when hunger, severe weather, oppression and legal apartheid forced their hand.

Perhaps the most remarkable and unexpected twist of the mid-thirteenth century was the death without male issue of all five of William Marshal II's sons by 1245. The subsequent partition of the lordship of Leinster in 1247 weakened the colonists and fractured landholding patterns, political authority and financial stability in many places, nowhere more so than Wexford (Sweetman 1875–86, vol. i, pp 439–40, no. 2949; vol. ii, pp 160–1, no. 933; Orpen 1968, vol. iii, 79–110; Colfer 2002a, 71–82; Empey 2017, 61–4). The legal redistribution of the Marshal purparty created a mosaic of disconnected liberties. The manors of Ross and the Island (also known as Hervey's Island and Greatisland) were granted to William Marshal's eldest daughter Maud, wife of Hugh Bigod, earl of Norfolk (Morris 2005; Sweetman 1875–86, vol. ii, pp 160–1, no. 933). As outlying manors of the lordship of Carlow, they were administered by officials and their security became more and more precarious in an increasingly volatile political landscape. Similarly, the de Mortimer manors of Clonmines and Taghmon were annexed to the liberty of Kildare and the de Bohun manor of Carnew became attached to Dunamase (Colfer 2002a, 72–4; 2004, 39; 2013, 72). The remainder of the liberty of Wexford was retained by the de Valences, but it too would be divided when Aymer de Valence died without an heir in 1324 (Phillips 1972, 240–4, 292–3, 337, map 2).

Meic Murchada power had been almost entirely extinguished by the Anglo-Normans by the end of the twelfth century, enabling the colonists to set about bedding in and expanding their control. This they did with great efficiency and success, but the defeated, disenfranchised and marginalised Irish had not gone away; they held out in the Blackstairs and Wicklow Mountains. Gradually they regrouped, accumulated an array of allies (including the O'Nolans, O'Tooles and O'Byrnes), constantly endeavouring to frustrate the settlers' efforts, and generally biding their time until the moment came for a full-scale recovery operation. Things were not black-and-white, however, and a series of complex relationships and partnerships served to muddy the waters. The Meic Murchada were, after all, related to the Marshals; indeed, in 1225 four Meic Murchada were killed in Connacht while on campaign with their cousin William Marshal II (O'Byrne 2007, 168). There was faction-fighting among the Meic Murchada too, and nor were they natural allies of the O'Tooles and O'Byrnes (Colfer 2002a, 229, 233). Some members of the family had become an integral part of the new political and economic landscape of medieval Wexford (they even christened their sons with settler names like Maurice, Gerald, William and Luke (O'Byrne 2007, 168)).

Nonetheless, by the mid-thirteenth century the Meic Murchada threat increased considerably. In some places they extracted protection money from the settlers. In the face of mounting pressure and the futility of their lot, several settler families chose to ally themselves with the native Irish. The crown sought to retrieve the situation through negotiation and by offering a retainer to Irish leaders in return for keeping the peace (Colfer 2013, 75–6, 80). The government employed Gaelic allies (often Meic Murchada: Colfer 2002a, 227, 233; Connolly 1998, 353, 390, 483, 484, 545). In the following years it is possible to see how the Meic Murchada fell into and out of royal favour. The account of Ross for 1279 notes the purchase for Art Mac Murchada of a robe with a fur-lined hood, and in 1280 he was presented by Roger Bigod with a robe, a cap, furs, money and a cask of wine (O'Byrne 2003, 29; 2007, 169). Later the same year his brother Muirchertach (king of Leinster) was imprisoned and several people were accused of 'harbouring Art Mac Murchada' (Colfer 2002a, 225; Hore 1900–11, vol. v, 94–5). Bigod planned to take the Meic Murchada brothers back to England and organised letters of safe passage for them (Colfer 2002a, 225). But the new justiciar had them murdered by government assassins at Arklow in 1282 (O'Byrne 2003, 73). There was comparative peace for the next twelve years or so.

The colonists' hand was weakened from the late thirteenth century by the departure of so many men from the colony to fight in the king's wars in Scotland, Wales and Flanders (and France, by the start of the Hundred Years' War in 1337) (for examples, see Lydon 1954; Connolly 1998, 234). Food and other resources were also being exported from Ireland to support the troops overseas, thus compounding the impotence of those left behind to defend their homes, their livelihoods and their families against a now-rampant Gaelic resurgence. The matter was exacerbated by the fact that convicted felons (of all ethnicities) were pardoned in return for joining the royal armies overseas. In 1282 New Ross exported corn, wine, fish, cattle, pigs and sheep to sustain the king's army in Wales (Colfer 2002a, 226); in 1295 £650 worth of corn was sent from New Ross to the troops in Gascony and the following year corn and beans were shipped to Bayonne for the army in France. In 1300 further shipments of victuals were sent to Gascony (Hore 1900–11, vol. v, 98), while in 1299, 1302, 1312 and 1324 food provisions (including corn and wine) were dispatched from New Ross for the war in Scotland (Connolly 1998, 150, 154, 170, 215, 294, 335, 592, 603). In 1303 and 1311 ships from Wexford were requisitioned for the king's war in Scotland (Hore 1900–11, vol. v, 101), in 1321–2 ships from New Ross and Wexford were required to transport men-at-arms to England (Hore 1900–11, vol. v, 104), and in 1324 all ships entering Wexford Harbour were seized and used to provision the king's expeditions in France (Colfer 2008, 58; see also Connolly 1998, 294; Hore 1900–11, vol. v, 105). This drain on resources was unrelenting through much of the century and ships at Wexford were again required to ship corn to England in the 1370s (Hore 1900–11, vol. v, 119–20). It was not just fighting men, food and other supplies, it was hard cash too; in 1303–4 the community of Co. Wexford handed over eighty marks to subsidise the king's war in Scotland, while the community of the borough of New Ross paid £40 (Anon. 1906, 70). In the 1290s, Ireland contributed the vast sum of almost £30,000 towards the construction of Edward I's castles in Wales (Colfer 2002a, 226). In 1294 famine, pestilence and faction-fighting again coalesced to generate a rebellion. The crown was unable to respond satisfactorily due to its commitments in overseas conflicts, and worse was yet to come.

The fourteenth century witnessed a range of famines, livestock epidemics, poor harvests, climatic deterioration, flooding and other natural disasters. The Bruce

Invasion coincided with the worst famine of the Middle Ages (Orpen 1968, vol. iv, 160–206; Armstrong 1923; McNamee 1997, 166–205; Lydon 1987c; Duffy 2002; Colfer 2002a, 231). Things were just about recovering for some communities when the Black Death hit Irish shores in 1348 (Kelly 2004). The plague spread quickly through ports, along trade routes and within and between towns – and so it affected the nucleated settler populace more than the more dispersed native Irish. It is estimated that the main outbreak and subsequent aftershocks depleted the colonial population by as much as 50 per cent (Colfer 2013, 77; Down 1987, 449–50). The Black Death respected no boundary and no authority, and in 1348 the bishop of Ferns himself succumbed to it (Hore 1900–11, vol. vi, 197; Colfer 2002a, 219). In 1349 the town of Old Ross suffered 'mortality from pestilence' from which it never recovered (Hore 1900–11, vol. i, 190; Colfer 2002a, 234; 2013, 77).

In *c.*1285, Greatisland was abandoned after being flooded by seawater, but the people returned and the mill was repaired the following year (Hore 1900–11, vol. iii, 210; Murphy 2007, 87). In 1325 several burgages in Wexford town were evacuated because they too had been inundated by the sea (Hore 1900–11, vol. v, 106), the muniments of St Selskar's were destroyed in a fire in 1355 (Gwynn and Hadcock 1970, 198), while subsidence of a property in the town was recorded in 1395–6 (Hore 1900–11, vol. v, 124). Bannow and Clonmines suffered when the channels there silted up (Bradley and King 1990, 14) and it is likely that both of these boroughs were ultimately abandoned due to drifting sand.

In the early years of the fourteenth century war was endemic in Ireland. The seneschal of the liberty of Wexford, Gilbert de Sutton, was killed by the Irish in 1305 (Colfer 2002a, 227), while a special meeting was called at Ross in 1312 by the king's council to make arrangements to suppress the rebels (Colfer 2013, 75). It was felt that Ireland was on the point of being lost 'unless God improved the situation' (Hartland 2018, 228). Even income from tax on beer dropped by a third in the 1320s due to the 'Irish war' (Hore 1900–11, vol. v, 105). In 1332/3 a payment of £10 was made to Art Mac Murchada for his good service, past and future, and a robe was given to his son, indicating that he had a role as an official (Connolly 1998, 353). At the same time, officers were sent to 'pacify certain discords which have arisen between the English and Irish' in Wexford (Connolly 1998, 353). Two years later the king's seneschal of Wexford, Robert Poer, was recompensed for going to Wexford with men-at-arms, hobelars and foot soldiers 'to pacify discords between the English and Irish in those parts … lest worse should happen to the king's faithful people there' (Connolly 1998, 378, 379, 385, 623; Hore 1900–11, vol. v, 110). In order to stem the tide of settlers abandoning Ireland, in 1343 a proclamation was issued to port towns that all ships were to be detained and only merchants were to be permitted to leave the country without the king's warrant (Hore 1900–11, vol. v, 112); this was reissued in 1382 (Hore 1900–11, vol. v, 123).

The crown's actions in attempting to save the colony became increasingly desperate. In 1356 Thomas de Asteley was paid £12

> because recently the Obryns of Dofre, Irish enemies and rebels of the king, with a great multitude of armed men, both mounted and foot, attacked and plundered the faithful people of Co. Wexford, and Thomas with a small force of men, fought and defeated them, completely recovered the booty, killed Mourgh Roth captain of the Obryns and William Omorth and three others of that nation and brought their heads before the king's council in Ireland as proof, granted to him as a reward, by the advice of the council, in consideration of his praiseworthy service and also of the fact that it had been proclaimed that whoever brought the head of any Irish captain to the king's court would receive an appropriate reward (Connolly 1998, 482; Smith 2018, 250–1).

Muirchertach Mac Murchada was executed in 1354, Domhnall Riabhach and Art died in prison in Trim Castle in 1362, while other Meic Murchada leaders were killed by the English in 1375 (Potterton 2005, 217, 226, 414; Colfer 2002a, 235). These deaths appear to have galvanised the resolve of the Meic Murchada and precipitated the emergence of a new force in the region. Art Mór Cáemánach Mac Murchada claimed to be king of Leinster and even had a seal made to demonstrate this (Lydon 1963, 146; Meirtneach 1978) (Figure 2.30). He provided the Irish with a strong new leader who catalysed their efforts and quickened the pace of recovery (Frame 1995; O'Byrne 2003, 103–18; Kavanagh 2003, 38–53). He skilfully negotiated his way through the politics of the time, receiving fees from the crown.

In the summer of 1375 certain keepers of the peace in Co. Wexford petitioned parliament that Philip Nyvell had been living for a long time among the Meic Murchada, Irish enemies, and that he had

> perpetrated homicides, burnings, robberies and many other wrongs at various times on the lieges of the said county in the company of the said Irishmen. Having treated with the said keepers and other marchers of the said county, he has now restored himself to the peace at their request, and later by his aid, ordinance and spying, sixty of the better men of the said Irish, with their horses, arms and their other goods worth £100 were killed and captured. By this, all that march, which was continually occupied by the said Irish before this time, is totally cleared of the said Irish for fear of the said Philip and because of the notoriety that he has in those parts.

In return for this 'good service', Nyvell was pardoned of 'all manner of seditions' (Crooks, PR 49 Ed. III, no. 128). It is hardly surprising that the chief chamberlain and his assistant, who were in Wexford the following summer to levy the king's debts and make extents of certain lands, were 'often in fear of their lives' (Connolly 1998, 537).

2.30 Art Mór Cáemánach Mac Murchada had a seal made to demonstrate his claim to the kingship of Leinster. It was probably similar to the great seal of his kinsman Domhnall Riabhach Mac Murchada (d. 1362), an impression of which is depicted here (SIGILLUM ◆ DONALL ◆ MEICM URACHA ◆ DA ◆ REGIS ◆ LAGEIE, after *Journal of the Royal Society of Antiquaries of Ireland*, vi (1994), 23)

Things had deteriorated to such a degree that in the autumn of 1394 Richard II became the first English king to visit Ireland in almost two centuries (Curtis 1927; Lydon 1963; McGettigan 2016). He arrived with an unprecedented force of eight thousand men in an attempt to stop the rot. In what was essentially a tacit admission of the failure of two centuries of attempted conquest and settlement, Richard granted most of the northern half of Wexford to John de Beaumont in 1395, having negotiated an agreement with the native Irish leaders to turn their attentions elsewhere. Neither side abided by the agreement and when Richard returned to Ireland in 1399 with his household knights and nobles he was defeated by the Irish and forced to return to England (where he was deposed, imprisoned and starved to death). Ever the opportunist, Art Mór Cáemánach stepped up his activities in Leinster and became even more of a thorn in the crown's side. In 1403 Henry IV gave permission for New Ross, by then described as being 'in the march and surrounded by Irish enemies', to pay a yearly tribute of ten marks to Mac Murchada and to trade freely with the Irish (something they had been prohibited from doing up to this point) (Colfer 2013, 82). If this was the state of affairs for New Ross, the county's largest and strongest walled settlement, then smaller enclaves like Carrick had no hope of survival.

The manor

As the Gaelic revival gathered momentum and instability spread generally, the core unit of Anglo-Norman settlement – the manor – came under increasing pressure. A grant was provided early in the fourteenth century towards the defence of the coastal manor of Glascarrig (Figure 2.31) from 'the malice of the Irish' (Colfer 2002a, 149, 153, 227; Mills 1914, 13). But the de Caunteton settlers, to whom the grant had been awarded, allied with the O'Byrnes in 1306 to carry out robbery, rebellion, cattle rustling and murder (Colfer 2002a, 227–9). In 1311 Glascarrig was devastated by the Meic Murchada, and most of the tenants fled; all forty burgages had fallen and were not rebuilt (Griffith 1956, 159; Colfer 2002a, 148–9, 228–9). The lands were described as being 'in the march and sterile' because nobody dared 'to put their hands on them' (Colfer 2002a, 228–9). In 1334 the lands were 'worth nothing because waste and uncultivated and among the Irish' (Colfer 2002a, 153; Crooks, CR 8 Ed. III, no. 116). Most of the manor centre at Glascarrig appears to have been lost to coastal erosion (Breen 2007; Colfer 2002a, 148–9; Gahan 2018).

Archaeological excavation of a thirteenth-century settlers' undefended farmstead (a house and associated field system) at Moneycross near Gorey concluded that the site had been abandoned after a short period of occupation (Schweitzer 2009; O'Keeffe 2015, 60, fig. 24). There was local pottery but no imported wares. A barbed-and-socketed iron arrowhead discovered at the site is likely to date from the thirteenth century (Schweitzer 2009, 181). In some places in Britain, moated sites on very marginal land appear to have functioned as hunting lodges (see O'Conor 1998, 61), and the Moneycross arrowhead may have been used in hunting, but it could also have had a military purpose. Among the arrowheads recovered during excavations at Ferns Castle were several armour-piercing examples of late thirteenth-/early fourteenth-century type, as well as part of a dagger (Sweetman 1979, 237–8).

The potential scale of the defences on a moated site is generally belied by the surviving denuded field remains. An indication of the former complexity of this monument type can be found in a range of medieval documents including details of the construction of the moated site at Ballyconnor/Mylerspark in Wexford in the mid-1280s (Colfer 1996; 2013, 59; ch. 3). According to Mark Gardiner and Kieran O'Conor (2017, 140), Coolamurry, 'if defended resolutely by its owners and farms servants, could have seen off more than just a few thieves, perhaps even a small raiding party'. They compare Coolamurry with less-well-defended moated sites elsewhere in Ireland, noting that 'moated sites in quite turbulent frontier zones needed stronger defences than ones in more peaceful areas' (141). The chance discovery in 1978 of a corroded double-edged medieval sword on the site of a recently destroyed moated site at Barmoney, c.10km north-west of Wexford town, is further evidence of the need for security in these locations (Halpin 1986, 200, 221). Just 3km to the south-west of Barmoney, excavations at the moated site on marginal ground at Camaross revealed

2.31 This motte was the focal point of the de Caunteton manor of Glascarrig. Much of the manor centre – and parts of the earthen defences – have slipped into the Irish Sea (image courtesy of Robert Shaw (Discovery Programme) and the Climate, Heritage and Environments of Reefs, Islands and Headlands (CHERISH) Project)

that primary occupation of the enclosure had taken place in the late thirteenth/early fourteenth century (Tierney 2009; Gardiner and O'Conor 2017, 137–9, 152; Eogan and Kelly 2016, 214). This was followed by a period of decline and neglect, destruction by fire and ultimately abandonment. Similarly, archaeological excavations next to the motte at the manorial village of Duncormick revealed evidence for an early thirteenth-century cereal-drying kiln and defended Anglo-Norman site that 'was later abandoned, or at least not significantly developed' (Dehaene 2009, 65). More generally, the sparsity of moated sites in the north of Co. Wexford can be viewed as a reflection of the early desertion of that part of the colony by the Anglo-Normans.

The borough

In the 1240s Wexford was worth more than all the other Marshal properties combined (Orpen 1968, vol. iii, 79–80). In the decades that followed, however, historical and archaeological evidence demonstrate the remarkable decline in value and population of Anglo-Norman Wexford. Gaelic resurgence affected the north of the county first, and already by the end of the thirteenth century the Irish had begun to recover large tracts of land there. They killed or evicted large numbers of settlers, reoccupying the lands themselves. The fact that so little is known about Anglo-Norman Gorey, for instance, apart from a brief reference in 1296 to 'the community of the town (*ville*) of Gory', is probably a reflection that this most northerly of Wexford's boroughs was evacuated at a very early stage (Hore 1900–11, vol. vi, 609; Moore 1996, no. 1451). Just 6km further south, the borough of Courtown was uninhabited by the 1280s 'because of the war', and was taken into the king's hand (Sweetman 1875–86, vol. ii, nos 1801, 2010; Colfer 2002a, 149, 230). John Roche offered to take it over (Colfer 2002a, 230), but early in the fourteenth century it was granted to a branch of the Meic Murchada who held it for the rest of the Middle Ages (Hore 1900–11, vol. vi, 642; Bradley and King 1990, 25).

Between 1245 and 1307 the value of the Marshal manor at Ferns dropped from £81 15*s.* to £38 16*s.* 6*d.* (Hore 1900–11, vol. vi, 6, 9; Sweetman 1875–86, vol. iv, no. 306). Accounts from 1296 state that there were almost fifty waste burgages there (Hore 1900–11, vol. v, 100; vol. vi, 192). Upgrades at Ferns Castle in the mid-to-late thirteenth century can probably be attributed to the de Valences and are likely – in part at least – to be a response to increasing threats from the Gaelic Irish (Colfer 2013, 62–5). Indeed, Tadhg O'Keeffe and Margaret Coughlan consider that Ferns Castle was built in its *entirety* by the de Valences after they took over the lands in 1247 (2003, 147). The fact that the de Valences were not themselves present in Wexford (appointing constables in their stead) meant that even major works of consolidation at their key castle were unlikely to stem the Gaelic revival in north Wexford. As the ancestral headquarters of the Uí Chennselaig and the Meic Murchada, as well as being a key military, economic, administrative and religious stronghold, Ferns was always going to be a primary target for the resurgent Irish.

The new century witnessed further deterioration and Ferns was captured during the Bruce Wars and again by the Leinster Irish in 1331 (Hore 1900–11, vol. vi, 195–6; Gwynn and Hadcock 1970, 175). The castle was said to be in poor repair in 1324, at which time the mill had been destroyed and the court no longer functioned; indeed the entire manor of Ferns was considered to be worthless, for it had been 'totally wasted by Irish felons' (Sharp and Stamp 1910, 326; Hore 1900–11, vol. vi, 9; Otway-Ruthven 1968, 252). Despite being confiscated from its absentee owners and having newly appointed constables (Colfer 2013, 65–6), in 1346–7 the castle was besieged and taken by the Irish (Connolly 1998, 421; Hore 1900–11, vol. vi, 11). They relinquished it for a few years but attacked it again in the mid-1350s, destroying much of it (Connolly 1998, 482–3), before capturing it once again *c.*1360, after it had been repaired, and holding on to it for the remainder of the Middle Ages (Hore 1900–11, vol. vi, 13; Bradley and King 1990, 50; Sweetman 1979; Moore 1996, no. 1440; Colfer 2002a, 219; Anon. 1906, 42). In 1385 Ferns was still worth nothing because it had been 'devastated by the Irish' (Dawes et al. 1974). Archaeological excavations at Ferns Castle in the 1970s revealed little evidence for occupation after the fourteenth

2.32 This motte castle was built by Strongbow at Old Ross, which developed as a busy manor in the thirteenth century. There were cattle, horses and 2,500 sheep, a rabbit warren, an oak wood, an orchard, a water mill, a variety of arable crops and a dairy

century, and David Sweetman surmised that 'the Irish resurgence of the middle of the fourteenth century probably would have terminated any attempt by the Normans to hold such outposts as Ferns' (1979, 240).

From the Prendergasts, Enniscorthy passed to the de Rochfords, who held it through the fourteenth century. In 1324 the manor was described as being waste and 'destroyed by the war of the Irish' (Hore 1900–11, vol. vi, 394; Moore 1996, no. 1436; Sharp and Stamp 1910). Later that century the manor struggled further at the hands of the Meic Murchada, who appear to have annexed it soon after that (Bradley and King 1990, 35–6). Just 5km downriver from Enniscorthy, the value of Edermine fell by almost 70 per cent due to war in the fourteenth century (Bradley and King 1990, 30; Brooks 1950, 45, no. 2; Sharp and Stamp 1910).

Ross became 'Old' Ross when 'New' Ross was established 12km to the west by William Marshal when the port of Waterford was taken into the king's hand. New Ross became the manorial caput and, while Old Ross continued to function, the old borough gradually contracted and faded in importance. Strongbow had constructed a motte castle at Old Ross (Figure 2.32) as the centre of his demesne manor and borough, and this earthwork castle was superseded by a (now-demolished) masonry

castle nearby in the thirteenth century. A rental of 58s. 10d. in 1280–1 suggests a
population of almost sixty burgesses (and about the same number of houses) (Hore
1900–11, vol. i, 9; Bradley and King 1990, 134). In 1307 it was recorded that the
buildings of the manor included an old (unroofed) hall surrounded by a wall, a smaller
unroofed hall, a chapel, a kitchen, a grange, a thatched sheep-fold, a garden and a
curtilage of pasture, all of no value because no one will rent (*conducere*) them (Sharp
and Stamp 1913; Hore 1900–11, vol. i, 170; Sweetman 1875–86, vol. v, pp 175–6,
no. 617; Mills 1914, 347). By 1349 Old Ross, 'on the borders of the enemy', had
witnessed 'divers persons killed, as often by frequent hostile invasions as by warlike
conflicts for the defence of the town, as by mortality from pestilence, impoverishment,
and even total destruction … the community are in such a state of unaccustomed
misery, poverty and helplessness … a great part of the men of the said town are ready
to leave and fly to foreign parts' (Hore 1900–11, vol. i, 190; Colfer 2013, 77). Later,
the mill was burned down by enemies, presumably the Kavanaghs (Hore 1900–11,
vol. i, 216; Bradley and King 1990, 135). So bad was the situation at Old Ross that it
was offered a very rare debt-forgiveness of one-third of a £100 debt to the crown on
the provision that the money saved would be used to defend the town and
surrounding countryside. Towards the end of the fourteenth century – perhaps in
response to this arrangement – Richard Brown (one of the burgesses) built a new mill
and a tower for his safety and for the defence of Old Ross (Hore 1900–11, vol. i, 216).

Ironically, perhaps, the construction of a defensive wall around New Ross was
carried out in response to a settler feud rather than an Irish attack, anticipated or
otherwise (O'Byrne 2007, 168). Infighting among the colonists (the de Burgh v.
FitzGerald dispute of the 1260s) was significant enough to merit inclusion in the 1265
Walling of New Ross poem (Hartland 2018, 228; Shields 1976; Busby 2017). There are
other signs of internal pressures and conflict in New Ross; by 1282 the school house
was being used to store hay (Mills 1892, 57), and the Fratres Cruciferi community
expired before 1295 when the brethren were killed by the townsmen of New Ross in
retaliation for a murder committed by one of their members. Their site was given to
the Franciscans (Gwynn and Hadcock 1970, 215; Ó Drisceoil 2017, 305–7; Colfer
2002a, 172, 209).

Despite the 1265 poem, the earliest-known murage grant for New Ross dates to
1374 (Thomas 1986; 1992, vol. ii, 176). It was issued in response to 'frequent attacks
by the Irish' and, while it was to last for twenty years, it was followed in 1378 by
further funding 'for repair of town, walls and port'. By 1381 the 'greater part of the
walls and towers were prostrated' and in 1392 a new twenty-year murage grant was
issued. This remarkable sequence of defensive funding initiatives at New Ross did not
stop Art Mór Cáemánach from burning the town in 1394 (O'Donovan 1848–51, *s.a.*
1394), and indeed further monies were invested in defence in the aftermath of that
attack and before yet another twenty-year grant was issued in 1400.

2.33 A house of Augustinian Canons Regular was established in Wexford town, probably in the early thirteenth century. It was dedicated to SS Peter and Paul but is more commonly referred to as Selskar Abbey. St Nicholas' Church at Carrick was granted to Selskar Abbey in 1418 (© National Monuments Service Photographic Unit)

By 1307, rents from Wexford town decreased by 35 per cent because 127 of the burgages were waste and the tenants had become paupers (Hore 1900–11, vol. v, 102). At least some of the destruction had been due to 'the war of the Irish' (Sharp and Stamp 1908, 22). A later inquisition (on the death of Aymer de Valence in 1324) noted two watermills, almost prostrated, and described 221½ burgages as vacant, waste and returning nothing 'because of the war' (Sharp and Stamp 1910; Hore 1900–11, vol. v, 105), which must have meant a further 40 per cent decrease in rental income from the 1307 figures. It is likely that the 'war' in question was the Bruce Invasion. There are references to the collection of murage taxes in Wexford in 1331 and 1381 for the repair of town's defences (Hore 1900–11, vol. v, 107, 122), while in 1334 the priory of St Selskar's (Figure 2.33) claimed that its lands and rents had been destroyed by the war of the Meic Murchada and other Irish, and the monks were about to abandon their house and dwell with their friends in the countryside (Otway-Ruthven 1968, 252). Law-and-order was clearly breaking down – hostages and criminals escaped from prison, there were reports of breaking and entering, and even the town pillory was broken in 1356 (Hore 1900–11, vol. v, 113, 114, 115). In 1306 the seneschal of Wexford was fined £5 for each escaped prisoner and hostage; his total bill was £40 (Anon. 1906, 100). In the mid-fourteenth century, further criminal activity in Wexford town included the theft of charters and other documents, robbery by certain men of Clonmines, and repeated complaints of people being 'insulted' (Hore 1900–11, vol. v, 109–11, 114). In 1373–4 the burgesses at Wexford were unable to pay rent because the town and neighbourhood had been burned and totally destroyed by the king's Irish enemies and rebels (Hore 1900–11, vol. v, 119) and in 1377 there were reports of the devastation and waste of the timber in the park of Wexford – especially the oak trees (Hore 1900–11, vol. v, 121). In 1400, in recognition that Wexford town had suffered so much (robberies, death of burgesses etc.), the king pardoned all royal debts owed by the town (Hore 1900–11, vol. v, 126). The challenges faced by the townspeople continued into the fifteenth century and in 1416 much of Wexford and its suburbs were burned again by the Meic Murchada (Hore 1900–11, vol. v, 129).

Despite the determination and efforts of the settlers at Greatisland (see above), the expenditure of considerable sums on repairs to the castle, and the construction of an enormous moated site (Moore 1996, no. 1036), the outlook for the settlement there was bleak; by 1307 the castle had lost its new roof and was worthless (Sharp and Stamp 1913; Hore 1900–11, vol. iii, 201–19). Increasingly overshadowed by New Ross, Greatisland failed to recover in the fourteenth century and was abandoned. The bishop's borough at Mayglass was almost certainly abandoned by the end of the Middle Ages (Bradley and King 1990, 94). The borough of Bannow was in decline by the early fourteenth century, rents had decreased by about 20 per cent and the thatched grange was 'almost prostrate' (Sharp and Stamp 1910; Moore 1996, no. 1423). Some of the demesne lands of the liberty of Wexford were devastated in the winter of 1296, and at that time the value of the liberty had decreased from £300 to £150 (Sharp and Stamp 1912). By July 1324 it was reported that lands across the county were waste and worthless (Sharp and Stamp 1910, 1912). At Edermine, certain burgesses who previously rendered £9 10s. yearly, now paid only 60s., 'on account of the war' (Sharp and Stamp 1910).

Notwithstanding its key location, it appears that Taghmon had no castle until much later in the Middle Ages, and this may have left the area more exposed (Colfer 2013, 48; Doyle 2016, 43–8). Already by 1306 there were reports of uncultivated land on the manor and woods being held by Irishmen (Sharp and Stamp 1913). The convent became derelict in about 1333 (Gwynn and Hadcock 1970, 324), and by 1389 Taghmon was referred to as being 'in the marches' (Hore 1900–11, vol. v, 419).

By 1324 the castle at Carrick was ruinous, vacant and valueless, and the borough had been 'destroyed by war' (Sharp and Stamp 1910; Hore 1900–11, vol. v, 33; ch. 4) and from this time the borough fades in significance so that by the end of the Middle Ages it was completely deserted (Bradley and King 1990, 66; Colfer 2002a, 145–7). In the same way that proximity to New Ross made survival difficult for the boroughs of Rosbercon and Old Ross and, in Meath, Newtown Trim failed because it was right beside Trim (Potterton 2005, passim), one could suggest that Carrick was destined to fail as soon as it was established so close to Wexford.

The church

Initially, lay tenants were not allowed on Cistercian lands, and so their vast estates were worked and managed by large numbers of lay brethren. The challenge of finding sufficient recruits proved insurmountable, however, and already by 1220 they were permitted to lease lands to the laity (Colfer 2002a, 189; 2004, 52). This was the thin end of the wedge; increasing political instability, compounded by the Black Death, meant that by the end of the fourteenth century the Dunbrody estates were farmed mostly by laymen (Colfer 2004, 52–3). While incursions from the native Irish threatened the monastic estates, a greater challenge for the religious communities seems to have been ongoing altercations between the various orders themselves. Dunbrody was involved in clashes with the Templars at Kilcloggan in 1286 (Sweetman 1875–86, vol. iii, p. 328, no. 666; Colfer 2002a, 198), and these lengthy and bitter land disputes continued into the following century (Colfer 2004, 48–9).

The relationship between Tintern and Dunbrody became especially difficult in the fourteenth century (Gwynn and Hadcock 1970, 131, 143; Lynch 2010, 5; Colfer 2002a, 192). At the same time, Tintern was involved in disputes with the Cistercians at Jerpoint, who had seemingly imprisoned several monks and stolen some horses from Tintern (Gwynn and Hadcock 1970, 142; Lynch 2010, 195). Tintern was also involved in disputes with Canterbury (Hore 1900–11, vol. v, 120), it was plundered by monks from St Mary's Abbey in Dublin (Lynch 2010, 195) and in 1277 the abbot was deposed for not attending the chapter general for many years (Gwynn and Hadcock 1970, 142). The evidence from fourteenth-century archaeological contexts at Tintern indicates a period of downsizing and contraction (Lynch 2010, 195–6), suggestive of a smaller community with fewer resources. Analysis of the human skeletal remains from Tintern demonstrates the range of injuries suffered by those who were buried there – mostly as a result of interpersonal violence: incised weapon wounds, fractured ribs, skulls and vertebrae, broken arms suffered as a result of self-defence, and sharp-force trauma to the head (O'Donnabhain 2010). Many of the injuries were 'not compatible with life' (O'Donnabhain 2010).

In 1340 the abbot of Dunbrody was deposed and in 1348 the temporalities were taken into the king's hand because 'proper hospitality was not maintained' (Gwynn and Hadcock 1970, 131). In 1390 the abbot and six monks were accused of assaulting a royal commissioner investigating acts of violence in the district (Gwynn and Hadcock 1970, 131). Apparently, they imprisoned him for over a fortnight until he promised to prosecute nobody. Neither Dunbrody nor Tintern were within the Mellifont affiliation, and in 1342 Dunbrody was allowed its independence from St Mary's in Dublin (Colfer 2004, 47). The Wexford Cistercians were thus cut off from

2.34 The fortified church at Killesk formed part of the estates of Dunbrody Abbey in the
Middle Ages. The entrance to the tower seen here, at the west end of the church,
was protected by a murder-hole above

their sister-houses in the area that would become the Pale, the part of eastern Ireland
most loyal to the crown in the later Middle Ages.

Evidence for growing security concerns is visible in the surviving architecture. The
crossing tower inserted at Dunbrody would have provided an element of security
(Moore 1996, no. 1318; Colfer 2004, 62, 79; 2013, 118–25)(Figure 1.8), while the
monastic estates were increasingly exposed to raiding and it is no surprise to find two
fortified churches there – Killesk and St Catherine's on the cliff-top at Nook, near
Duncannon (Colfer 2013, 122). Situated within a prehistoric promontory fort (Moore
1996, nos 225, 1283), the church of St Catherine, which serviced the religious needs
of the lay-brethren working on the grange, was small but thick-walled, battered and
equipped with a battlemented wall-walk (Moore 1996, no. 1283; Hore 1900–11, vol.
iii, 250–6). The church at Killesk (Figure 2.34) was mentioned in 1370. The surviving
building has a vaulted and battered tower, a murder-hole over the entrance, a wall-walk
and (very unusually for a church) an oubliette (Colfer 2013, 125; Moore 1996, no.
1257; Hore 1900–11, vol. iii, 237–40).

A vaulted tower with stepped parapets and lookout platforms was added to the
church of Selskar Abbey in Wexford town in the fourteenth century (Moore 1996,
no. 1481; Colfer 2013, 109, 118–19, 124). The defended tower at Templetown was

2.35 The crossing tower appears to have been added to the priory church at Clonmines in the fourteenth century, in a pattern familiar in other parts of the county at that time (image courtesy of Cóilín Ó Drisceoil (Kilkenny Archaeology))

probably built by the Hospitallers in the fourteenth century as a response to increasing security threats locally as well as more widely across the colony (Moore 1996, no. 1302; Colfer 2002a, 206; 2004, 60; 2013, 124–5). Such pressures seem to have been behind the fortification of other churches in the south of the county at this time too. The large parish church at Bannow, for instance, probably built in about 1200 and dedicated to Mary, had battlements, a wall-walk, vaulted porches, buttresses and a bellcote added (by Tintern?) in the fourteenth century (Moore 1996, no. 1424; Corlett and Kirwan 2016; see also Bradley and Murtagh 2003, 215). Not far from Bannow, a crossing tower was added to the priory church at Clonmines (Moore 1996, no. 1432) (Figure 2.35), where the west end of the parish church was also provided with a defensive tower (Hore 1900–11, vol. ii, 200; Moore 1996, no. 1430). The medieval parish church of Kilmannan had an unbattered four-storey west-end tower added (Moore 1996, no. 1437; Colfer 2013, 124–5), probably in the fourteenth century. The tower was vaulted and had a murder-hole and bellcote (Moore 1996, no. 1437). While the church itself does not survive, the tower is still standing.

It is hard to know how effective were these security measures. We get a glimpse of the scale of the devastation of the churches and ecclesiastical properties in later medieval Wexford by perusing the extents made of the buildings, lands, rents and other properties of the religious houses across the county in January 1541 (White 1943, 353–76). Dunbrody: 'War of the Kavaners and other Irish … value nothing above repairs … waste by war of the Irishman … long been waste and unprofitable … vacant … lands being waste'; Tintern: 'worth nothing above repairs … now waste by rebellion of the Irish called the Cavaners … lands not fully occupied … all waste … detained without right … pays nothing … tenement now waste … mill unoccupied for want of repairs'; New Ross (Franciscan): 'church and kitchen can be thrown down'; Clonmines: 'tenement thrown down and waste'; Horetown: 'buildings worth nothing above repairs … 4 cottages now waste by war of the Irish Caverners … a carucate of land waste'; Wexford (Selskar): 'buildings worth nothing above repairs … lands waste by the Kavaners and unprofitable … tenement [in Wexford town] waste'; Wexford (Franciscan): 'church and all other buildings in the precinct can be thrown down'; Ferns: 'church and hall worth nothing above repairs … lands waste and unprofitable by war of the Kaverners … lands not well occupied by reason of war'; Glascarrig: 'buildings worth nothing above repairs … lands now waste by war of the Irish and le Kavaners … lands unsown … waste'.

The castle

The stone castles of Wexford came under increasing pressure in the late thirteenth century and major repairs had to be made to the castle at Greatisland in the hot dry summer of 1286 (Colfer 2013, 52, 56; Mills 1892, 57). Ten stone (64kg) of lead was imported from Wales for the roof repairs, as well as timber, mortar, slates, lime, nails, tin, tiles and turf to melt the lead. By 1307 both it and the castle at Old Ross had been abandoned, and within less than twenty years Wexford Castle and Carrick Castle were also in bad repair (Hore 1900–11, vol. v, 104; Sharp and Stamp 1910; 1913). In 1324 valuables were removed from Wexford Castle (Hore 1900–11, vol. v, 105; Colfer 2008, 88), and ten years later further repairs were needed there (Hore 1900–11, vol. v, 110). An enquiry carried out after the death of Aymer de Valence in 1324 found that Carrick Castle was then in ruins and Ferns Castle was ruinous too, because 'totally wasted by Irish felons' (Sharp and Stamp 1910).

When war in the north of the county forced the bishop to flee the diocesan capital at Ferns, the high-status late fourteenth-century castle at Fethard (Figure 2.36) became an episcopal residence. Indeed, the castle may have been built from scratch for Bishop Thomas Denne in about 1375 (Colfer 2002a, 219–20), making Fethard one of the very few castles built in Wexford in the fourteenth century. The presence of this castle and the bishop and his port seem to have ensured that Fethard survived when all about it failed (Colfer 2004, 36).

2.36 Fethard Castle is a rarity in Wexford – a castle built in the fourteenth century. It may have been constructed for Thomas Denne, bishop of Ferns, as an episcopal residence *c.*1375 when instability further north in the county led him to abandon Ferns itself. The castle has undergone many alterations over the centuries

Given the political turmoil and general instability of the time, it has always seemed odd that so few new castles were built in Wexford in the fourteenth century. Now that the date of the earliest tower houses has been pushed back into the fourteenth century (Barry 1995; Bradley and Murtagh 2003, 213–16; Hodkinson 2005; Jordan 1991), however, it seems likely that some of the 137 or so Wexford examples were built at this time, somewhat earlier than previously thought (for example, Colfer 1987, 89–92; 1988, 11; 2004, 79, 82; 2013, 106–17; but see also Cairns 1987; Barry 1993; O'Keeffe 1997; Sweetman 2000). For instance, in 1305 David de Caunteton was given a grant towards the construction of a fortalice on his manor of Glascarrig 'to resist the malice of the Irish' (Colfer 2002a, 149, 153, 227; Mills 1914, 13; O'Keeffe 2015, 262–4); could this have been a tower house? The Dennes' castle of Kayer is referred to in 1374 and, while there is no way to be sure, it too may have been a tower house (Colfer 2013, 106). Perhaps more compelling, towards the end of the fourteenth century, Richard Brown (a burgess of Old Ross) built a tower for his safety and for the defence of the borough (Hore 1900–11, vol. i, 216). A tower house next to (or sometimes within) a moated site is not an unusual sight in Wexford, and it suggests that the occupants of the latter built and moved to the former as they came under more sustained threat.

A second Pale?

Already by the 1320s much of northern Wexford was back in the hands of the Irish and, like the manorial tenants, the frontier moved steadily southwards (Colfer 2002a, 226). Proximity to Irish strongholds, challenging terrain and distance from secure ports made it impossible for the remaining colonists to survive and by the end of the century the north of the county was fully under the control of the Gaelic Irish. Even the bishop of Ferns moved his residence from Ferns south to New Ross at the start of the fourteenth century (Gwynn and Hadcock 1970, 101). The settler population was generally confined to the southern baronies of Forth, Bargy and Shelburne. As well as being further from Gaelic heartlands and closer to international trade routes, this part of the county was naturally defended by the sea on the east, west and south, and by Forth Mountain and the Corock and Owenduff rivers to the north, and so it became an enclave for the beleaguered colonists. As the very first land grants issued to the Anglo-Normans in Ireland, these baronies were also more densely settled and encastellated from the earliest years of the colony.

The existence of a 'Gaelic north' and an 'Anglo-Norman' south is reflected in the concentration of defensive earthworks (especially moated sites, ringworks and mottes) across the middle of Wexford, the 'interface' or marches between Irish and English (see Colfer 2002a, 53–5, 92, fig. 33; 2004, 35 (and fig. 8), 78; 2008, 48, fig. 16; 2013, 48–50, 56–9, 70–83; Gardiner and O'Conor 2017, 141). The density of Anglo-Norman settlement in the south of the county is reflected in the distribution of townland names with the suffix '-town' (Jones Hughes 1970, 247–50, fig. 15.1; Colfer 2002a, 125, 245; 2004, 79; 2008, 62, fig. 9; 2013, 81, 83) – nowhere else in Ireland beyond Dublin's hinterland has such a concentration of this type of place-name. Indeed, the concentration of 'English' place-names more generally in Ireland is nowhere more pronounced than in the south-east of Wexford (Jones Hughes 1970, 250–2, fig. 15.2). In relation to Bargy, Jones Hughes points out that 'such a range of English names are found nowhere else in Ireland' (1970, 252). Another indicator of the early abandonment of the north of the county is that place-names with the element 'court' (an early manor house) plus an Irish component are concentrated in that area (Colfer 2013, 115–16).

The settler community in the south-east became increasingly isolated from Dublin and the rest of the colony. So isolated was this community that a unique dialect emerged; *Yola* ('old'), which was still spoken in the nineteenth century (and of which some vocabulary remains in use), was derived from Middle English as spoken by the Anglo-Norman settlers in the twelfth and thirteenth centuries (Dolan and Ó Muirithe 1996; Colfer 2002a, 125, 245; ch. 3). By the fifteenth century, south Wexford really was a 'second Pale' (Nicholls 1982, 401; Colfer 2008, 60).

2.37 When Hervey de Montmorency became a monk of Christ Church, Canterbury, he granted some of his Wexford properties to the prior and chapter there, and thus initiated a connection between Canterbury and Tintern Abbey that would last long beyond his lifetime. Pictured here is an impression of the seal of Tintern attached to a warranty between the abbey and Canterbury Cathedral Priory dated 15 June 1245. The inscription reads SIGILLUM ABATT DE VOTO, 'the seal of the abbot of de Voto [Tintern]' (© Canterbury Cathedral Archives, CCA/Chant/I/232)

BIBLIOGRAPHY

Aalen, F., Whelan, K. and Stout, M. 1997. *Atlas of the Irish rural landscape.* Cork.

Aberg, F. 1978. *Medieval moated sites.* London.

Anon. 1906. *The thirty-eighth report of the deputy keeper of the public records and keeper of the state papers in Ireland.* Dublin.

Armstrong, O. 1923. *Edward Bruce's invasion of Ireland.* London.

Bailey, M. 2002. *The English manor, c.1200–1500.* Manchester.

Barry, T. 1977a. *The medieval moated sites of south-eastern Ireland: counties Carlow, Kilkenny, Tipperary and Wexford.* Oxford.

Barry, T. 1977b. 'The medieval moated sites of County Wexford'. *Journal of the Old Wexford Society*, 6 (1976–7), 5–17.

Barry, T. 1987. *The archaeology of medieval Ireland.* London and New York.

Barry, T. 1988. 'Medieval moated sites in Ireland: some new conclusions on their chronology and functions'. In Mac Niocaill, G. and Wallace, P. (eds), *Keimelia: studies in medieval archaeology and history in memory of Tom Delaney*, 525–35. Galway.

Barry, T. 1993. 'The archaeology of the tower house in late medieval Ireland'. In Anderson, H. and Wienberg, T. (eds), *The study of medieval archaeology*, 211–17. Stockholm.

Barry, T. 1995. 'The last frontier: defence and settlement in late medieval Ireland'. In Barry, T., Frame, R. and Simms, K. (eds), *Colony and frontier in medieval Ireland: essays presented to J.F. Lydon*, 217–28. London.

Barry, T. 2003. 'The defensive nature of Irish moated sites'. In Kenyon, J. and O'Conor, K. (eds), *The medieval castle in Ireland and Wales: essays in honour of Jeremy Knight,* 182–93. Dublin.

Barry, T. 2016. 'Reflections on the moated sites of Wexford'. In Doyle, I. and Browne, B. (eds), *Medieval Wexford: essays in memory of Billy Colfer*, 202–10. Dublin.

Bourke, E. 1995. 'Life in the sunny south-east: housing and domestic economy in Viking and medieval Wexford'. *Archaeology Ireland*, 9:3, 33–6.

Bradley, J. 1988. 'Anglo-Norman sarcophagi from Ireland'. In Mac Niocaill, G. and Wallace, P. (eds), *Keimelia: studies in medieval archaeology and history in memory of Tom Delaney*, 74–94. Galway.

Bradley, J. and King, H. [1990]. 'Urban Archaeology Survey, part 11: County Wexford'. Unpublished report prepared for the OPW, Dublin.

Bradley, J. and Murtagh, B. 2003. 'Brady's Castle, Thomastown, Co. Kilkenny: a 14th-century fortified town house'. In Kenyon, J. and O'Conor, K. (eds), *The medieval castle in Ireland and Wales: essays in honour of Jeremy Knight*, 194–216. Dublin.

Breen, C. 2007. 'An eroding earthwork castle in Wexford'. In Manning, C. (ed.), *From ringforts to fortified houses: studies on castles and other monuments in honour of David Sweetman*, 65–74. Dublin.

Brooks, E. 1950. *Knights' fees in counties Wexford, Carlow and Kilkenny*. Dublin.

Busby, K. 2017. *French in medieval Ireland, Ireland in medieval French: the paradox of two worlds*. Turnhout.

Byrne, M. 1995. 'The results of a resistivity survey undertaken at Clonmines, Co. Wexford'. *Journal of the Wexford Historical Society*, 15 (1994–5), 67–73.

Byrne, P. 2018. 'Tile found in Ferns may date back to Strongbow'. *Gorey Guardian*, 18 August.

Caffrey, P. 2016. 'The visual culture of the Hospitaller Knights of the Priory of Ireland'. In Browne, M. and Ó Clabaigh, C. (eds), *Soldiers of Christ: the Knights Hospitaller and the Knights Templar in medieval Ireland*, 151–66. Dublin.

Cairns, C. 1987. *Irish tower houses: a Co. Tipperary case study*. Athlone.

Cloney, S. 1989. 'Some stone artifacts of south-west Wexford'. *Journal of the Wexford Historical Society*, 12 (1988–9), 92–7.

Cloney, S. 1997. 'A Templar's tomb'. *Journal of the Wexford Historical Society*, 16 (1996–7), 165–6.

Colfer, B. 1985. 'The tower of Hook'. *Journal of the Wexford Historical Society*, 10 (1984–5), 69–78.

Colfer, B. 1987. 'Anglo-Norman settlement in County Wexford'. In Whelan, K. and Nolan, W. (eds), *Wexford, history and society: interdisciplinary essays on the history of an Irish county*, 65–101. Dublin.

Colfer, B. 1988. 'County focus: Wexford'. *Archaeology Ireland*, 2.1, 8–11.

Colfer, B. 1991. 'Medieval Wexford'. *Journal of the Wexford Historical Society*, 13 (1990–1), 4–29.

Colfer, B. 1996. 'In search of the barricade and ditch of Ballyconnor, Co. Wexford'. *Archaeology Ireland*, 10:2, 16–19.

Colfer, B. 2002a. *Arrogant trespass: Anglo-Norman Wexford, 1169–1400*. Wexford.

Colfer, B. 2002b. 'The ethnic mix in medieval Wexford'. *History Ireland*, 10:1, 19–23.

Colfer, B. 2004. *The Hook Peninsula, County Wexford*. Cork.

Colfer, B. 2007. 'The Cistercians in County Wexford'. In Cunningham, G. (ed.), *The Roscrea Conference: commemorating forty conferences, 1987–2007*, 21–8, Roscrea.

Colfer, B. 2008. *Wexford: a town and its landscape*. Cork.

Colfer, B. 2010a. 'Medieval boom and bust: the rise and fall of Bannow and Clonmines'. *Journal of the Bannow Historical Society*, 2, 57–62.

Colfer, B. 2010b. 'Medieval Enniscorthy: urban origins'. In Tóibín, C. and Rafferty, C. (eds), *Enniscorthy: a history*, 83–97. Wexford.

Colfer, B. 2013. *Wexford castles: landscape, context and settlement*. Cork.

Connolly, P. 1998. *Irish exchequer payments, 1270–1446*. Dublin.

Connolly, P. and Martin, G. (eds). 1992. *The Dublin Guild Merchant roll, c.1190–1265*. Dublin.

Corlett, C. 2012. 'Two Romanesque fonts in Wexford'. *Archaeology Ireland*, 26:4, 17–19.

Corlett, C. 2015. 'Seventeenth-century monument at Killag, Co. Wexford'. *Archaeology Ireland*, 29:1, 24–5.

Corlett, C. 2018. 'A knight on the tile'. *Archaeology Ireland*, 32:4, 23–4.

Corlett, C. and Kirwan, S. 2016. 'The medieval parish church at Bannow, Co. Wexford'. In Doyle, I. and Browne, B. (eds), *Medieval Wexford: essays in memory of Billy Colfer*, 262–91. Dublin.

Cotter, C. 1987. 'Excavations at the site of MacMurrough Castle, near New Ross, Co. Wexford'. *Journal of the Wexford Historical Society*, 13 (1986–7), 33–49.

Crooks, P. (ed.). *CIRCLE: a calendar of Irish chancery letters* (http://chancery.tcd.ie).

Culleton, B., de Vál, S. and Culleton, E. 1994. *Treasures of the landscape: County Wexford's rural heritage*. Wexford.

Culleton, E. 1999. *Celtic and early Christian Wexford, AD400–1166*. Dublin.

Culleton, E. and Colfer, W. 1975. 'The Norman motte at Old Ross: method of construction'. *Journal of the Old Wexford Society*, 5 (1974–5), 22–5.

Cunningham, G. 1987. *The Anglo-Norman advance into the south-west midlands of Ireland, 1185–1221*. Roscrea.

Curtis, E. 1927. *Richard II in Ireland, 1394–5, and submissions of the Irish chiefs*. Oxford.

Dawes, M., Devine, M., Jones, H. and Post, M. 1974. 'Inquisitions post mortem, Richard II'. In *Calendar of Inquisitions post mortem, vol. 16: Richard II* (London). *Online* www.british-history.ac.uk/inquis-post-mortem/vol16 (accessed 3 April 2019).

Deevy, M. 1996. 'Ring brooches in medieval Ireland'. *Archaeology Ireland*, 10:2, 8–10.

Deevy, M. 1998. *Medieval ring brooches in Ireland: a study of jewellery, dress and society*. Bray.

Dehaene, G. 2009. 'Medieval rural settlement beside Duncormick motte, Co. Wexford'. In Corlett, C. and Potterton, M. (eds), *Rural settlement in medieval Ireland in the light of recent archaeological excavations*, 59–65. Bray.

Dolan, T. and Ó Muirithe, D. 1996. *The dialect of Forth and Bargy, Co. Wexford, Ireland*. Dublin.

Doran, L. 2012. 'New Ross: from European archetype to town "situated in the marches"'. In Ní Ghrádaigh, J. and Byrnes, E. (eds), *The march in the islands of the medieval west*, 79–96. Leiden and Boston.

Down, K. 1987. 'Colonial society and economy'. In Cosgrove, A. (ed.), *A new history of Ireland, vol. ii: medieval Ireland, 1169–1534*, 439–91. Oxford.

Downham, C. 2018. *Medieval Ireland*. Cambridge.

Doyle, I. 2016. '"Telling the dancer from the dance": the archaeology of early medieval Wexford'. In Doyle, I. and Browne, B. (eds), *Medieval Wexford: essays in memory of Billy Colfer*, 35–61. Dublin.

Dryburgh, P. and Smith, B. (eds). 2005. *Handbook and select calendar of sources for medieval Ireland in the National Archives of the United Kingdom*. Dublin and London.

Duffy, S. 2002. *Robert the Bruce's Irish wars: the invasions of Ireland, 1306–1329*. Stroud, Gloucestershire.

Eames, E. and Fanning, T. 1988. *Irish medieval tiles: decorated medieval paving tiles in Ireland with an inventory of sites and designs and a visual index*. Dublin.

Empey, A. 2017. 'The evolution of the demesne in the lordship of Leinster: the fortunes of war or forward planning?'. In Bradley, J., Ó Drisceoil, C. and Potterton, M. (eds), *William Marshal and Ireland*, 41–77. Dublin.

Eogan, J. and Kelly, B. 2016. 'New roads to medieval Wexford'. In Doyle, I. and Browne, B. (eds), *Medieval Wexford: essays in memory of Billy Colfer*, 211–40. Dublin.

Fegan, G. 2009. 'Discovery and excavation of a medieval moated site at Coolamurry, Co. Wexford'. In Corlett, C. and Potterton, M. (eds), *Rural settlement in medieval Ireland in the light of recent archaeological excavations*, 91–108. Bray.

FitzPatrick, E. and Ó Drisceoil, C. 2016. 'The landscape and law school settlement of the O'Doran brehons, Ballyorley, Co. Wexford'. In Doyle, I. and Browne, B. (eds), *Medieval Wexford: essays in memory of Billy Colfer*, 383–415. Dublin.

Flynn, J. and Grennan, T. 2016. 'What does the Kilmokea enclosure enclose?'. In Doyle, I. and Browne, B. (eds), *Medieval Wexford: essays in memory of Billy Colfer*, 62–72. Dublin.

Frame, R. 1995. 'Two kings in Leinster: the crown and the MicMhurchadha in the fourteenth century'. In Barry, T., Frame, R. and Simms, K. (eds), *Colony and frontier in medieval Ireland: essays presented to J.F. Lydon*, 155–75. London.

Furlong, N. 1968. 'The town that died'. *Journal of the Old Wexford Society*, 1, 35–42.

Gahan, S. 2018. 'Drone survey explores secrets of medieval Glascarrig village'. *Gorey Guardian*, 7 July.

Gardiner, M. and O'Conor, K. 2017. 'The later medieval countryside lying beneath'. In Stanley, M., Swan, R. and O'Sullivan, A. (eds), *Stories of Ireland's past: knowledge gained from NRA roads archaeology*, 133–52. Dublin.

Gilbert, J. (ed.). 1884. *Chartularies of St Mary's Abbey, Dublin, with the register of its house at Dunbrody, and Annals of Ireland*. 2 vols. London.

Glasscock, R. 1970. 'Moated sites, and deserted boroughs and villages: two neglected aspects of Anglo-Norman settlement in Ireland'. In Stephens, N. and Glasscock, R. (eds), *Irish geographical studies in honour of E. Estyn Evans*, 162–77. Belfast.

Glasscock, R. 1971. 'Rural settlement in Ireland'. In Beresford, M. and Hurst, J. (eds), *Deserted medieval villages: studies*, 279–301. London.

Graham, B. 1985. 'Anglo-Norman manorial settlement in Ireland: an assessment'. *Irish Geography*, 18, 4–15.

Griffith, M. (ed.). 1956. *Calendar of the justiciary rolls … Ireland, I to VII years of Edward II*. Dublin.

Gwynn, A. and Hadcock, R. 1970. *Medieval religious houses: Ireland*. Dublin.

Hadden, G. 1969. 'The origin and development of Wexford town, part 3: the Norman period'. *Journal of the Old Wexford Society*, 2, 3–12.

Hartland, B. 2018. 'The height of English power: 1250–1320'. In Smith, B. (ed.), *The Cambridge history of Ireland, vol. i: 600–1550*, 222–43. Cambridge.

Halpin, A. 1986. 'Irish medieval swords, c.1170–1600'. *Proceedings of the Royal Irish Academy*, 86C5, 183–230.

Hayden, A. 2000. 'Hook Lighthouse, Hook Head, Co. Wexford'. In Bennet, I. (ed.), *Excavations 1999: summary accounts of archaeological excavations in Ireland*, 303, no. 882. Bray.

Hodkinson, B. 2005. 'Thom Cor Castle: a 14th-century tower house in Limerick city'. *Journal of the Royal Society of Antiquaries of Ireland*, 135, 119–29.

Hore, P. 1900–11. *History of the town and county of Wexford*. 6 vols. London.

Hore, P. 1910. 'Ferns, County Wexford'. *Journal of the Royal Society of Antiquaries of Ireland*, 40, 297–315.

Hunt, J. 1974. *Irish medieval figure sculpture, 1200–1600: a study of Irish tombs with notes on costumes and armour*. 2 vols. Dublin.

Jones Hughes, T. 1970. '*Town* and *baile* in Irish place-names'. In Stephens, N. and Glasscock, R. (eds), *Irish geographical studies in honour of E. Estyn Evans*, 244–58. Belfast.

Jones, D. (trans.). 2011. *Friars' tales: thirteenth-century exempla from the British Isles*. Manchester.

Jordan, A. 1991. 'Date, chronology and evolution of the County Wexford tower houses'. *Journal of the Wexford Historical Society*, 13 (1990–1), 30–82.

Kavanagh, A. 2003. *The Kavanaghs: kings of Leinster*. Dublin and Wexford.

Kelly, M. 2004. *A history of the Black Death in Ireland*. Stroud, Gloucestershire.

Kiely, J. and Lyttleton, J. 2004. '56–60 Main Street South, Wexford'. In Bennet, I. (ed.), *Excavations 2002: summary accounts of archaeological excavations in Ireland*, 523, no. 1935. Bray.

Knight, J. 2007. 'Medieval imported building stone and utilised stone in Wales and Ireland'. In Manning, C. (ed.), *From ringforts to fortified houses: studies on castles and other monuments in honour of David Sweetman*, 143–54. Bray.

Leask, H. 1951. *Irish castles and castellated houses*. Dundalk.

Lydon, J. 1954. 'The hobelar: an Irish contribution to medieval warfare'. *The Sword*, 2:5, 12–16.

Lydon, J. 1963. 'Richard II's expeditions to Ireland'. *Journal of the Royal Society of Antiquaries of Ireland*, 93, 135–49.

Lydon, J. 1987a. 'A land of war'. In Cosgrove, A. (ed.), *A new history of Ireland, vol. ii: medieval Ireland, 1169–1534*, 240–74. Oxford.

Lydon, J. 1987b. 'The expansion and consolidation of the colony, 1215–54'. In Cosgrove, A. (ed.), *A new history of Ireland, vol. ii: medieval Ireland, 1169–1534*, 156–78. Oxford.

Lydon, J. 1987c. 'The impact of the Bruce Invasion, 1315–27'. In Cosgrove, A. (ed.), *A new history of Ireland, vol. ii: medieval Ireland, 1169–1534*, 275–302. Oxford.

Lydon, J. 1987d. 'The years of crisis, 1254–1315'. In Cosgrove, A. (ed.), *A new history of Ireland, vol. ii: medieval Ireland, 1169–1534*, 179–204. Oxford.

Lynch, A. 1990. 'Summary of archaeological excavations, 1982–1994'. In *Tintern Abbey County Wexford: Cistercians and Colcloughs eight centuries of occupation*, 16–19. Saltmills.

Lynch, A. 2010. *Tintern Abbey, Co. Wexford: Cistercians and Colcloughs, excavations, 1982–2007.* Dublin.

Lyons, M. 1981. 'An account for the manor of Old Ross, September 1284 to September 1285 (part i)'. *Decies: Old Waterford Society*, 18 (Sept.), 33–40.

Lyons, M. 1982. 'An account for the manor of Old Ross, September 1284 to September 1285 (part ii: textual appendix)'. *Decies: Old Waterford Society*, 19 (Jan.), 18–31.

Mac Niocaill, G. 1961. 'Documents on the suppression of the Templars in Ireland'. *Analecta Hibernica*, 24, 183–226.

Magahy, I. 2016. 'Rebuilding Bannow: mapping the abandoned town of Bannow'. In Doyle, I. and Browne, B. (eds), *Medieval Wexford: essays in memory of Billy Colfer*, 312–30. Dublin.

Marshall, S. and McMorran, T. 2016. 'People and places: a bird's-eye view of medieval Old Ross'. In Doyle, I. and Browne, B. (eds), *Medieval Wexford: essays in memory of Billy Colfer*, 241–61. Dublin.

McCormick, F. 2010. 'The faunal remains'. In Lynch, A., *Tintern Abbey, Co. Wexford: Cistercians and Colcloughs, excavations, 1982–2007*, 227–31. Dublin.

McCutcheon, C. 2009. 'The pottery'. In Fegan, G. 2009. 'Discovery and excavation of a medieval moated site at Coolamurry, Co. Wexford'. In Corlett, C. and Potterton, M. (eds), *Rural settlement in medieval Ireland in the light of recent archaeological excavations*, 91–108. Bray.

McCutcheon, C. with Papazian, C. 2010. 'The medieval pottery'. In Lynch, A., *Tintern Abbey, Co. Wexford: Cistercians and Colcloughs, excavations, 1982–2007*, 148–58. Dublin.

McCutcheon, S. 1998. 'New Ross Main Drainage Scheme, New Ross, Wexford'. In Bennet, I. (ed.), *Excavations 1997: summary accounts of archaeological excavations in Ireland*, 193, no. 601. Bray.

McEneaney, E. 1979. 'Waterford and New Ross trade competition, *c*.1300'. *Decies: Old Waterford Society*, 12 (Sept.), 16–24.

McGettigan, D. 2016. *Richard II and the Irish kings*. Dublin.

McLoughlin, C. (forthcoming). 'Medieval Wexford: the evidence from archaeological excavations'. In Potterton, M. and Corlett, C. (eds), *Towns in medieval Ireland in the light of recent archaeological excavations*. Dublin.

McLoughlin, C. and Stafford, E. 2016. 'Excavation of the remains of an early thirteenth-century house at the Thomas Moore Tavern, Cornmarket, Wexford'. In Doyle, I. and Browne, B. (eds), *Medieval Wexford: essays in memory of Billy Colfer*, 342–64. Dublin.

McNamee, C. 1997. *The wars of the Bruces: Scotland, England and Ireland, 1306–1328*. East Linton, Scotland.

Meirtneach, M. 1978. 'Art Mac Murchadha Caomhánach (1357 go 1417)'. *The Past*, 12, 33–8.

Mills, J. 1892. 'Accounts of the earl of Norfolk's estates in Ireland, 1279–1294'. *Journal of the Royal Society of Antiquaries of Ireland*, 22, 50–62.

Mills, J. (ed.). 1914. *Calendar of the justiciary rolls … Ireland, Edward I, part ii: xxxiii to xxxv years*. London.

Moore, M. (comp.). 1996. *Archaeological inventory of County Wexford*. Dublin.

Moran, J. 2007. 'Windmill Lane, New Ross, Wexford'. In Bennet, I. (ed.), *Excavations 2004: summary accounts of archaeological excavations in Ireland*, 470, no. 1820. Bray.

Morris, M. 2005. *The Bigod earls of Norfolk in the thirteenth century*. Gateshead.

Moss, R. 2010. 'Stone with diaper ornament'. In Lynch, A., *Tintern Abbey, Co. Wexford: Cistercians and Colcloughs, excavations, 1982–2007*, 127–8. Dublin.

Mullins, C. 2003. 'Rathaspick, Co. Wexford: possible medieval settlement adjacent to church site'. In Bennet, I. (ed.), *Excavations 2001: summary accounts of archaeological excavations in Ireland*, 405–6, no. 1315. Bray.

Murphy, M. 2007. 'The profits of lordship: Roger Bigod, earl of Norfolk, and the lordship of Carlow, 1270–1306'. In Doran, L. and Lyttleton, J. (eds), *Lordship in medieval Ireland: image and reality*, 75–98. Dublin.

Murphy, M. 2009. 'Agriculture and rural settlement in medieval Wexford: revisiting the documentary sources'. *Group for the Study of Irish Historic Settlement: newsletter*, 13 (2008), 1–6.

Murphy, M. 2015. 'Manor centres, settlement and agricultural systems in medieval Ireland, 1250–1350'. In Murphy, M. and Stout, M. (eds), *Agriculture and settlement in Ireland*, 69–100. Dublin.

Murphy, M. 2016. 'From swords to ploughshares: evidence for Templar agriculture in medieval Ireland'. In Browne, M. and Ó Clabaigh, C. (eds), *Soldiers of Christ: the Knights Hospitaller and the Knights Templar in medieval Ireland*, 167–83. Dublin.

Murphy, M. and Potterton, M. 2010. *The Dublin region in the Middle Ages: settlement, land-use and economy*. Dublin.

Murphy, P. 2016. 'Medieval rabbit farming and Bannow Island'. In Doyle, I. and Browne, B. (eds), *Medieval Wexford: essays in memory of Billy Colfer*, 292–311. Dublin.

Murtagh, B. 2016. 'The medieval Tower of Hook: a review of its dating and history'. In Doyle, I. and Browne, B. (eds), *Medieval Wexford: essays in memory of Billy Colfer*, 124–80. Dublin.

Ní Dhonnchadha, M. 2002. 'Inis Teimle, between Uí Chennselaig and the Déissi'. *Peritia: Journal of the Medieval Academy of Ireland*, 16, 451–8.

Nicholls, K. 1982. 'Anglo-French Ireland and after'. *Peritia: Journal of the Medieval Academy of Ireland*, 1, 370–403.

Nicholson, H. 2016. 'A long way from Jerusalem: the Templars and Hospitallers in Ireland, c.1172–1348'. In Browne, M. and Ó Clabaigh, C. (eds), *Soldiers of Christ: the Knights Hospitaller and the Knights Templar in medieval Ireland*, 1–22. Dublin.

Noonan, D. 2007. 'North Quay, New Ross, Wexford'. In Bennet, I. (ed.), *Excavations 2003: summary accounts of archaeological excavations in Ireland*, 533, no. 2025. Bray.

Ó Drisceoil, C. 2017. '*Pons Novus, villa Willielmi Marescalli*: New Ross, a town of William Marshal'. In Bradley, J., Ó Drisceoil, C. and Potterton, M. (eds), *William Marshal and Ireland*, 268–314. Dublin.

Ó Súilleabháin, M., Downey, L. and Downey, D. 2017. *Antiquities of rural Ireland*. Dublin.

O'Brien, K. 2015. 'A third Romanesque font from County Wexford'. *Archaeology Ireland*, 29:2, 41–2.

O'Byrne, E. 2003. *War, politics and the Irish of Leinster, 1156–1606*. Dublin.

O'Byrne, E. 2007. 'The MacMurroughs and the marches of Leinster'. In Doran, L. and Lyttleton, J. (eds), *Lordship in medieval Ireland: image and reality, 1170–1340*, 160–92. Dublin.

O'Conor, K. 1998. *The archaeology of medieval rural settlement in Ireland*. Dublin.

O'Doherty, R. 1982. 'Tomb fragments at Rosbercon'. *Old Kilkenny Review*, 2:4, 380.

O'Donnabhain, B. 2010. 'The human remains'. In Lynch, A., *Tintern Abbey, Co. Wexford: Cistercians and Colcloughs, excavations, 1982–2007*, 105–25. Dublin.

O'Donovan, J. (ed.). 1848–51. *Annals of the kingdom of Ireland by the Four Masters*. 7 vols. Dublin.

O'Keeffe, T. 1985. 'The castle of Tullow, Co. Kildare'. *Journal of the County Kildare Archaeological Society*, 16:5, 528–9.

O'Keeffe, T. 1997. *Barryscourt Castle and the Irish tower house*. Kinsale.

O'Keeffe, T. 2000. *Medieval Ireland: an archaeology*. Stroud, Gloucestershire.

O'Keeffe, T. 2015. *Medieval Irish buildings, 1100–1600*. Dublin.

O'Keeffe, T. and Carey Bates, R. 2016. 'The abbey and cathedral of Ferns, 1111–1253'. In Doyle, I. and Browne, B. (eds), *Medieval Wexford: essays in memory of Billy Colfer*, 73–96. Dublin.

O'Keeffe, T. and Coughlan, M. 2003. 'The chronology and formal affinities of the Ferns donjon, Co. Wexford'. In Kenyon, J. and O'Conor, K. (eds), *The medieval castle in Ireland and Wales: essays in honour of Jeremy Knight*, 133–48. Dublin.

O'Sullivan, M. 1962. *Italian merchant bankers in Ireland in the thirteenth century*. Dublin.

Oksanen, E. 2012. *Flanders and the Anglo-Norman world, 1066–1216*. Cambridge.

Orpen, G. 1968. *Ireland under the Normans*. 4 vols. Reprint. Oxford.

Otway-Ruthven, A. 1968. *A history of medieval Ireland*. London.

Phillips, J. 1972. *Aymer de Valence, earl of Pembroke, 1307–1324: baronial politics in the reign of Edward II*. Oxford.

Potterton, M. 2005. *Medieval Trim: history and archaeology*. Dublin.

Roche, R. 1987. 'Forth and Bargy: a place apart'. In Whelan, K. and Nolan, W. (eds), *Wexford, history and society: interdisciplinary essays on the history of an Irish county*, 102–21. Dublin.

Schweitzer, H. 2009. 'A medieval farmstead at Moneycross Upper, Co. Wexford'. In Corlett, C. and Potterton, M. (eds), *Rural settlement in medieval Ireland in the light of recent archaeological excavations*, 175–88. Bray.

Scott, A. and Martin, F. (eds). 1978. *Expugnatio Hibernica by Giraldus Cambrensis*. Dublin.

Seymour, St John D. 1929. *Anglo-Irish literature, 1200–1582*. Cambridge.

Shanahan, B. and O'Conor, K. (forthcoming). 'Rindown, Co. Roscommon: recent investigations of the medieval town'. In Corlett, C. and Potterton, M. (eds), *Towns in medieval Ireland in the light of recent archaeological excavations*. Dublin.

Sharp, J. and Stamp, A. 1908. 'Inquisitions post mortem, Edward II'. In *Calendar of Inquisitions post mortem, vol. 5: Edward II* (London). *Online* www.british-history.ac.uk/inquis-post-mortem/vol5 (accessed 23 March 2019).

Sharp, J. and Stamp, A. 1910. 'Inquisitions post mortem, Edward II'. In *Calendar of Inquisitions post mortem, vol. 6: Edward II* (London). *Online* www.british-history.ac.uk/inquis-post-mortem/vol6 (accessed 21 March 2019).

Sharp, J. and Stamp, A. 1912. 'Inquisitions post mortem, Edward I'. In *Calendar of Inquisitions post mortem, vol. 3: Edward I* (London). *Online* www.british-history.ac.uk/inquis-post-mortem/vol3 (accessed 3 April 2019).

Sharp, J. and Stamp, A. 1913. 'Inquisitions post mortem, Edward I'. In *Calendar of Inquisitions post mortem, vol. 4: Edward I* (London). *Online* www.british-history.ac.uk/inquis-post-mortem/vol4 (accessed 3 April 2019).

Shields, H. 1976. 'The walling of New Ross: a thirteenth-century poem in French'. *Longroom: Bulletin of the Friend of the Library, Trinity College Dublin*, 12 & 13 (autumn 1975–spring 1976), 24–33.

Shine, L. 2018. 'Reconstructing Rosbercon: from modern suburb to medieval settlement'. In Bevivino, M., Bhreathnach, E. and Shine, L. (eds), *Discovery Programme Reports, 9: a research miscellany*, 147–59. Dublin.

Smith, B. 2018. 'Disaster and opportunity: 1320–1450'. In Smith, B. (ed.), *The Cambridge history of Ireland, vol. i: 600–1550*, 244–71. Cambridge.

Stafford, E. (forthcoming). 'A feast or famine: medieval New Ross in the light of recent investigations'. In Corlett, C. and Potterton, M. (eds), *Towns in medieval Ireland in the light of recent archaeological excavations*. Dublin.

Stalley, R. 1971. *Architecture and sculpture in Ireland, 1150–1350*. Dublin.

Stalley, R. 1987. *The Cistercian monasteries of Ireland*. London and New Haven, CT.

Stalley, R. 1997. 'Sculptured stone'. In Hurley, M. and Scully, O. with McCutcheon, S. (eds), *Late Viking Age and medieval Waterford: excavations, 1986–1992*, 400–3. Waterford.

Stout, G. 2016. 'The abbey of the port of St Maria, Dunbrody, Co. Wexford: an architectural study'. In Doyle, I. and Browne, B. (eds), *Medieval Wexford: essays in memory of Billy Colfer*, 97–123. Dublin.

Sweetman, D. 1979. 'Archaeological excavations at Ferns Castle, County Wexford'. *Proceedings of the Royal Irish Academy*, 79C10, 217–45.

Sweetman, D. 1999. *Medieval castles of Ireland*. Cork.

Sweetman, D. 2000. *The origin and development of the tower house in Ireland*. Kinsale.

Sweetman, H. (ed.). 1875–86. *Calendar of documents relating to Ireland, 1171–1307*. 5 vols. London.

Thomas, A. 1986. 'Financing town walls in medieval Ireland'. In Thomas, C. (ed.), *Rural landscapes and communities: essays presented to Desmond McCourt*, 65–91. Dublin.

Thomas, A. 1992. *The walled towns of Ireland*. 2 vols. Dublin.

Tierney, M. 2009. 'Excavating feudalism? A medieval moated site at Carrowreagh, Co. Wexford'. In Corlett, C. and Potterton, M. (eds), *Rural settlement in medieval Ireland in the light of recent archaeological excavations*, 189–200. Bray.

Toy, S. 1939. *Castles: their construction and history*. London.

Waterman, D. 1970. 'Somersetshire and other foreign building stone in medieval Ireland, c.1175–1400'. *Ulster Journal of Archaeology*, 3rd ser., 33, 63–75.

Whelan, K. 2018. *Religion, landscape and settlement in Ireland, from Patrick to present*. Dublin.

White, N. 1943. *Extents of Irish monastic possessions, 1540–1541, from manuscripts in the Public Record Office, London*. Dublin.

Wren, J. 2010. 'Roof tiles'. In Lynch, A., *Tintern Abbey, Co. Wexford: Cistercians and Colcloughs, excavations, 1982–2007*, 138–44. Dublin.

CHAPTER THREE

Town and county: the archaeology of medieval Wexford

EMMET STAFFORD

INTRODUCTION

The life experiences of the twelfth- and thirteenth-century population of Wexford town and county can be investigated by examining those medieval sites and artefacts that are still scattered across the modern landscape. Such an examination can give us an appreciation for the development of domestic and political life in Ireland in the early years following the arrival of the Anglo-Normans in 1169.

By investigating the past through an analysis of physical remains, archaeology gives us the opportunity to check the veracity of historical accounts and to counter modern cultural assumptions, some of which are based on the opinions of early historians influenced by the writings of medieval chroniclers such as Giraldus Cambrensis (Gerald of Wales) – a first-generation Anglo-Norman who visited Ireland in the late twelfth century.

To understand medieval society, its myriad remains must be broken down into manageable sections. Elements of the past that have left a visible trace in the archaeological record of Co. Wexford include rural and urban settlement, trade, religion and agriculture, each of which is discussed below.

RURAL SETTLEMENT

Rural settlement before the arrival of the Anglo-Normans is typically considered to focus on the ringforts or raths which are still a common feature of the Irish countryside (Figure 3.1). Ringforts, which are enclosed or defended farmsteads of the early medieval period, are one of the most common archaeological monuments in the Irish countryside and upwards of forty-five thousand have been identified on the island of Ireland (Ó Súilleabháin et al. 2017, 125). The archaeological inventory for Co. Wexford records six hundred known ringforts (Moore 1996, 28) and it can be assumed that more were once in use throughout the county.

Although ringforts are often perceived as the quintessential native Irish settlement, an insular response to the cultural practice of cattle raiding, their construction actually

3.1 The surviving ringfort at Grange Lower, north Co. Wexford

reached its peak before the late tenth century and seems to have been on the wane well before the arrival of the Anglo-Normans (Stout 1997, 29). Oak timbers recovered from one of the few dated ringforts in Co. Wexford, at Robinstown Great/Templenacroha, were cut down in the mid-eighth century (Moore 1996, 42 (no. 379)). The reasons for the shift away from ringfort settlement toward a less enclosed form of settlement are not entirely clear but may indicate a more peaceful or centrally controlled society with a decrease in violent raids across territorial boundaries. This may be reflective of a more effective control of territory by powerful kings such as Diarmait Mac Murchada, leader of the Uí Chennselaig territory which roughly equates to modern Co. Wexford, in the immediate pre-Anglo-Norman period (Colfer 2002, 1). The decline in ringfort construction may also be indicative of a shift in importance away from pastoral agriculture concentrated on the rearing of cattle and toward cereal production in the centuries prior to the arrival of the Anglo-Normans (Monk 2015).

Landscape analysis in Co. Wexford indicates that ringforts were far from a 'one-size-fits-all' monument. As was the case at Grange Lower near Rathnure (Figure 3.1), most were univallate, meaning that the domestic farmyard at the centre of the site was enclosed by just one bank of earth and a defensive ditch. Other more socially significant sites such as that investigated at Tomona, near Kiltealy, and the surviving monument at Bolinrush, near Bunclody, were surrounded by two and even three banks of earth (Moore 1996, 33 (no. 284), 43 (no. 387)). These bivallate and trivallate ringforts were not necessarily larger than their single-ditched neighbours; the trivallate ringfort at Bolinrush has an internal diameter of just 24m. Nor could they be

3.2 Shrouded in trees, the 9m-high motte at Salville/Motabeg outside Enniscorthy is almost invisible in the landscape

interpreted as being more defensive. Rather, the single, double and triple ditches surrounding the ringforts appear to have indicated the social class of the residents, with a multivallate site such as Bolinrush perhaps being occupied by a local lord known as the *Aire Forgaill* (Stout 1997, 111–13). Irrespective of social class, daily life within ringforts revolved around agricultural production. Although cattle rearing was a central part of the Irish economy, other agricultural activities such as cereal drying have been recorded in the vicinity of ringfort sites such as Raheenagurren West in Wexford (Doyle 2016, 38).

After the arrival of the Anglo-Normans, ringforts were joined in the Irish countryside by defensive features such as ringworks, like Carrick itself, as well as mottes and their associated baileys. Although those mottes seem like simple earthen mounds today, nothing like them preceded the late twelfth century in Ireland and their appearance was an indication of a changing political reality. The motte castle was not unique to Ireland and was such a common symbol of Norman conquest that the construction of a motte is included in the Bayeux Tapestry depiction of William the Conqueror's preparations for the Battle of Hastings. Surrounded by a palisade, and topped by a wooden or stone tower, mottes were an imposing statement in the landscape and it is no coincidence that they were often built adjacent to the monasteries that were among the few nucleated settlements in the twelfth-century Irish countryside.

Motte castles have been recorded at various sites in Co. Wexford including at Salville/Motabeg where the 9m-high mound is situated on a high point overlooking the River Slaney, suggesting that the motte had an important role in controlling the navigable waterway of the river (Figure 3.2). At Old Ross archaeological investigations around the 9m-high motte have traced the development of the site from a defensive mound to a fully developed medieval town complete with a stone castle (Marshall and McMorran 2016, esp. 257–61)(Figure 2.32).

The motte-and-baileys of the twelfth-century conquest are not the direct equivalent of the pre-Anglo-Norman ringfort. The function of the defended farmstead was directly replaced by moated sites. Like ringforts, moated sites tend to be situated in areas of good-quality farmland and consist of a deep ditch or moat surrounding an earthen bank with a substantial gated entrance. Unlike ringforts, moated sites tend to be square or rectangular in plan and were generally, although not exclusively, occupied in the thirteenth and fourteenth centuries by Ireland's new Anglo-Norman colonists (Ó Súilleabháin et al. 2017, 157; O'Conor 1998, 87). Thanks to Anglo-Norman record keeping, much is known about these structures and their residents. The construction of a new moated site at Ballyconnor in Wexford is recorded in the Bigod manorial accounts of 1283–4. The detailed account of that seven-hundred-year-old project includes the wages paid to the carpenters who constructed the farmyard's fence and gate. At that time, a day's wages for a carpenter was just four pennies (Hore 1900–11, vol. i, 28). Historical analysis by the late Billy Colfer suggested that the Ballyconnor moated site is the same monument as the large moated site in modern Mylerspark near New Ross (Colfer 2002, 94).

Archaeological investigations at various moated sites have revealed physical evidence of similar defences as those recorded in the Bigod accounts. At Coolamurry in Co. Wexford excavations in advance of road construction revealed a defensive ditch 4–5m wide surrounding an enclosed area divided in half to separate agricultural from domestic activities (Eogan and Kelly 2016, 215)(Figure 2.1). Excavations at the same site, in central Co. Wexford at the frontier between Anglo-Norman and Irish territory, revealed the defensive nature of the site's architecture where the remains of a timber drawbridge were likely to have been complemented by a wooden gate tower at the site's entrance. Radiocarbon dating one of the beams used to support the access bridge suggested that it was constructed in the late thirteenth or early fourteenth century (ibid., 216).

The moated site was generally the centre of a medieval landholding occupied and farmed by a substantial peasant or minor Anglo-Norman knight (O'Conor 1998, 61).

3.3 Pottery and metallurgical waste recovered from the vicinity of the ringfort at Harristown, south Co. Wexford

Archaeological excavations have shown that in some locations moated-site builders deliberately chose to occupy the site of an earlier ringfort, thus providing a continuity of settlement pattern in the rural landscape after 1169. Although no excavations have yet shown this to be the case in Co. Wexford, the excavation of a site at Baunogephlure in neighbouring Co. Carlow uncovered a substantial trivallate ringfort that was re-ordered by the construction of a large moated site in the late twelfth or thirteenth century (Stafford and McLoughlin 2011, 294–5).

Although not re-modelled as moated sites, limited investigations in Co. Wexford have shown that at least two ringforts, at Kinnagh and at Harristown in the south of the county, were not abandoned in the late twelfth century and were the sites of domestic and agricultural activity into the thirteenth and fourteenth centuries (McLoughlin 2004; 2015). Pottery recovered from within the ringfort at Kinnagh and in the immediate vicinity of the ringfort at Harristown was similar to the Leinster Cooking Ware recovered during medieval excavations in Wexford town (McLoughlin and Stafford 2016, 354, 362; Figure 3.3). Small quantities of furnace waste recovered from the investigation of the Harristown site suggested that industrial activities such as metalworking were also taking place there during the medieval period.

URBAN SETTLEMENT

In common with the continuing use of certain rural settlement sites into the thirteenth century, urban settlement patterns in Wexford display a continuation and gradual development rather than a complete shift after 1169.

In May 1169, Robert Fitz Stephen landed, with about five hundred foreign soldiers, at Bannow Bay on the south coast of Wexford (see ch. 1). Soon after landing, Fitz Stephen, together with the local forces of Diarmait Mac Murchada, are recorded as marching directly to the town of Wexford, suggesting that both parties considered the town to be of economic and strategic significance (Orpen 1968, vol. i, 150).

In 1169, Wexford was a Hiberno-Norse town occupied by the descendants of the raiding Vikings who had plundered the monasteries and settlements of ninth-century Ireland before settling as sea-faring traders in the port towns they established at Wexford, Waterford, Dublin, Limerick and Cork (Colfer 2008, 30). Archaeological investigations, as well as the writings of the twelfth-century chronicler Giraldus Cambrensis, suggest that Wexford was a small D-shaped settlement measuring perhaps 400–600m along the waterfront of Wexford Harbour. Surrounded by a defensive bank and ditch, and perhaps a timber palisade, the town was substantial enough to withstand an initial assault by Mac Murchada and Fitz Stephen before the townspeople agreed to the mediated surrender described by Giraldus. After the surrender, Wexford was granted by Mac Murchada to Fitz Stephen and his brother Maurice Fitz Gerald making Wexford the very first Anglo-Norman town in Ireland (Scott and Martin 1978, 33–5).

Following the initial Anglo-Norman take-over there is no direct evidence that Fitz Stephen displaced the existing residents of Wexford town. The archaeological evidence from Wexford suggests that property boundaries remained constant in the southern end of the town from the late twelfth through to the fourteenth century (Bourke 1995, 33–6). Rather than evicting the existing Hiberno-Norse residents, Giraldus records that the townspeople submitted to Mac Murchada and that he accepted four hostages from them as assurance of their fidelity.

With the original residents still in place, however, Fitz Stephen was understandably cautious of his new holding and Giraldus records that in late 1169 and early 1170 he 'built a fortress on a steep crag, about two miles from Wexford, called Carrick in the vernacular' (Scott and Martin 1978, 53; ch. 4, below). Fitz Stephen's ringwork at Carrick is the earliest named and dated Anglo-Norman fortification in Ireland and it still stands in the Irish National Heritage Park (INHP; see ch. 4, below, for a complete

3.4 (*above*) The 1.4m-wide town wall uncovered at Clifford Street, Wexford town, in 2018 (photograph courtesy of Catherine McLoughlin)

3.5 (*left*) The surviving town gate adjacent to Selskar Abbey, Wexford town

history). Together with Enniscorthy and Dunanore, the Carrick ringwork is one of a series of three early Anglo-Norman fortifications on the transport network provided by the River Slaney.

Life in Wexford town did of course change after 1169, but the change does not seem to have been immediate. The existing town defences evolved from a simple earthen bank and ditch to a more effective stone wall, substantial elements of which survive. Recent archaeological investigations in the southern part of the town have shown the thirteenth-century wall to be as much as 1.4m wide at the base and constructed of lime-mortared locally quarried stone (Catherine McLoughlin, pers. comm.; see Figure 3.4). Eventually Wexford's urban area was extended when the northern part of the town was walled at some point in the late twelfth or early thirteenth century. Portions of that wall stand to a height of 6m, making it a substantial defensive feature (Moore 1996, 162 (no. 1478)).

In addition to their defensive role, medieval town walls in Ireland functioned as indicators of economic and cultural status, with the burgesses or townspeople living inside the walls enjoying greater rights than the rural dwellers living outside. The development of town walls was financed through taxes and tolls which were paid by residents, consumers and traders who moved through defended gates from the

3.6 A domestic hearth uncovered at 84 and 86 South Main Street, Wexford town

agricultural hinterland into the medieval town. By at least 1331, and presumably earlier, murage taxes were being collected for the maintenance of Wexford's town wall and its five gates (Hore 1900–11, vol. v, 107). Although the approximate location of Wexford's town gates is known, none has been archaeologically investigated. Only one gate tower, a private entrance once associated with Selskar Abbey, still stands (Figure 3.5).

Although Giraldus refers to suburbs outside the walled town existing in 1169, no archaeological evidence for such extra-mural settlement has yet been found in Wexford. Inside the town walls, however, pre-Anglo-Norman settlement has been identified at two South Main Street sites in what appears to be the core of the Hiberno-Norse town. Most interestingly the continuity of settlement suggested by Giraldus is supported by the limited archaeological evidence, which indicates that the house types constructed inside the urban area remained quite consistent before and after the Anglo-Norman arrival in 1169.

At the junction of South Main Street and Bride Street archaeological excavations by Ed Bourke revealed that, from the eleventh century, house types were of a modest size and constructed of the same post-and-wattle materials, and to a similar plan, as those in Hiberno-Norse Dublin (Bourke 1988). The same excavations revealed a very similar form of construction being used in the thirteenth and fourteenth centuries. Excavations by the author at 84 and 86 South Main Street and in the Cornmarket area of Wexford town also show a consistency in domestic construction between the mid-twelfth and later thirteenth centuries (McLoughlin and Stafford 2010; 2016; Figure 3.6).

The post-and-wattle house uncovered in the Cornmarket was rectangular in plan, approximately 5.4m wide by at least 6m long (McLoughlin and Stafford 2016, 344).

The house had a simple internal layout where an open fire was located in the middle of a central aisle which ran the length of the house from the front door to the back. On either side of the aisle, low timber structures provided seating and working space during the day and sleeping space at night. Despite the architectural simplicity of these spaces, the artefacts recovered during the excavation of the site indicated a rich material culture that included wooden barrels, fragments of chainmail and, like the developed ringfort sites of rural Wexford, substantial quantities of locally produced pottery. Evidence of international contact in the form of pottery imported from England, France and the Low Countries was also discovered (ibid., 354).

Post-and-wattle structures with a simple internal layout reminiscent of Norse Dublin may not be the only houses occupied in Anglo-Norman Wexford, but they are the only ones so far uncovered that were built before the mid-thirteenth century, a hundred years after the Anglo-Norman conquest of the town. Archaeological investigations at North Main Street have uncovered a more substantial stone house, built at that time on land reclaimed from the sea (Sheehan 2002).

The continuity of construction techniques and property boundaries in post-1169 Wexford indicates the survival of a settled population after the arrival of the Anglo-Normans. That survival is mirrored by a continuity of dedication in the pre-Anglo-Norman parishes of SS Iberius, Mary, Patrick and Doologue into the later medieval period (Colfer 2008, 33). In the late twelfth and early thirteenth centuries new people were moving to Wexford and the town was expanding but the resident population of the town appears to have remained at least partially, if not largely, in place. A document dating to 1283 supports this evidence by recording the survival of a Hiberno-Norse population in the county after the Anglo-Norman conquest: 'in the time of the Marshals [the early thirteenth century] there were within the county of Wexford five score foreign oustmen, very rich, having many beasts'. By 1283, however, cultural change had overtaken this remnant population, leaving 'not more than forty oustmen … having a little property' (Hore 1900–11, vol. v, 93).

TRADE

When Mac Murchada and Fitz Stephen assaulted Wexford in 1169 they were seeking to control a place not just of strategic value but one which had an established value as an international trading port. The Hiberno-Norse town of Wexford was part of a late Viking Age trading network that stretched westward to Iceland, Greenland and North America and eastward to continental Europe, Istanbul and the Far East. Giraldus records that when Fitz Stephen and his men attacked Wexford they burned any ships they found in the harbour. The international nature of Wexford's contacts is specifically mentioned as one of those ships had 'come from Britain to trade and was laden with wheat and wine' (Scott and Martin 1978, 35).

Although international trade was not a new concept to Ireland, the new association with Anglo-Norman Britain intensified trade between the two islands after 1169. Economic profiteering was after all the main motivation of the Anglo-Norman colonists. Archaeological excavations throughout Wexford town have shown that during the thirteenth and fourteenth centuries 30 to 40 per cent of the pottery in use in the town was imported into Ireland (McLoughlin and Stafford 2016, 355). Most of these imported pots, represented in excavation by fragments of broken vessels, either came directly from south-western Britain or were associated with the French wine trade from Bordeaux. Other pottery recovered from excavations in the medieval town was imported from Normandy, Utrecht and Flanders (ibid., 354).

After the arrival of the Anglo-Normans the big change in Co. Wexford's urban settlement pattern was not what the houses or lifestyles looked like but how numerous the towns became. In 1169, the main towns in Ireland could be counted on one hand; Dublin, Wexford, Waterford, Cork and Limerick, all of which had been founded by the Hiberno-Norse descendants of Viking raiders.

By the early fourteenth century, however, Co. Wexford alone had more recorded towns than all of pre-Anglo-Norman Ireland (ch. 2). Diarmait Mac Murchada's settlement at Ferns, where his 'stone house' had been destroyed by his enemies in 1166, continued to develop from its proto-urban roots (Stout 2017, 262). Other urban sites, mostly located along the riverine and coastal trading networks, included the Anglo-Norman town of Enniscorthy, the new town of Carrick, which developed around Robert Fitz Stephen's ringwork (ch. 4), the enlarged Hiberno-Norse town of Wexford, the new foundations of Old Ross, Taghmon, Clonmines, Bannow and Greatisland as well as the great port of New Ross (Colfer 2002, 131–82).

New Ross, the largest walled town in Ireland, at thirty-nine hectares, was far larger than even the expanded town of Wexford, which reached a maximum walled extent of twenty-five hectares – as such the town deserves special mention here. A poem written in medieval French dated to 1265 records the walling of the town by the townspeople who were concerned for their collective security (Seymour 1929, 23–8). Portions of the medieval town wall survive, and its circuit can be traced in the street pattern of the modern town, which is located on the eastern bank of the River Barrow. New Ross was a planned town founded in the early thirteenth century by Diarmait Mac Murchada's granddaughter Isabella de Clare and her husband William Marshal, earl of Pembroke and lord of Leinster, as a port for their Irish estates (Thomas 1992, vol. ii, 175–9). The town has an exceptionally large medieval parish church dedicated to St Mary and experienced rapid growth in its first century of existence. For a period in the late thirteenth century New Ross appears to have been the most prolific trading port in Ireland. The state tax records for the export of wool, skins and leather certainly support this interpretation (Colfer 2002, 180). Archaeological investigations within the town have revealed the same variety of traded goods as uncovered in Wexford but the early promise of the town does not seem to have been fulfilled by continued growth. Although excavations along the waterfront and in the northern core of the town have revealed extensive archaeological deposits, large areas toward the south-eastern limit of New Ross have proven to be relatively archaeologically sterile, almost as if the extensive town wall was built to accommodate a growth that was stifled by economic and cultural pressures in the fourteenth century (Stafford forthcoming). By 1349, after the arrival of the Black Death, New Ross appears to have been approaching total ruin with a contemporary account claiming that 'the community … are in such an unaccustomed state of misery, poverty and helplessness … that a great part of the men … are ready to leave and fly to foreign parts' (Hore 1900–11, vol. i, 190).

RELIGION

All of the new and expanded towns and settlements came complete with their own churches and parishes, often dedicated to the favoured saints of the Anglo-Norman settlers, such as Anne, Catherine, James and Nicholas. Many of these church sites are still visible long after the settlements they once served have been lost to war, famine and economic collapse. At Bannow, the site of the first Anglo-Norman landing in 1169, a parish church dedicated to St Mary was built by the year 1200. That church still stands long after the town it once served was reduced to a series of parched cropmarks only visible in a grass field after the long hot summer of 2018 (Figure 3.7).

The medieval churches that continue to dot the Irish countryside have led to the understanding that the Anglo-Normans introduced the parish system to Ireland. Certainly, the alleged anarchy and antiquity of pre-Anglo-Norman Christianity in Ireland was one of Henry II's defences of his conquest of the island, and in this he was supported by an 1155 Papal Bull of Adrian IV (Ó Corráin 2017, 98). Although the authenticity of *Laudabiliter* has been debated, it appears to have given Henry papal support to invade Ireland in order to impose a continental European church system (ibid., 100).

In reality, however, Ireland's post-1169 parish network appears to have been a progression, rather than a wholly new introduction, of a developing insular system that had been the subject of debate at Irish church synods from at least 1111 when the matter was discussed at Ráth Breasail near Cashel. In 1152, at the Synod of Kells, the Irish diocesan system was at least nominally ratified into a system of thirty-six sees with four archbishoprics at Armagh, Dublin, Cashel and Tuam (Ó Corráin 2017, 96).

Archaeological evidence for the development of pre-existing ecclesiastical sites in Wexford can be seen in churches such as St Dubhain's at Hook Head and at Mayglass, where evidence of Hiberno-Romanesque architecture can be seen amid the later medieval fabric (Figure 3.8). Aerial photography has also shown that several medieval

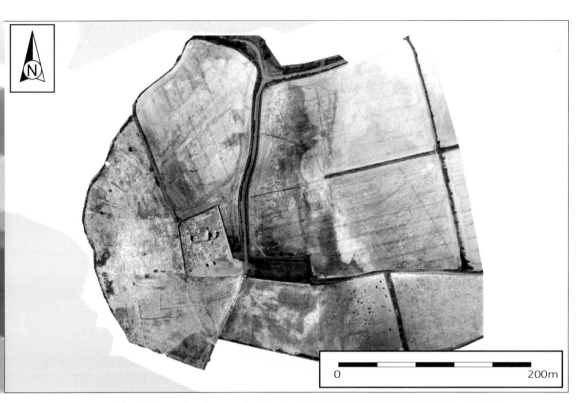

0   200m

3.7 (*above*) The medieval town of Bannow visible as parch marks in the grass during the dry summer of 2018 (photograph courtesy of Simon Dowling)

3.8 (*right*) The Hiberno-Romanesque doorway in the southern wall of Mayglass parish church

parish churches, such as those at Grange in Kilmore and Killegney near Clonroche, are centred on large ecclesiastical enclosures typical of early medieval church sites in Ireland (Moore 1996, 128 (no. 1243), 130 (no. 1256)).

Similar changes were occurring in the pre-Anglo-Norman monastic system, where innovators like Malachy of Armagh and Diarmait Mac Murchada were bringing the continental orders to monastic sites like Mellifont, Baltinglass and Ferns from the 1140s (Stout 2017, 248). In Ferns the Augustinian abbey established by Mac Murchada can still be seen immediately to the south of the thirteenth-century cathedral established by John St John, the first Anglo-Norman bishop of the diocese (Hore 1900–11, vol. vi, 185). As was the case with the explosion of urban settlement in Wexford after the arrival of the Anglo-Normans, the building of large monastic houses, often centred on vast estates bequeathed by lords such as William Marshal to the Cistercian order, became more commonplace in the late twelfth and thirteenth centuries. In Wexford alone, the houses of Tintern de Voto and Dunbrody are a visible reminder of the wealth and prestige of these religious foundations.

AGRICULTURE

Ireland is an agricultural nation; it was not until the 1960s that census returns showed more of the Irish population living in urban settlements than in the countryside (Redmond 2000, 16). As economic profiteers, it was the produce of the countryside that the Anglo-Normans sought in Ireland. In the twelfth and thirteenth centuries the population of Europe was growing strongly, and that population needed to be clothed and fed from the farmland controlled by a developing system of feudal lordship and international trade (Stout and Murphy 2015, xxii).

The condition of pre-Anglo-Norman agriculture in Ireland has often been perceived as entirely pastoral, with herds of cattle clustered around scattered ringforts. Despite this perception, tillage was an important part of Irish rural life before the arrival of the Anglo-Normans. Wheat and barley had been grown in Ireland since the prehistoric period and archaeological evidence suggests that oats had become the dominant cereal crop of early medieval Ireland (Monk 2015, 322). Archaeological excavations at Raheenagurren West and chance discoveries at Greatisland have uncovered evidence of cereal drying and milling in pre-Anglo-Norman Wexford. The cereal-drying kilns excavated at Raheenagurren West appear to have been in use at some stage between the early ninth and early thirteenth centuries (Doyle 2016, 38). At Greatisland a grinding stone and the oak flume (or sluice) of a watermill were uncovered within the boundaries of an early medieval monastic site (Monk 2015, 313; Moore 1996, 45 (no. 400)). Although the general area of Greatisland was developed after 1169 into the site of an Anglo-Norman borough and port town, it is likely that

3.10 (*above*) Metal fixing, typical of Scandinavian boat-building technology, recovered from 84 and 86 South Main Street, Wexford town

3.9 (*right*) A medieval funerary slab featuring a, now-indistinct, thirteenth-century-style vessel in the graveyard of Selskar Abbey, Wexford town (after Hore 1900–11, vol. v, 75)

the watermill associated with the early medieval monastery was in use at roughly the same time as the kilns at Raheenagurren West.

In the years following 1169 the Anglo-Normans did develop a system of agricultural excess and international trade, which increased throughout the thirteenth century (Murphy 2015, 99–100). In the early years of the Anglo-Norman colony the trading vessels coming in to and out of Wexford Harbour looked very similar to those of the Hiberno-Norse inhabitants of the town. With overlapping clinker-built hulls, steering oars toward the stern and large square sails, little differentiated the thirteenth-century trading vessels from the *knarrs* of the late Viking Age. Although archaeological investigations have not yet recovered any such vessels from the waters around Wexford, their basic outline can be traced in the decoration of a medieval funerary slab in Selskar Abbey in Wexford town (Figure 3.9). Fragmentary evidence of earlier vessels, in the form of clenched nails likely to have held Hiberno-Norse planked vessels together, were recovered from the early medieval shoreline during the excavations at numbers 84 and 86 South Main Street in Wexford town (Figure 3.10; McLoughlin and Stafford 2010). Gradually, however, as the quantities of agricultural produce exported from Ireland increased so did the scale and draught of visiting ships. Archaeological investigations in the port towns of Wexford and New Ross have shown how the waterfronts of both towns were progressively reclaimed during the later medieval period to allow larger, deeper-draught vessels to come alongside the towns' quays (McLoughlin forthcoming; Ó Drisceoil 2016, 289–94).

Although the export of agricultural produce became an increasingly significant part of the Irish economy after 1169, it was not an entirely new departure for the Irish countryside, particularly in the Wexford heartland of Diarmait Mac Murchada's kingdom. It has been pointed out that much of the wealth generated by Mac Murchada in the pre-Anglo-Norman era may have come from the international sale of the royal tributes presented to him by his subjects (Swift 2015, 95–102). This view is supported by Giraldus' remark that Ireland 'is pleased to send the hides of animals and the skins of flocks and wild beasts overseas'. In an early form of cultural stereotyping, Giraldus notes that much of the returning cargo was made up of vast quantities of wine, so much so that one would scarcely notice that grapes were not cultivated in Ireland (ibid., 100).

Much of that early trade must have flowed through Wexford town, the only identified pre-Anglo-Norman trading port in the county. Wexford is situated just 30km south of Mac Murchada's capital at Ferns, and most of that distance lies along the navigable length of the River Slaney down which exportable products could easily have been transported. By the mid-twelfth century the Hiberno-Norse towns, although culturally distinct, were very much a part of Irish society and, at least nominally, were under the control of kings like Mac Murchada. In 1165 it may have been Mac Murchada who contracted out the Dublin sailing fleet to Henry II to transport his troops along the Welsh coastline during a period of conflict there (Swift 2015, 96). This pre-existing relationship may explain why Mac Murchada was in a position to approach Henry for aid when he lost control of his own Leinster kingdom in 1166.

Although twelfth-century Ireland was already a place capable of producing agricultural excesses, one significant change to the Irish landscape rendered by the new Anglo-Norman style of agriculture was a move away from pastoralism toward tillage farming throughout the thirteenth century. Historical and archaeological investigations have suggested that as much as 70 per cent of demesne land farmed in Anglo-Norman Ireland was under tillage (Murphy 2015, 88). Archaeological investigations at Camaross in Wexford revealed a probable kiln associated with the drying of those crops during the later medieval period. The kiln contained charred remnants of oat and wheat grains and was associated with a moated site. The excavation revealed pottery (Leinster Cooking Ware, imported Redcliffe pottery and local Wexford-type pottery) similar to the material recovered during excavations in Wexford town (Eogan and Kelly 2016, 218).

COLONISTS

The 1169 arrival of the Anglo-Normans in Wexford developed and altered the pre-existing Irish and Hiberno-Norse patterns of urban and rural settlement, international exchange, religious practices and even agricultural productivity. These developments are visible in the modern archaeological record as town walls, moated sites, pottery, quay fronts, ruinous churches and field patterns.

Perhaps the biggest change in Wexford society after 1169 was one that is less visible in the archaeological landscape. Farmers of the moated sites and residents in new towns like New Ross and Bannow were colonists. Those places were settled by French-, English- and Welsh-speakers with names like Stafford, Roche, Devereux and Furlong (Colfer 2002, 130). The descendants of those early Anglo-Norman colonists became the principal landholders in Wexford and the south-east of Ireland. In south Wexford, where those surnames are still common, the impact of the newcomers was so intense that the entirely unique language or dialect of Yola eventually developed in the baronies of Forth and Bargy (ibid., 125).

CONCLUSION

Archaeology, through the study of material culture, gives us an insight into the changing lifestyles of the people of medieval Wexford. Perhaps for the average resident of medieval Wexford the greatest changes between the late twelfth and early thirteenth century were not in the material culture, architecture and social practices of everyday life, but in the organisation of hierarchical society. When Diarmait Mac Murchada died in 1171, Wexford and the traditional kingdom of Leinster came under the control of Mac Murchada's Anglo-Norman son-in-law Richard de Clare, more commonly referred to as Strongbow. In 1189/90 Strongbow was in turn succeeded by his own son-in-law William Marshal (Empey 2017, 56–8). As this new generation of Anglo-Norman lords took control of Wexford and the lordship of Leinster the motte-and-bailey and ringwork campaign castles of the late twelfth century were replaced by the masonry castles still visible in the modern landscape.

Outside Wexford town, Robert Fitz Stephen's ringwork at Carrick was replaced by a masonry structure in the early thirteenth century (ch. 4). That castle, like others in Wexford, has long since been removed, leaving a footprint visible only to excavating archaeologists. Other castles, however, such as those built by the Marshal family at

Mac Murchada's capital of Ferns and by the Prendergasts at the Slaney ford of Enniscorthy, are still standing. Those castles, among the most lasting archaeological features of the medieval period, remain imposing reminders of the changed reality of the Irish cultural landscape in the thirteenth century.

BIBLIOGRAPHY

Bourke, E. 1988. '1988:67 Bride Street/South Main Street, Townparks, Wexford'. In Bennett, I. (ed.), *Excavations 1988: summary accounts of archaeological excavations in Ireland*, www.excavations.ie/report/1988/Wexford/0000833/, accessed 25 November 2018.

Bourke, E. 1995. 'Life in the sunny south-east: housing and domestic economy in Viking and medieval Wexford'. *Archaeology Ireland*, 9:3, 33–6.

Colfer, B. 2002. *Arrogant trespass: Anglo-Norman Wexford, 1169–1400*. Wexford.

Colfer, B. 2008. *Wexford: a town and its landscape*. Cork.

Doyle, I. 2016. '"Telling the dancer from the dance": the archaeology of early medieval Wexford'. In Doyle, I. and Browne, B. (eds), *Medieval Wexford: essays in memory of Billy Colfer*, 35–61. Dublin.

Empey, A. 2017. 'The evolution of the demesne in the lordship of Leinster: the fortunes of war or forward planning?'. In Bradley, J., Ó Drisceoil, C. and Potterton, M. (eds), *William Marshal and Ireland*, 41–77. Dublin.

Eogan, J. and Kelly, B. 2016. 'New roads to medieval Wexford'. In Doyle, I. and Browne, B. (eds), *Medieval Wexford: essays in memory of Billy Colfer*, 211–40. Dublin.

Hore, P. 1900–11. *History of the town and county of Wexford*. 6 vols. London.

Marshall, S. and McMorran, T. 2016. 'People and places: a bird's-eye view of medieval Old Ross'. In Doyle, I. and Browne, B. (eds), *Medieval Wexford: essays in memory of Billy Colfer*, 241–61. Dublin.

McLoughlin, C. (forthcoming). 'Medieval Wexford: the evidence from archaeological excavations'. In Corlett, C. and Potterton, M. (eds), *Towns in medieval Ireland in the light of recent archaeological excavations*. Dublin.

McLoughlin, C. 2004. 'Archaeological testing, Kinnagh, Co. Wexford'. Unpublished archaeological report, licence 03E1448.

McLoughlin, C. 2015. 'Archaeological assessment report, Harristown, Co. Wexford'. Unpublished archaeological report, licence 15E0339.

McLoughlin, C. and Stafford, E. 2010. 'Archaeological excavation report, 84 and 86 South Main Street, Wexford'. Unpublished archaeological report, licence 05E0612.

McLoughlin, C. and Stafford, E. 2016. 'Excavation of the remains of an early thirteenth-century house at the Thomas Moore Tavern, Cornmarket, Wexford'. In Doyle, I. and Browne, B. (eds), *Medieval Wexford: essays in memory of Billy Colfer*, 342–64. Dublin.

Monk, M. 2015. 'Early medieval agriculture in Ireland: the case for tillage'. In Purcell, E., MacCotter, P., Nyhan, J. and Sheehan, J. (eds), *Clerics, kings and Vikings: essays on medieval Ireland in honour of Donnchadh Ó Corráin*, 309–22. Dublin.

Moore, M. 1996. *Archaeological inventory of County Wexford*. Dublin.

Murphy, M. 2015. 'Manor centres, settlement and agricultural systems in medieval Ireland, 1250–1350'. In Murphy, M. and Stout, M. (eds), *Agriculture and settlement in Ireland,* 69–100. Dublin.

Ó Corráin, D. 2017. *The Irish church and its reform and the English invasion.* Dublin.

Ó Drisceoil, C. 2016. '*Pons Novus, villa Willielmi Marescalli*: New Ross, a town of William Marshal'. In Bradley, J., Ó Drisceoil, C. and Potterton, M. (eds), *William Marshal and Ireland,* 268–314. Dublin.

Ó Súilleabháin, M., Downey, L. and Downey, D. 2017. *Antiquities of rural Ireland.* Dublin.

O'Conor, K. 1998. *The archaeology of medieval rural settlement in Ireland.* Dublin.

Orpen, G. 1968. *Ireland under the Normans.* 4 vols. Reprint. Oxford.

Redmond, A. 2000. *That was then, this is now: change in Ireland, 1949–1999.* Dublin.

Seymour, St John D. 1929. *Anglo-Irish literature, 1200–1582.* Cambridge.

Scott, A. and Martin, F.X. (eds). 1978. *Expugnatio Hibernica by Giraldus Cambrensis.* Dublin.

Sheehan, C. 2002. '2002:1934: Shaw's, 62–68 Main Street North, Wexford'. In Bennett, I. (ed.), *Excavations 2002: summary accounts of archaeological excavations in Ireland,* www.excavations.ie/report/2002/Wexford/0009252/, accessed 25 November 2018.

Stafford, E. and McLoughlin, C. 2011. 'Partial excavation of a modified ringfort at Baunogephlure, Co. Carlow'. In Corlett, C. and Potterton, M. (eds), *Settlement in early medieval Ireland in the light of recent archaeological excavations,* 289–300. Dublin.

Stafford, E. (forthcoming). 'A feast or famine: medieval New Ross in the light of recent investigations'. In Corlett, C. and Potterton, M. (eds), *Towns in medieval Ireland in the light of recent archaeological excavations.* Dublin.

Stout, M. 1997. *The Irish ringfort.* Dublin.

Stout, M. 2017. *Early medieval Ireland, 431–1169.* Dublin.

Stout, M. and Murphy, M. 2015. 'Introduction'. In Murphy, M. and Stout, M. (eds), *Agriculture and settlement in Ireland,* xvi–xxx. Dublin.

Swift, C. 2015. 'Follow the money: the financial resources of Diarmait Mac Murchada'. In Purcell, E., MacCotter, P., Nyhan, J. and Sheehan, J. (eds), *Clerics, kings and Vikings: essays on medieval Ireland in honour of Donnchadh Ó Corráin,* 91–102. Dublin.

Thomas, A. 1992. *The walled towns of Ireland.* 2 vols. Dublin.

CHAPTER FOUR

A history of Carrick

DENIS SHINE & CATHERINE McLOUGHLIN

INTRODUCTION

Carrick is an unusual monument in that while being of outstanding importance to the history of the nation, it has passed into and out of both public consciousness and academic enquiry (Barry 1983; Bennett 1985). The remains of the monument consist of a large earthwork enclosure perched on top of the edge of a cliff adjacent to the River Slaney. The site was 're-identified' by Terry Barry in the 1980s and included on his list of ringwork castles (Barry 1983, 303) but has variously been recalled, rejected or confused with the mid-sixteenth-century Roches' Castle, on the north bank of the Slaney (in Ferrycarrig townland) (Colfer 2013, 38, 185). While past authorities have identified the site and while it best matches the location given in near-contemporary accounts (Orpen 1892, lines 1775–9, 1395–9; Scott and Martin 1978, 53, 298n58, 306–7n118), it is only in the last generation or so that the monument has been confirmed as a ringwork (Barry 1983, 303) and has been the focus of archaeological investigation (Bennett 1985; Shine et al. 2018). Past historical summaries give good accounts of the site (for example, Bennett 1984, 1985; Hore 1900–11, passim; Jeffrey 1979), but our understanding of both Carrick and its medieval landscape has been added to significantly in recent years. The purpose of this chapter is to present a summary of the historical importance of Carrick.

SITE DESCRIPTION

Carrick ringwork is located in the Irish National Heritage Park (INHP) in the townland of Newtown (barony of Shelmalier West) (NGR in ITM 701328, 623185; see Figure 4.1). The ringwork is c.4km west of Wexford town on a cliff face that reaches a height of almost 30m and falls dramatically toward the River Slaney. The remains of the ringwork comprise a large sub-circular enclosure defined by a massive ditch and earthen bank. The ringwork was sundered from its surrounding landscape in the 1980s due to the construction of the modern N11 road (for a more detailed description of the site, see ch. 5).

4.1 Site location on 2005 Ordnance Survey orthographic aerial photograph (© Ordnance Survey Ireland/Government of Ireland – copyright permit MP004218)

PRE-ANGLO-NORMAN ARCHAEOLOGICAL EVIDENCE

There is no confirmed archaeological evidence for occupation at Carrick before its 1169 foundation date. A collared urn burial (RMP WX037–029) was located within Newtown townland, *c.*200m south-east of the ringwork. This burial, discovered in 1984, consisted of the rim of a collared urn and a small sample of cremated bone, probably representing an older adolescent (Moore 1996, 10 (no. 86); Sikora 2011). No other prehistoric activity has been discovered in the immediate vicinity of the site; however, a small number of flint artefacts have been found during the current excavations at Carrick, as well as in previous investigations (Bennett 1984; 1985), and these may indicate earlier occupation (see ch. 5).

ROBERT FITZ STEPHEN AND THE ARRIVAL OF THE ANGLO-NORMANS

The historical significance of the coming of the Anglo-Normans has been discussed extensively, both for the country generally (for example, Duffy 1997) and for Wexford specifically (for example, Colfer 2002; ch. 1, above). In this chapter, we present Carrick's history, including wider regional or national events only where needed to add context to the overall narrative.

Carrick's foundation is well documented in two of the earliest sources for the Anglo-Norman 'landing' and conquest, *Expugnatio Hibernica: The conquest of Ireland* by Giraldus Cambrensis (Gerald of Wales) (Scott and Martin 1978) and the anonymously written *Song of Dermot and the earl* (the *Song*) (Orpen 1892). Giraldus was Anglo-Norman and related to key figures in the invasion (including his uncle Robert Fitz Stephen), meaning his writings are undoubtedly underpinned with Anglo-Norman propaganda and derision of the Irish (Martin 1969). This near contemporary account, however, written in 1189, remains the most useful document for tracing Carrick's early history.

In May 1169 Robert Fitz Stephen, accompanied by his nephews Meiler Fitz Henry and Miles Fitz David, along with Hervey de Montmorency (Strongbow's uncle), landed with three ships in Bannow Bay (Scott and Martin 1978, 31; ch. 1, above). Giraldus places this force at 30 knights, 60 men wearing mail and 300 foot-archers (Scott and Martin 1978, 31). The next day Maurice de Prendergast arrived with a further ten men-at-arms and a body of archers, making a complete force of not more than six hundred, who were joined by five hundred of Mac Murchada's troops (Colfer 2002, 29; 2013, 23–4). The combined force of approximately 1,100 men attacked and defeated the Norse-Irish town of Wexford, after which Mac Murchada renewed his promise to grant Wexford town and its dependent territories, equivalent to the barony of Forth, to Robert Fitz Stephen and his half-brother Maurice Fitz Gerald (who was yet to arrive) (Colfer 2002, 30; 2013, 24; Hore 1900–11, vol. v, 20; Scott and Martin 1978, 36). Hervey de Montmorency was also granted two cantreds (Bargy and Shelburne) in southern Wexford.

Robert Fitz Stephen came from a family of split loyalties, with Giraldus calling him 'a knight, sprung from two races' (Scott and Martin 1978, 28); he was a son of Nest, a Welsh princess, and Stephen, the constable of Aberteifi (Cardigan) and loyal supporter of Henry I. Fitz Stephen himself supported Henry II on his invasion of Wales in 1157. In 1165 Fitz Stephen's first cousin Rhys ap Gruffydd led a Welsh revolt against the English, including placing Fitz Stephen's castle under siege. Fitz Stephen was forfeited to Rhys by his own men and imprisoned, a state he still occupied when approached by Diarmait Mac Murchada (Scott and Martin 1978, 29). A mediated agreement was struck whereby Fitz Stephen chose to leave Wales and assist Mac Murchada, in the hope of promised endowments on a new frontier (Cohen 2006).

Immediately following the landing and battle for Wexford, Fitz Stephen accompanied Mac Murchada on a series of short campaigns around Leinster (for example, see Scott and Martin 1978, 41). In early autumn 1169 his half-brother Maurice Fitz Gerald arrived in the country, putting in at Wexford with 10 knights, 30 mounted archers and 100 foot archers (Scott and Martin 1978, 51). Fitz Stephen sent troops to support Fitz Gerald and Mac Murchada, who was emboldened by the new arrivals, in their march and siege on Dublin. Fitz Stephen himself stayed in Wexford

4.2 (*above*) Aerial view of the River Slaney with the old bridge before the construction of the new N11 road in the 1980s. The building of this road had a significant impact on the integrity of this medieval archaeological site and landscape (see Figure 4.3, below). The restoration work had not yet taken place at Roches' Castle either (image courtesy of Irisheye)

4.3 (*below*) Carrick ringwork, on an escarpment face overlooking the Slaney. The original ferry crossing would have been between these two points, close to the line of the current bridge

4.4 Dunanore ringwork, showing the scale of the fortifications

to fortify the region and built a wooden 'ringwork' or 'campaign fort' on top of a large rock, directly overlooking a strategic point on the River Slaney (Figures 4.2, 4.3). The castle, referred to as 'chastel sur Slane' in the *Song* (Orpen 1892, line 1777), has been attributed to Fitz Gerald in some accounts, including in the *Song* (Jeffery 1979, 102). As recorded by Giraldus, however, it was undoubtedly Fitz Stephen who built it – improving the natural defences of the cliff by 'artificial means' (Scott and Martin 1978, 53).

Fitz Stephen's castle is archaeologically classified as a ringwork (Barry 1983), but as late as the 1970s a sign at the site erroneously identified it as a promontory fort (Jeffery 1979, 105). Ringworks have been increasingly recognised within the landscape in recent decades (see Arbuthnot 2011), including notable examples such as Carrick and Hugh de Lacy's 'house' in Trim, Clonmacnoise in Co. Offaly, and Dunanore in Wexford, to name just a few (see, for example, Hayden 2011; Sweetman 1978). Generally being simple and efficient to construct, they can exceed 60m in diameter, but are usually smaller (McNeill 1997). Of twenty-nine Anglo-Norman earthworks identified by Colfer in Wexford (2002, 53–64; 2013, 38–51), nine are thought to be ringworks (including others on 'promontories' at Dunanore (Figure 4.4), Templetown, Toberfinnick, Castlesow and Ballyhoge), although only Ferrycarrig (Bennett 1985; Shine et al. 2018) and Ferns (Sweetman 1978; 1979; 1999) have been excavated. Carrick is one of only a handful of earthworks associated with seignorial caputs, or headquarters, to be recorded in historical records (Colfer 2002 53–64; 2013, 38–51).

THE SIEGE

Giraldus records that Fitz Stephen's ringwork was subject to a siege in 1171 (Scott and Martin 1978, 81). The site's garrison was weakened after Fitz Stephen sent thirty-six men to the aid of Strongbow in Dublin (Hore 1900–11, vol. v, 30; Jeffrey 1979, 103). Seizing their chance, the Irish retook the town of Wexford and Fitz Stephen fled to his stronghold at Carrick. The garrison was attacked by Domhnall, son of Diarmait, with a supposed, but probably exaggerated force of up to three thousand men (Scott and Martin 1978, 85). Giraldus notes that the garrison were 'in the midst of their enemies, trapped in a most ill-fortified castle, which was enclosed by flimsy wall of branches and sods' (Scott and Martin 1978, 81). Despite a speculated defensive Anglo-Norman force of only five knights and a few archers, the garrison held until the Irish, resorting to 'falsehood and deceit', tricked Fitz Stephen into surrender by bringing bishops to the gates who claimed that Dublin had fallen (Scott and Martin 1978, 85). They promised that Rory O'Conor had routed the Anglo-Norman forces, including his half-brother Maurice Fitz Gerald, encouraging Fitz Stephen to leave and return to Wales. Giraldus records how Strongbow had actually broken the siege to come to Fitz Stephen's aid, but on arrival in Wexford found the town burnt and Fitz Stephen imprisoned with hostages on Begerin Island in Wexford Harbour (the modern north slob lands); he dared not assist him for fear of the hostages being executed (Hore 1900–11, vol. v, 31; Lewis 1837, 279; Scott and Martin 1978, 306–7n118). Giraldus does not mention the site of Carrick again after this event. The *Song* also records the siege, when Fitz Stephen's men were 'utterly betrayed, killed, cut to pieces and brought to shame' (Orpen 1892, line 1778). As with Giraldus' account, the *Song* does not refer to Carrick again after the siege.

The historical accounts indicate that in 1171 the site consisted of a bank and fosse (ditch), with a wooden palisade ('flimsy wall of branches'). A wooden castle, and potentially a wooden gatehouse, are also likely to have been erected at this time (between 1169 and 1171). Hore (1900–11, vol. v, 32) speculates further that Fitz Stephen, in nearly two years of occupancy, would have completed something stronger than 'an earthen rampart and stockade' and may have erected a stone structure or keep at the site. The fact that the castle resisted a siege indicates a well-fortified stronghold at this time. It seems unlikely, however, that stone structures (later recorded in the thirteenth century) would have been built by this time, considering both the instability of the new colony and Fitz Stephen's distraction with Mac Murchada's campaigns in his early career in Ireland.

Fitz Stephen himself was handed over to Henry II in Waterford in October 1171, who relieved him of Wexford and his lands and imprisoned him in Reginald's Tower (Scott and Martin 1978, 95). He was soon released and recruited into the royal household – first being assigned duties in the garrison of Dublin in April of 1172

under Hugh de Lacy, before later entering the services of Strongbow. Fitz Stephen was
recalled by the king in 1173 and helped put down rebellions in England, only to be
recalled in 1177, when he was rewarded for his service with a speculative land grant of
the kingdom of Desmond in Cork (Hore 1900–11, vol. v, 31; Scott and Martin 1978,
185). Fitz Stephen is thought to have died in 1183, leaving no living male heir.

DEVELOPMENT OF A BOROUGH

After the departure of Fitz Stephen there is a gap in the known history of Carrick, but
the area, along with Wexford town, was given to Strongbow as a seignorial manor in
August 1173, following a campaign of service in Normandy (Colfer 2002, 49; Hore
1900–11, vol. v, 32; Jeffrey 1979, 104). Hore (1900–11, vol. v, 32) speculates that
Strongbow or William Fitz Audelin, a seneschal of Wexford appointed after
Strongbow's death in 1176, commenced building in stone at the site. He also suggests
that the stone castle is more likely to have been built between 1189 (when William
Marshal, the earl of Pembroke, became the lord of Leinster following marriage to
Isabella de Clare, Strongbow's daughter) and 1231, when William Marshal II died, and
the castle is first recorded. Carrick was home to one of six early thirteenth-century
stone castles in the county – the others were at Wexford town, Ferns, Old Ross, the
Island and Enniscorthy (Colfer 2013, 51; ch. 2, above).

The construction of a stone castle at Carrick is most likely to have begun when
other Marshal castles in the region were being built; for example, Carlow was
commenced *c.*1210–15 (O'Conor 1997, 13–16) and Carrick and other Marshal castles
may have been completed in the period *c.*1222–5 when Marshal II had service to the
king cancelled to allow him to fortify castles in Ireland.

William Marshal I died in 1219 and William Marshal II died in 1231. The stone
castle of Carrick-on-Slaney is first recorded at the time of William II's death, when the
king ordered that castle constables, including Carrick, give up custody of the castles to
the king's bailiff (Orpen 1968, vol. iii, 59). In Wexford, the castles of Ross and the
Island were also placed into the king's hands, as were Carlow and Odagh; Ferns was
held in dower for the countess of Pembroke (Colfer 2002, 71; 2013, 51). Carrick is
recorded again in 1231–4, as 'Kastrum de Karrick', the caput of the manor of Carrick,
by Richard Marshal (William II's younger brother) in his disafforestation charter.
Richard died in 1234 and was succeeded by Gilbert Marshal who was killed in a
tournament in 1241. When his remaining brothers Walter and Anselm died in 1245
the male Marshal line was extinguished, and in 1247 Leinster was divided between the
five daughters of William Marshal I (Orpen 1968, vol. iii, 75).

Marshal's second daughter Johanna, who was married to Warren de Munchensy,
was granted the burgh and body of Wexford in 1245, including the manor of 'Karrac'

(Hore 1900–11, vol. v, 32). Carrick is next recorded in 1247 when Joan de Valence (daughter of Johanna and Warren de Munchensy), married to William de Valence, was given possession of 'Karrec', then worth £23 15s. (Hore 1900–11, vol. v, 38; Orpen 1968, vol. iii, 86). The de Valence lands in Wexford consisted of the liberty of Wexford, including Wexford town and the seignorial manors of Rosslare, Carrick, Ferns, Bannow and the detached manor of Odagh (in Kilkenny) (Colfer 2002, 74).

Carrick was constituted as a borough, or town, at some stage during the thirteenth century, as an inquisition to the extent of Joan de Valence's lands upon her death in 1307 records burgages and burgesses there (Colfer 2002, 70; Orpen 1968, vol. iii, 88; see Table 4.1). Quite a large town appears to have developed, as the rents at an average of 1s. a piece indicate 111 houses in the borough surrounding the castle (Hore 1900–11, vol. v, 33); other assets included a ferry and two watermills. The inquisition of 1307 appears to record a *c.*50 per cent decrease in Carrick's value since 1247.

Table 4.1 Extent of Joan de Valence's assets at Carrick in 1307 (after Hore 1900–11, vol. v, 33; see also Jeffrey 1979, 33, 102)

Description	£	s.	d.
One castle with two carucates and 20 acres of land in demesne	3	0	0
Rent of burgages there	5	11	9
Rent of one free tenement	0	2	0
Two watermills	1	10	0
Profits of pasturage and underwood at 'Colunagh' (Cullentra)	0	10	0
Perquisites of the hundred court	0	2	0
The ferry	0	10	0
Total	*11*	*5*	*9*

The location of Carrick borough remained unknown until relatively recently. Bradley and King (1990, 71) suggested that the town existed either at the site of the ringwork/castle or, less likely, beside Roches' Castle. Colfer (2002, 145) also speculated that it must be close to the ringwork/castle site or St Nicholas', Carrick's parish church.

St Nicholas' Church is located *c.*900m to the south of Carrick ringwork. All that remains of the site is an overgrown small rectangular structure (Moore 1996, 123–4 (no. 1208); see Figure 4.5) within a D-shaped enclosure. A granite font (RMP WX037–030003) is also extant at the site (for a survey of the graveyard, see Cantwell 1981–3). Lewis (1837, 280) and later Hore (1900–11, vol. v, 34) record that only stone foundations survived at the site in the mid-nineteenth and early twentieth centuries; tree roots erode these few courses today. The first recorded cleric was Nicholas Talbot, appointed to Carrick by the crown in 1385 (Leslie 1936, 161). The

4.5 St Nicholas' Church, Carrick's parish church, showing the remaining church walls, which are heavily overgrown

church was granted to the monastery of Selskar in 1404 by Sir John Talbot (Bradley and King 1990, 70). Hore (1900–11, vol. v, 180) records that in about 1551 John Parker obtained all the possessions of the monastery of Selskar (except for the tithes) for a nominal rent of 15*s.* 3*d.*; this included farm lands in Carge (Carrick) for 8*d.* In 1635 the church is recorded as belonging to John Wadding, of Wadding's Castle, Wexford.

The site of the borough was confirmed as being to the north of St Nicholas' Church and to the south-east of Carrick ringwork during archaeological test excavations in 2006 (McLoughlin 2006); the borough is separated from the ringwork/castle, and likely partly truncated, by the modern N11 road. The results of the test excavations and of a geophysical survey at Carrick borough in 2018 (Green 2018) are described in detail by McLoughlin and Green below (ch. 6). Excavations revealed a number of sub-soil cut features, including a large ditch, which contained sherds of locally produced medieval pottery. The location of the archaeological features along with an examination of the historic mapping suggests that the medieval town extended to a length of 400m. The work indicates that the borough, or at least a portion of it, is directly south of the townland of Park. Park itself is significant, the name reflecting the presence in the medieval period of an Anglo-Norman deer park at the site. This park is discussed by Beglane below (ch. 7), so only brief mention follows here (see also Beglane 2010; 2012; 2015; 2017).

The townland of Park runs directly east from Carrick ringwork along the estuary's southern bank and originally contained the deer park of the borough. Deer parks are an Anglo-Norman introduction to Ireland, consisting of an artificially enclosed park with high earthen banks and ditches and/or a wall or palisade (Beglane 2015; Murphy and O'Conor 2006). The parks were stocked with preferred prey species, such as fallow deer, as at Carrick, which were imported from the thirteenth century onward (McCormick and Murray 2017, 208). Fallow, while not rare, are unusual in medieval Ireland, generally being limited to the east of the country and the highest tier of Anglo-Norman lordly society (Beglane 2012, xviii). Beglane (2012, 257–89; 2015, 15; see also ch. 7, below) recorded forty-six medieval deer parks in Ireland, selecting Carrick for a historical, cartographic and survey-based case study. She identified a key reference to Carrick deer park in the aforementioned disafforestation charter on the forests of Ross and Taghmon, sometime between 1231 and 1234 (2012, 257; Orpen 1934, 56; ch. 7, below):

> Now of the forest around Tauchmune [Taghmon] I have deforested outside the metes and bounds hereunder-written, that is to say, from the place where the river which flows between the castle of Karrich [and] the park [into] the Slaney, and by that river ascending to my mill on that river.

This charter makes Carrick one of the earliest referenced parks in the country, with Beglane (2015, 28) proposing that it was constructed by one of the two William Marshals – between 1189 and 1231. William Marshal II is known to have been gifted twenty fallow does by the king in 1225, which were to be brought to Ireland to stock a park(s), which conceivably included Carrick (Beglane 2012, 247; 2015, 28; 2017). References to 'two carucates and 20 acres [105 hectares] of appurtenant land in demesne' and 'two carucates [97 hectares] of arable pasture land' in the afore-mentioned inquisitions of 1307 and 1324 may refer to the original park area (Beglane 2012, 267; 2015, 28); if so, Carrick park had reverted to agricultural use by the early fourteenth century.

Other important known elements of the settlement of Carrick included the ferry and mills – although little is known about either. The ferry was located at an extremely strategic point at the only crossing between Enniscorthy and the Irish Sea (Figure 4.6); as such, it developed as an important source of revenue to the town from the thirteenth century onward. In 1307 it was worth 10s. per annum, but by 1324 had its value wiped out – possibly as a result of the Bruce Invasion. The Roches (or de Rupes) controlled the ferry from this time until at least the seventeenth century. It was not replaced until the end of the eighteenth century, when the bridge was constructed. The mills are mentioned in 1307, 1399 and 1519 (Hore 1900–11, vol. v, 33, 133). Two potential mill sites can be identified, one to the east of the ringwork where the River Carrig joins the Slaney, and one to the west of the ringwork, along an unnamed stream that is now part of the INHP (see Figure 4.6).

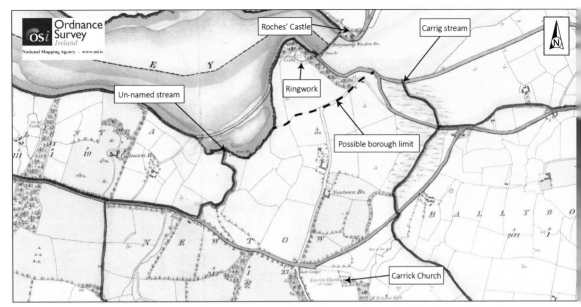

4.6 The first-edition Ordnance Survey map (1841) showing the medieval landscape of Carrick, before the construction of the modern road. The possible limit of Carrick borough is hypothesised (see ch. 6 for more detail). The ferry crossing would have taken a similar line (shown) to the bridge across the Slaney (© Ordnance Survey Ireland/Government of Ireland – copyright permit MP004218)

DECLINE

It was not just the ferry that lost value by the fourteenth century; the settlement of Carrick generally appears to have been in decline at that time. The inquisition of 1324, on the lands of Joan's son, Aymer de Valence (earl of Pembroke), records the 'Castle of Carryk' as ruinous and valued at nothing; this inquisition also mentions a ruinous hall and chapel within an 'enclosure' (or *classum*) at the Carrick ringwork (Bradley and King 1990, 66; Hore 1900–11, vol. v, 33). A total of 110 burgages were still recorded at this time but the value of the site had dropped to £11, with the 'tenants destroyed by war' (Colfer 2002, 76; see Table 4.2). Aymer de Valence died in 1324, with lands in Wexford (and elsewhere) ultimately left in dower to his wife Mary (or Maude) de Valence. This included lands at Carrick with the manor then valued at £9 17*s*. 4*d*., except for 40*d*. for the woods at Colynath (Cullentra), which were assigned to Wexford Castle (Hore 1900–11, vol. v, 106). Hore (1900–11, vol. v, 105) speculates that approximately sixty acres (24 hectares) of the Park in the manor of Carrick were appurtenant to Wexford Castle at this time.

The decline of the town in the early fourteenth century mirrors both Wexford's and the national experience, whereby the Anglo-Norman colony was in retreat due to

Table 4.2 Extent of Aymer de Valence's assets at Carrick in 1324 (after Hore 1900–11, vol. v, 33)

Description	£	s.	d.
One castle and two carucates of land in demesne	2	0	0
A wood containing one carucate		?	
A pasture called 'le Gortyn'		?	
Close to the castle a parcel of land which used to be worth 3s. 4d. per annum, but then owing to the war		nil	
110 burgages for which the burgesses paid as rent	5	10	0
3 burgages waste for want of tenants		nil	
The ferry, which used to be worth 2 marks, but then (owing to war)		nil	
Two watermills, owing to the poverty of the tenants and injuries caused by the war, worth not more than	2	0	0
Total	*11*	*10*	*8*

Table 4.3 References to Carrick in the late fourteenth/early fifteenth century (after Hore 1900–11, vol. v, 33, 129, 130)

Date	Description
1399	Reymund Flemyng is recorded as the executor of the will of Dionisius Roche, 'the late farmer of two-third parts of the water-mill at Carrick and the park of Wexford'
1402	John Barry is recorded as the farmer of the manor and a chapel called 'Insula Barry'
1406	John Topp is recorded as custodian of the manor of Carrick, then valued at only £5 per annum
1408	John Chevers, Wm White and Maurice Beddeford were 'distrained to account for all the lands and tenements of the Manor of "Carryk"'
1413	Nicholas Brown and Nicholas, son of David, Senot (Synnott) are accused by John Toppe of intrusions into the manor
1416	John Chevers applies for 'attachment … for the possessions of the late Sir Gilbert Talbot the manors … of Wexford, Balmaschalre, Rosclare, Atharte, Ballymore, Ballinacaryn, Fernes, Edyrdrom (Edermine) and Carryk (Ferry Carrig)'
1420	The dower of Lady Beatrix, widow of Sir Gilbert Talbot, now in the king's hands due to her absence. Among other possessions, she held the castle of Carrick with two tofts called 'the Mille places' of Carrick with the watercourse belonging thereto

Table 4.4 References to Carrick in the sixteenth century (after Hore 1900–11, vol. v, 34, 133)

Date	Description
1519	During an inquisition at the castle of Wexford into a feud among the Roches, the parishioners and burgesses of Carrick were mentioned 'as accustomed to have a provost and hold a court amongst the burgesses'. The watermill is also recorded as rented by John Devereux FitzJohn, Walter Devereux and Nicholas Keating. The ferry is held by the lord of the liberty, although William Keating was accused of collecting monies for passage
1538	William St Loo, seneschal of Wexford, records the Kavanaghs have wasted the manor of 'Karryck'
1554	John Parker is recorded as possessing two arable acres in the 'Villat of Carge, alias Carrycke', valued at 2s. per annum
1575	Lancelot Allford sold to Richard Synnott the 'park of Wexford', consisting of sixty acres (24.3 hectares) from the manor of Carrick
1581	Thomas, earl of Ormond, was granted (among other lands) 'the scite and precincts of an old castle of the manor of Carge, containing half an acre, and two acres of pasture near the said castle'

numerous factors including the Bruce Invasion (1315–18), resurgent Gaelic leadership and plague and famine (see ch. 2). In particular the Black Death, which arrived in Dublin and Drogheda in 1348, hastened the decline of urban centres, including towns in Wexford such as the Island, Bannow, Clonmines and Carrick (Colfer 2002, 234); this followed a series of famines (1316–17), cattle murrains (1321, 1324, 1325) and crop failures (1328, 1330, 1331) through the first and second quarters of the fourteenth century (Bennett 1985, 31). Wexford castles, including Carrick, Ross and the Island, were all recorded as abandoned or derelict by the early fourteenth century (Colfer 2002, 70; 2013, 53). Wexford town itself reported 127 waste burgage plots in 1307 and a castle in bad repair by 1323 (Hore 1900–11, vol. v, 102–4). Carrick borough is recorded regularly around the time of the reign of Henry IV (1399–1413), as outlined in Table 4.3.

Carrick, although burned and ruined, is still recorded as an asset in 1420 in an inquisition by Henry V (Hore 1900–11, vol. v, 34). Jeffrey (1979, 103) refers to another un-named inquisition in 1421 (quite possibly the 1420 inquisition referred to by Hore), which records the castle as still standing. Carrick is recorded reasonably regularly in the sixteenth century (see Table 4.4).

The last known reference to Carrick Castle itself is contained in Hooker's translation of a passage in *Expugnatio*, referring to the construction of Fitz Stephen's ringwork:

The said Carricke (as it is written) is distant from the town of Wexford about two English miles, and standeth on a high rocke, and is environed on two sides by the river which floweth to Wexford towne, and it is verie deepe and navigable, the other two sides are upon the maine land, which is a verie fertile soile, and in height almost equal with the Castell. It was first made of rods and turffes, according to the manner in those daies, but since builded with stone, and was the strongest fort then in those parts of the land: but being a place not altogether sufficient for a prince, and yet it was thought too good and strong for a subject, it was pulled down, defaced and raced, and so dooth still remain (Holinshed 1587, 11).

This note is valuable evidence both that the castle was at least partially pulled down prior to Holinshed's time in the sixteenth century, and that ruins remained at the site. Similarly, references from the sixteenth century to Carrick burgesses are informative, as they indicate that an active settlement continued in existence after the fourteenth-century decline of Carrick. The nature and form of this is uncertain as excavations on the borough site (ch. 6) found no artefacts that post-dated the thirteenth century.

Carrick is not mentioned in the list of the principal castles of the county in the time of Queen Elizabeth (post-1603), as it was ruinous (Hore 1900–11, vol. v, 34; Bennett 1985, 32); nor is it listed in the Civil Survey of 1654 (Jeffrey 1979, 103–4). In 1610 an inquisition taken in Wexford recorded the death of John Roche, who held the ferry of Carige (Carrick) through military service to the earl of Shrewsbury; another inquisition in 1635 stated that Walter Roche held the ferry (Hore 1900–11, vol. v, 28). In 1618 an inquisition in Wexford recorded that the late Philip Devereux was seised of lands and assets in Wexford town and county, including a three-and-a-half-acre park (1.4 hectares), called Whitt's Park, in the parish of Carrick (Hore 1900–11, vol. v, 234). In 1635 Carrick was visited by Sir William Brereton on his travels around Wexford and Ireland. He took the ferry at Carrick, recording the surrounding landscape as burnt and in drought (Hawkins 1844, 393). He also records Park as approximately one mile (1.6km) from the ferry and leased to a Mr Hardye (from a William Synode), who had an estate on it for about thirteen years. The last significant event to take place at the site was a meeting of the Confederated Catholics of Co. Wexford, in October 1642 (Bennett 1989, 59). Hore (1900–11, vol. v, 253) records the meeting on the hill of Carrick as one for the 'principal gentry and burgesses to consider the state of affairs, the stagnation of trade, and the distress and poverty so prevalent in the whole county'. Hore (ibid.) questions the meeting's date given in chancery inquisitions (3 October 1642), speculating that it occurred in 1641 – shortly before the rebellion outbreak.

FINAL DESTRUCTION

It is not known exactly when the castle was pulled down although, as previously stated, it was referred to as 'defaced and raced' in 1587 (Holinshed 1587, 11). Buildings undoubtedly stood on the site well past this date, with several references to the castle being 'quarried' through the eighteenth and nineteenth centuries. The first-edition Ordnance Survey map (1841) shows a subtle dotted rectangular feature surviving within the ringwork, inferring a ruinous building at the site in the mid-nineteenth century (Figure 4.6). By the time author P.R. Hanrahan (1866, 90) described the site in his historical fiction novel, however, he stated that '[Fitz Stephen's fortification] occupied the site on the high cliffs on the right bank, not a vestige of which now remains'. While it is impossible to ascertain if Hanrahan's account accurately records an absence of buildings at the site, it is tempting to speculate that much of the above-ground remains were quarried between 1840 and 1866 to coincide with the construction of a round tower commemorating the Crimean War (Figure 4.7; ch. 9).

The round tower is not representative of the only quarrying episode at the site, which is likely to have occurred more organically over centuries. Hore (1900–11, vol. v, 34) recorded that when Belmont House was constructed in about 1800 cut stones from the castle were used. The site of this house, which is no longer extant, is just over 1km south of Carrick. Jeffrey (1979, 102), citing *The People* newspaper from 1889, records that no trace of Carrick (which he refers to as Shan-a-court) exists, as it was 'entirely demolished more than 160 years ago and the materials used in the construction of Belmont Mansion'. Jeffrey (1979, 103) also cites a Miss Adams writing in 1904, who recorded further that mills at Carrick were also 'demolished to supply stones for the building of the old mansion of Belmont by the earl of Donoughmore'. According to Bennett (1985, 32), older local residents who recalled Belmont were unaware of any connection to the castle of Carrick.

Lewis (1837, 280) recorded Belmont House as the residence of Charles Arthur Walker, stating that it was also built of stone from Carrick; he mentions Belmont's views of several other elegant mansions (including Sanders Court, Barntown House, Park House, Janeville, Bettyville and other villas) – which might also be built from 'Carrick stone'. A courtyard and out-buildings (National Inventory number 15703733) associated with Belmont House survive 250m to the west of the house site. These are recorded as dating to 1700–1840. The geology of these buildings has recently been assessed, and the results are described below (ch. 9).

Destruction of the castle may also have been undertaken to 'quarry' stone for Wexford Bridge (built 1795). O'Donovan (1840, 357) recorded the 'castle over the River Slaney in the townland of Newtown … [its] stones were carried away to build the stone part of the Bridge of Wexford'. Ferrycarrig Bridge, like Wexford Bridge, was designed by Lemuel Cox – under an act passed in 1794 that empowered subscribers

4.7 The round tower at Carrick, which impacted the subsurface archaeology of the site and was built from remaining medieval ruins (see chs 5, 9). The ringwork bank is seen under excavation in the foreground

to raise £7,000 for the bridge construction (Hore 1900–11, vol. v, 22). The bridge, constructed of American Oak, with a portcullis on the southern side and toll houses on both sides, opened in 1795. It survived until 1912 – although it was closed for repair in 1901 – when it was replaced by a concrete bridge, which was itself replaced in 1980 by the current bridge. It is credible that stone from the castle was drawn to construct Ferrycarrig Bridge, although it could also have been brought to Wexford town.

Finally, in 1857 a replica early medieval round tower (RMP WX037—028001) was constructed in the middle of the ringwork as a memorial to those who died in the Crimean War (1854–6) (see Bennett 1989; ch. 9, below). Remaining stone at the site is likely to have been used in this tower, possibly bringing to an end any upstanding buildings at Carrick. The tower was completed in July 1858, with the foundation stone laid by the lord lieutenant, the earl of Carlisle, on Thursday 8 October 1857 (*Wexford Independent*, 10 October 1857). The ceremony was recorded at length in the

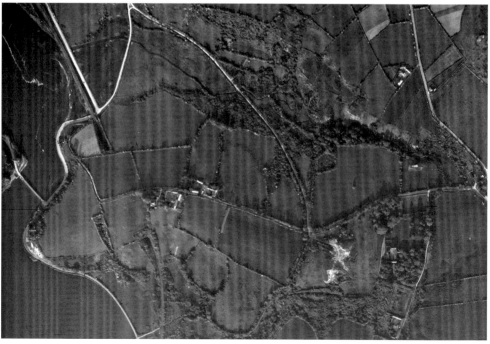

Carrick Castle, on the river Slaney Co. of Wexford,

4.8 (*opposite top*) Modern aerial photography showing the location of Carrick ringwork (left, white circle) and the field containing archaeology associated with Carrick borough (right, white trapezoid), as confirmed in archaeological testing and geophysics (see ch. 6). The image highlights the scale of the modern road's impact on Carrick's potential subsurface archaeology and the disconnect it has created in the medieval landscape here

4.9 (*opposite bottom*) Carrick ringwork and the surrounding landscape, prior to the construction of the modern road (© Military Archives, file V176_000880)

4.10 (*above*) Carrick and the River Slaney as shown in Gabriel Beranger's painting 'Carrick Castle on the River Slaney, in the county of Wexford' from the late eighteenth century (© Royal Irish Academy MS3C30(73))

Wexford Independent; Mayor John Coghlan described the tower 'as a testimonial in honour of the brave and lamented men of this country, who have offered up their lives at the shire of duty during the late war'. References were made in speeches to the location being the 'ancient fort of Carrig', notably by a Mr Walker, the vice-lieutenant of the county. He also drew connections to King John, citing Carrick as the location of a 'fortified palace' that retains the name John's Place (see ch. 9 for a full description).

THE MODERN PERIOD

In 1837 the parish of Carrick was recorded as containing 2,538 acres (1,027 hectares) and having 1,054 inhabitants (Lewis 1837, 279–80). Lewis describes the parish as being of good-quality tillage land, containing quarries of good building stone; one of which was used to construct St Peter's College in Wexford. In the later nineteenth century Carrick was dissected by the Wexford railway line, which was opened as far as Carcur, just outside Wexford town, in 1870 (Jenkins 2001, 97).

Over a century later, in 1981, land containing both the site and the INHP was acquired by Wexford County Council in advance of the construction of the new N11 route (also called the Rosslare Road and Wexford Ring Road). The road opened in 1988 after eight years of construction that radically altered the landscape surrounding Carrick ringwork/castle, as a cutting approximately 80m wide and 25m deep was excavated (Figure 4.8). This excavation separated the castle of Carrick from the settlement and borough that had developed around it (Figure 4.9). The road left an 'island' of marshy land, used for both tillage and pasture in living memory, to the west of the new road, which was developed as the INHP (Bennett 1985, 26; Culleton 1980, 51–2). Since 1987 the INHP has been open to the public as an open-air museum that recreates key stages in Ireland's past (see ch. 10).

In advance of both the road and the park opening, archaeological excavations were conducted at the site of the ringwork, but not within the road catchment. The first was undertaken by Isabel Bennett (licence number E000282) in 1984 (Bennett 1984; 1985), followed by Claire Cotter in 1986/7 (Cotter 1987; 1988); a minor excavation was also undertaken at the site in 2014 by Emmet Stafford (licence number 14E0411) (Stafford 2015). These excavations are described elsewhere in this volume (see ch. 5). In January of 2018 the Irish Archaeology Field School (IAFS) and INHP launched a major new archaeological research initiative – *Digging the Lost Town of Carrig Project* – the work of which is described in detail below (ch. 11).

BIBLIOGRAPHY

Arbuthnot, E., 2011. 'The ringwork castles of medieval Leinster and Meath'. PhD, TCD.

Barry, T. 1983. 'Anglo-Norman ringwork castles: some evidence'. In Reeves-Smyth, T. and Hammond, F. (eds), *Landscape archaeology in Ireland*, 295–314. Oxford.

Beglane, F. 2010. 'Deer and identity in medieval Ireland'. In Kucera, M. and Kunst, G.-K. (eds), *Using animals to construct human identities in medieval Europe*, 77–84. Vienna.

Beglane, F. 2012. 'Parks and deer hunting: evidence from medieval Ireland'. PhD, NUI, Galway.

Beglane, F. 2015. *Anglo-Norman parks in medieval Ireland*. Dublin.

Beglane, F. 2017. 'Forests and chases in medieval Ireland, 1169–c.1399'. *Journal of Historical Geography*, 59, 90–9.

Bennett, I. 1984. 'Archaeological excavations at Newtown td, Co. Wexford'. Unpublished archaeological report.

Bennett, I. 1985. 'Preliminary archaeological excavations at Ferrycarrig ringwork, Newtown td, Co. Wexford'. *Journal of the Wexford Historical Society*, 10, 25–43.

Bennett, I. 1989. 'The Crimean War memorial, Ferrycarrig, Co. Wexford: a precisely dated round tower'. *Archaeology Ireland*, 3:2, 58–60.

Bradley, J. and King, H. [1990]. 'Urban Archaeology Survey, part 11: County Wexford'. Unpublished report prepared for the OPW, Dublin.

Cantwell, B. 1981–3. 'Memorials of the dead: east Wexford'. Vol. 6 of 11. Unpublished survey in Wexford County Library.

Cohen, J. 2006. *Hybridity, identity and monstrosity in medieval Britain: on difficult middles*. New York.

Colfer, B. 2002. *Arrogant trespass: Anglo-Norman Wexford, 1169–1400*. Wexford.

Colfer, B. 2008. *Wexford: a town and its landscape*. Cork.

Colfer, B. 2013. *Wexford castles: landscape, context and settlement*. Cork.

Cotter, C. 1987. 'Ferrycarrig, Newtown, ringwork'. In Cotter, C. (ed.), *Excavations 1986: summary accounts of archaeological excavations in Ireland*, p. 37, no. 79. Dublin.

Cotter, C. 1988. 'Ferrycarrig, Newtown, ringwork'. In Bennett, I. (ed.), *Excavations 1987: summary accounts of archaeological excavations in Ireland*, p. 30, no. 56. Dublin.

Culleton, E. 1980. *The south Wexford landscape*. Dublin.

Duffy, S. 1997. *Ireland in the Middle Ages*. Dublin.

Green, A. 2018. 'Newtown, Ferrycarrig, Wexford: geophysical report (consent no./detection licence 18R0099)'. Unpublished technical report issued to IAFS.

Hanrahan, P. 1866. *Eva or the buried city of Bannow*. Wexford.

Hawkins, E. (ed.). 1844. *Travels in Holland, the United Provinces, England, Scotland and Ireland by Sir William Brereton*. Manchester.

Hayden, A. 2011. *Trim Castle, Co. Meath: excavations 1995–1998*. Dublin.

Holinshed, R. 1587. *The first and second volumes of chronicles … now newly augmented … to the year 1586 by John Hooker alias Vowell gent and others*. 3 vols. London.

Hore, P. 1900–11. *History of the town and county of Wexford*. 6 vols. London.

Jeffrey, W. 1979. 'The castles of Co. Wexford'. Notes presented to Wexford County Library by Old Wexford Society. Unpublished.

Jenkins, J. 2001. *The port and quays of Wexford, 800–2000AD: an industrial, commercial and social history*. Wexford.

Leslie, J. 1936. *Ferns clergy and parishes*. Dublin.

Lewis, S. 1837. *A topographical dictionary of Ireland: comprising the several counties, cities, boroughs, corporate, market and post towns, parishes and villages*. 2 vols. London.

Martin, F.X. 1969. 'Gerald of Wales, Norman reporter on Ireland'. *Irish Quarterly Review*, 58, 245–56.

McCormick, F. and Murray, E. 2017. 'The zooarchaeology of medieval Ireland'. In Albarella, U., Rizzetto, M., Russ, H., Vickers, K. and Viner-Daniels, S. (eds), *The Oxford handbook of zooarchaeology*, 195–213. Oxford.

McLoughlin, C. 2006. 'Archaeological testing report, Newtown, Co. Wexford (archaeological licence 05E1405)'. Unpublished technical report issued to James and Rita Codd.

McNeill, T. 1997. *Castles in Ireland: feudal power in a Gaelic world*. London.

Moore, M. 1996. *Archaeological inventory of County Wexford*. Dublin.

Murphy, M. and O'Conor, K. 2006. 'Castles and deer parks in Anglo-Norman Ireland'. *Journal of the American Society of Irish Medieval Studies*, 1, 53–70.

O'Conor, K. 1997. 'The origins of Carlow Castle'. *Archaeology Ireland*, 41, 13–16.

O'Donovan, J. 1840. *Ordnance Survey letters*. Dublin.

Orpen, G. (ed.). 1892. *The song of Dermot and the earl*. Oxford.

Orpen, G. (ed.). 1934. 'Charters of Earl Richard Marshal of the forests of Ross and Taghmon'. *Journal of the Royal Society of Antiquaries of Ireland*, 64, 54–63.

Orpen, G. 1968. *Ireland under the Normans*. 4 vols. Reprint. Oxford.

Scott, A. and Martin, F.X. (eds). 1978. *Expugnatio Hibernica by Giraldus Cambrensis*. Dublin.

Shine, D., Mandal, S., Hayes, C. and Harris, M. 2018. 'Finding Carrig'. *Archaeology Ireland*, 32:2, 35–40.

Sikora, M. 2011. 'Newtown, Co. Wexford, E1189'. In Cahill, M. and Sikora, M. (eds), *Breaking ground, finding graves: reports on the excavations of burials by the National Museum of Ireland, 1927–2006*. 2 vols. Vol. 1, 596–8. Dublin.

Stafford, E. 2015. 'Report on works at the Crimean War memorial, Newtown, Co. Wexford'. Unpublished technical report for WCC (licence 14E0411).

Sweetman, D. 1978. 'Archaeological excavations at Trim Castle, Co. Meath, 1971–4'. *Proceedings of the Royal Irish Academy*, 78C6, 127–98.

Sweetman, D. 1979. 'Archaeological excavations at Ferns Castle, County Wexford'. *Proceedings of the Royal Irish Academy*, 79C10, 217–45.

Sweetman, D. 1999. *Medieval castles of Ireland*. Cork.

CHAPTER FIVE

New investigations at the Carrick ringwork site

DENIS SHINE, RICHARD REID, STEPHEN MANDAL,
ASHELY GREEN & RICHARD CLUTTERBUCK

INTRODUCTION

Archaeological excavation resumed at the Carrick ringwork in 2018 after a hiatus of more than thirty years (see Shine and Mandal 2018). This chapter details the inaugural season of Irish Archaeological Field School (IAFS) excavations, which occurred over four weeks in January and February and six weeks in June and July. The objective of the 2018 excavation, and associated works, was clearly defined, and restricted to two main aims: a) to clear the site of overgrowth and define the monument's full form; and b) to re-expose the cuttings originally excavated by Claire Cotter in the 1980s before undertaking targeted excavation, in advance of environmental sampling and radiometric dating.

The excavation was incorporated into a full programme of archaeological research, so that Carrick and its relationship and importance to the surrounding region might be better understood. As part of this programme, several non-invasive surveys were undertaken, namely geological, geophysical, landscape assessment and 3D Lidar scanning. The surveys added greatly to our knowledge of the site, in advance of larger-scale investigations in 2019 and future years.

CARRICK LANDSCAPE

Carrick ringwork is located in the northern limits of the Irish National Heritage Park (INHP) in the townland of Newtown (barony of Shelmalier West) (NGR in ITM 701328, 623185). Today the area is referred to as Ferrycarrig, although Ferrycarrig is the name of the townland on the northern side of the River Slaney, directly across from Newtown. The ringwork is approximately 4km west of Wexford town at the head of a 'promontory' that extends into the Slaney; this headland reaches a height of almost 30m and falls dramatically in a sheer cliff toward the Slaney. The remains of the ringwork comprise a large sub-circular enclosure defined by a massive ditch and earthen bank extending to approximately 70m (east to west) by 30m (north to south) (Figure 5.1). It is possible that the enclosed area was originally larger, as erosion is

5.1 Carrick ringwork at the point excavation commenced in January 2018. Note the difference in vegetation on the east and west limits of the monument (i.e., either side of the footbridge)

known to occur of the escarpment face to the site's north and west. The ringwork was separated from its surrounding medieval setting by the construction of the N11 road in the 1980s (see also ch. 4).

The defining attribute of the site for Carrick ringwork is its location on a promontory. The monument is sited at a pinch-point in the River Slaney – a natural place for crossing by ferry and by bridge for travellers from Wexford town to Enniscorthy and Dublin (Figure 5.2). The promontory area is the location of both Carrick Castle and the medieval borough of Carrick, which were situated within the medieval parish of the same name. The promontory is flanked on either side by two streams flowing into the Slaney. Those who controlled the promontory and the ferry point were able to control travel by land and water from Wexford town into the heart of the county. The parish church dedicated to St Nicholas was located in the centre of the medieval parish, which extended from the Slaney south to the uplands of Shelmalier and Forth Commons (Figure 5.2). The modern civil parish of Carrick contains fifteen townlands, with much the same outline as the parish mapped on the seventeenth-century Down Survey. Notably, the site of Carrick ringwork is in a separate division called 'Ballandsland', consisting of seventeen acres (6.9 hectares) of arable and pasture (Figure 5.4). This boundary may be significant to Carrick as it could denote the original boundary of the borough (for a full discussion, see ch. 6).

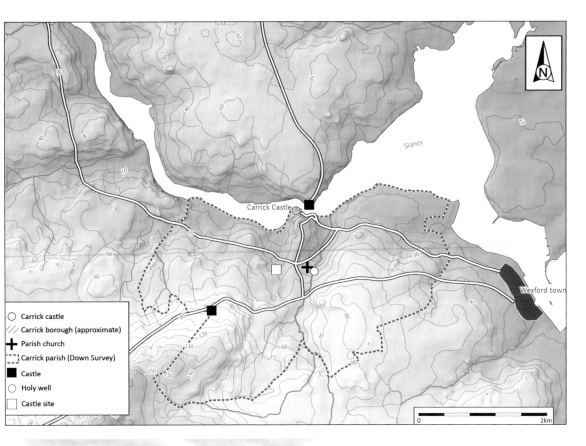

Carrick castle

/// Carrick borough (approximate)

✚ Parish church

Carrick parish (Down Survey)

■ Castle

○ Holy well

□ Castle site

5.2 (*above*) The topography of the landscape surrounding the Carrick site, showing the location of significant monuments identified during landscape assessment

5.3 Carrick ringwork at the head of a promontory overlooking the River Slaney

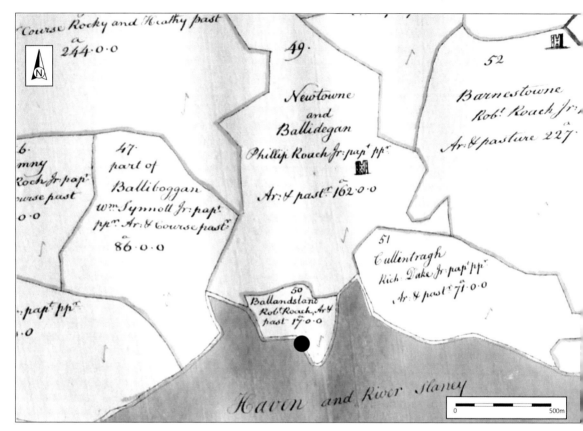

5.4 The Down Survey map, showing the site of 'Ballandsland' and Carrick ringwork
(© National Library of Ireland MS 725)

CARRICK GEOLOGY AND SOILS

The history of Carrick is, to a large extent, dominated by its geology, which has not only influenced its siting, but also provided the raw material of which the settlement was built. As such, an understanding of the local geology is important to better comprehend the archaeological site (see Figures 5.5 and 5.6; see also Table 5.1).

Carrick ringwork is located on a high ridge of Cambrian Age sediments and meta-sediments (Figure 5.5). The hill comprises two similar geological formations separated by a north-west to south-east trending fault. The bedrock consists of thickly bedded grey-green meta-greywackes with minor layers of slaty mudstones. In the northern-most portion of the hill, including the cliff on which the ringwork is perched, the greywackes are interbedded with chlorite phyllites and thinly laminated siltstones.

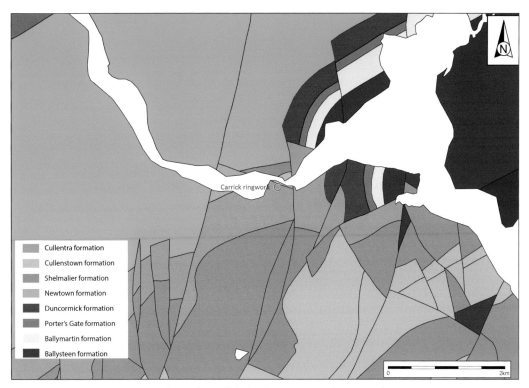

5.5 The geology of the landscape surrounding Carrick

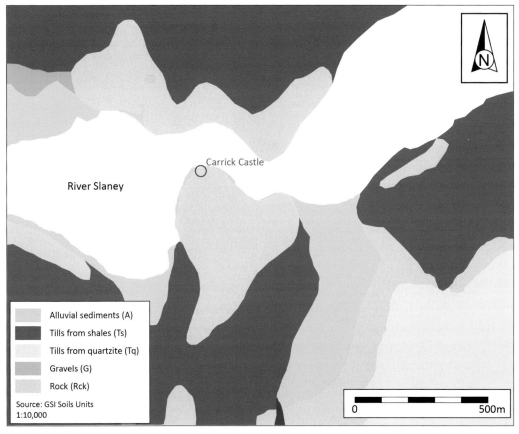

5.6 The soils of the landscape surrounding Carrick

In the region of the ringwork, a wide variety of rock types of differing age are represented, including Cambrian Age quartzites and greywackes and younger, Carboniferous Age, sandstones, limestones and shales.

The site at Carrick has only a thin covering of glacial till, the hill having been scarped by the effects of past glaciations. Bedrock is relatively close to the surface (marked Rck on Figure 5.6). Alluvial sediments (A) relating to the retreat of the ice sheets occur immediately to the east and on the north cliff face of the site. There are tills (Ts) composed of Lower Palaeozoic shales to the south, north and east. To the south-east occur tills (Tq) derived from quartzites, and gravels (G) derived from sandstones, while shales occur to the west.

Table 5.1 Geological formations in the area of the Carrick ringwork (after Tietzsch-Tyler and Sleeman 1994; see Figure 5.5)

Formation	Code	Description
Cullentra	CA	Thickly bedded grey-green meta-greywackes with minor layers of slatey mudstones
Cullenstown	CN	Green and occasionally purple, coarse- to fine-grained grey-wackes interbedded with chlorite phyllites and thinly laminated siltstones
Shelmalier	SH	Quartzites
Newtown	NN	Grey-green meta-greywackes and slates
Duncormick	DC	Red and grey conglomerates and sandstones of Old Red Sandstone facies
Porter's Gate	PG	Sandstone, shale and thin limestone
Ballymartin	BT	Limestone and dark grey calcareous shale
Ballysteen	BA	Dark muddy limestone and shale

PREVIOUS ARCHAEOLOGICAL INVESTIGATIONS

Prior to the commencement of the *Digging the Lost Town of Carrig Project* and the current investigations, archaeological excavations had been undertaken at Carrick ringwork on three occasions in 1984, 1986/7 and 2014 (see Figure 5.7). The largest of these, by Claire Cotter, will be reported in due course by the excavator; previous excavations by Isabel Bennett have been reported previously (Bennett 1984, 1985) and are here only briefly summarised.

The first excavations occurred in 1984 when several cuttings, including one through the ringwork, were excavated by Bennett in advance of the construction of

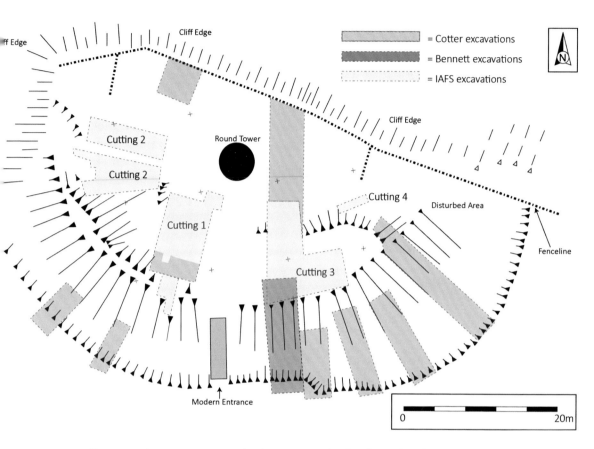

5.7 Previous and current excavations that have uncovered archaeology (after Shine et al. 2018)

the INHP. A central cutting in the ringwork was placed through the fosse. Within the cutting the entirety of the fosse fill, measuring 1.9m deep by 5.2m wide, was removed. The fosse was found to contain several fills – including a notable basal fill of burnt material (ash and charcoal) and a mortar-rich layer, which may relate to the construction of stone buildings at the site. Bennett (1985, 40) remarked on the paucity of finds from the fosse, offering an explanation that this may indicate regular cleaning of the site, possibly by disposing of refuse into the adjacent River Slaney. Except for modern pottery, only four sherds (two medieval and two post-medieval), five pieces of glass and eleven pieces of unidentified corroded iron were recorded. A piece of possible worked flint and a clay pipe fragment were also collected from the topsoil. Vegetation, and some topsoil, was also removed off the ringwork bank, revealing a wall, which Bennett speculated could run across much of the site. A small piece of corroded iron was found adhering to the wall surface and a few pieces of 'melted glass' were found adjacent to the wall's facing. Immediately outside the wall five possible post-holes were recorded, which were tentatively interpreted as evidence of the original twelfth-century palisade (see Bennett 1985 for a full discussion of the excavation).

Further excavations were undertaken by Cotter in 1986 and 1987 (Cotter 1987; 1988; see also Shine et al. 2018). The works were funded by Wexford County Council and the Social Employment Scheme, as part of works within the INHP. A total of six cuttings were excavated through the ditch in 1986, with a further four excavated on the interior of the site in 1987. The excavations revealed a burnt structure, possibly of sill-beam construction, in the western part of the interior. The associated finds suggested a late twelfth- or early thirteenth-century date. The stone footings of a building were revealed in the south-eastern sector. The building, which was interpreted as part of the stone castle, seems to have been placed at an angle against the wall previously exposed by Bennett (1985). The excavations indicated that the interior of the ringwork had been heavily disturbed, probably during the construction of the mid-nineteenth-century round tower (ch. 9). The series of cuttings excavated through the ditch indicated a maximum depth of *c*.2m and width of 5.4m. The ditch was crowned by a high bank composed of up-cast boulder clays, and a possible revetment wall was recorded on the inside of the enclosing bank. In comparison to Bennett's excavation, a large number of artefacts were recorded. Approximately 1,655 sherds of medieval pottery were recovered mainly from a midden deposit abutting the western bank. Almost all the finds were from the later twelfth to thirteenth century and were predominantly pottery, which included a broad variety of locally produced potteries and French and English imports. More unusual finds were also recovered including arrow heads, a silver long-cross penny, an iron battle-axe, a short-cross halfpenny, a horse stirrup and a barrel padlock.

Finally, excavations were undertaken at the base of the Crimean War monument (round tower) to facilitate the placement of lightning conductor mats for the monument in 2014 by Emmet Stafford (2015). The excavation was confined to two very discrete cuttings at the base of the war memorial. No archaeological remains were uncovered.

IAFS EXCAVATIONS

In January 2018, the IAFS, under the direction of Denis Shine and Stephen Mandal, commenced archaeological excavations at the site as part of an international field school (licence 17E0318). The three internal cuttings that contained archaeology in the 1980s were re-exposed and re-recorded. A new cutting (Cutting 4) was also opened (see Figure 5.8). Much of the site was also cleared of vegetation, which had grown since the conclusion of the 1980s dig; mature overgrowth was felled by INHP staff in advance of the dig, with smaller vegetation removed by the archaeological team using hand tools. Prior to this work all the old cuttings were virtually indiscernible. The re-exposed cuttings (Cuttings 1, 2 and 3) were recorded as follows:

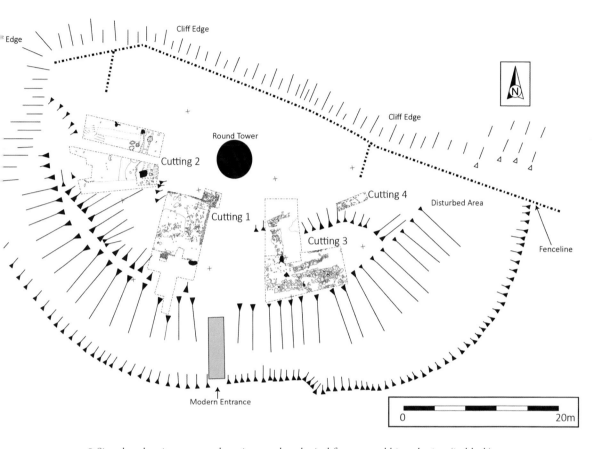

5.8 Site plan showing excavated cuttings, archaeological features and bioturbation (in black)

Cutting 1 is rectangular (measuring 10.2m by 6.2m), at the southern interior edge of the ringwork. A narrow extension (measuring 4.9m by 90cm) extended from the main cutting through the bank of the ringwork. This extension had eroded significantly since the 1980s and was widened to 2.5m, over a distance of 3.4m, to expose a clean bank section from which to obtain datable material. A small extension (measuring 2.5m by 2.25m) was also excavated at the north-east corner of Cutting 1, to investigate the junction of two possible walls.

Cutting 2 is in the western half of the enclosure. It was originally excavated as part of the 1980s excavation programme and consisted of two areas divided by a 1m-wide baulk. In total, Cutting 2 measures 11.9m by 10.1m at maximum extent.

L-shaped Cutting 3, which is in the eastern half of the ringwork, measures 13.2m by 11m at maximum extent. It was originally excavated by Cotter as an extension to an initial cutting excavated by Bennett. The cutting is divided into two distinct portions; the southern part lies across the top of the enclosure bank, while the northern portion is in the lower interior of the enclosure. An arbitrary vertical cut was created in the 1980s between these two areas.

A new cutting – Cutting 4 – was opened in 2018. It measures 4m by 1m and was oriented along a roughly east-to-west axis. This exploratory cutting is east of the other cuttings in an area undisturbed by the 1980s excavations.

Each of the previously opened cuttings (Cuttings 1–3) was found to be wholly or partially covered with a plastic membrane, which was covered with backfill after the 1980s excavation. The backfill and membrane were removed from Cuttings 1 and 2 in January 2018 and from Cutting 3 in June 2018, revealing the 1980s excavation surface. The cuttings were then cleaned and recorded. The exposed archaeology – at the point the 1980s excavation concluded – can be best surmised and grouped as follows:

Bank and fosse

The enclosing bank and fosse are the earliest confirmed archaeological features on the site, being historically dated to 1169 (Orpen 1892, lines 1775–9, 1395–9; Scott and Martin 1978, 81; see also ch. 4, above). A full section through the bank, excavated in the 1980s, remained open and this was extended, cleaned down and fully recorded; the base of this section was deepened to reveal a total bank height of 2.15m. The external ditch measured 2m in depth by 5.6m in width, giving a total defensive height of 4.15m from the base of the ditch to the crown of the bank. In addition, an enclosing palisade is attested in historical accounts (Orpen 1892, lines 1775–9, 1395–9; Scott and Martin 1978, 81), with possible evidence of such encountered in previous archaeological excavations (Bennett 1984; 1985).

The bank was composed of four basic layers of sterile boulder clays, up-cast from the digging of the ditch, covered by a slumped bank collapse(s) as well as relict and modern topsoil (Figure 5.9). The deposits all overlay the presumed twelfth-century ground surface, a sandy silt flecked with charcoal, which was extensively sampled and floated to obtain datable material. A sample of this charcoal returned a date of 880–980 cal. AD, providing a *terminus post quem* for the overlying bank (see Table 5.2). Further excavation and a full programme of radiometric dating will be required to see if this intriguing date is an indication of anthropogenic activity at Carrick prior to the arrival of the Anglo-Normans.

Table 5.2 Radiocarbon dates obtained for Carrick in 2018. Calibration after OxCal 4.1 (Bronk Ramsay 2009) using the IntCal09 dataset (Reimer et al. 2009)

Laboratory code	Material	Sample no.	Radiocarbon age (BP)	Calibrated age (95.4% probability) (cal. BC/AD)
Wk-47789	Charcoal	1023	1120±15	AD880–980
Wk-44399	Charcoal	2019	892±15	AD1040–1210

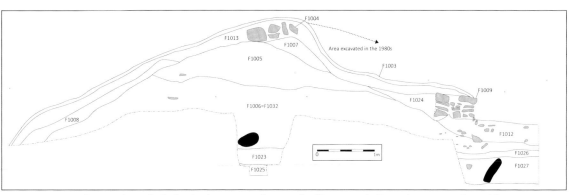

5.9 Section through the bank, showing southern wall of Structure A (F1009), remains of possible 'curtain wall' (F1004) and bioturbation (in black)

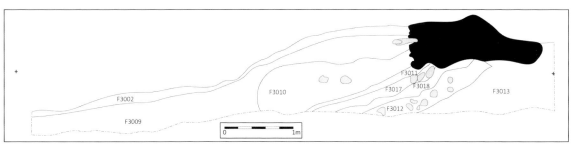

5.10 East baulk of Cutting 3, showing original bank (F3013), as well as overlying mortar layers (F3011 and F3018), relict topsoil layer (F3017) and bank extension (F3012); bioturbation is shown in black

The bank is crowned by a deposit of large stones, which could be the fragmentary remains of a curtain wall. While this suggestion requires further investigation, the stones sat upon a clearly levelled redeposited boulder clay that may represent a deliberate level platform upon which to build an enclosure. A better-preserved wall, interpreted as a possible curtain wall in previous excavations, was recorded in Cutting 3. This wall measures up to 1.8m wide and 10.2m long but survives to a maximum of only two courses, with generally only a single course surviving. No foundation cut was identified for the wall, which, based on current knowledge, appears to be constructed directly on the earliest deposit of bank material identified in Cutting 3.

Two internal extensions to the bank were observed in the section faces of Cuttings 2 and 3. In Cutting 3 (Figures 5.10, 5.11) the bank had been extended inward by 80cm through the addition of redeposited boulder clay. Two mortar deposits/dumps and a relict topsoil (total depth 30cm) accumulated over the original bank but beneath this redeposited extension. Further excavation will aim to clarify the function of this 'extension'; the mortar indicates it could be associated with a demolition or construction period. On current knowledge, it is speculated that the inward extension of the bank derives from levelling, or raking inward, a convex bank to create a level platform in advance of constructing the curtain wall.

5.11 Southern baulk of Cutting 3, showing walls SB2 and SB3 in the foreground

5.12 Students holding ranging rods in excavated post-holes in Cutting 2 for illustrative purposes

In Cutting 2 the 'extension' was significantly larger, extending the bank inward by 2.3m, again through the deposition of two boulder clays. The construction of internal platforms in ringworks may have been undertaken to accommodate structures, with ringworks frequently recorded as congested – almost 'claustrophobic' – places internally (Arbuthnot 2011, 127).

Twelfth-century structures

The earliest internal features are the ephemeral remains of probable twelfth-century wooden structures. The excavations revealed three new post-holes in Cutting 2, and re-exposed one post-hole and three shallow cut features from the 1980s excavation programme (Figure 5.12). While it was possible to relocate some post-holes identified in the 1980s, the cutting has been badly impacted by bioturbation in the intervening period. The post-holes (averaging 14cm in diameter by 24cm in depth) were covered by a patchy charcoal layer, interpreted as deriving from one major burning event. This charcoal has been dated to 1040–1210 cal. AD (with a 57.8% probability of dating from AD1120–1210). These post-holes, while small, may represent the first Anglo-Norman structures in the country!

Stratigraphically, the next features appear to be compacted ground surfaces, of currently indeterminate date. Similar deposits are recorded in Cuttings 1 and 4, which appear to represent a larger medieval ground surface across the ringwork. In Cutting 4 this 'surface' is sealed by an occupation layer containing much medieval pottery. This occupation layer is cut by a linear feature of unknown function, whose fill contained two sherds of medieval pottery. In Cuttings 1 and 4 the ground surface is overlain by rubble-like deposits. In the case of Cutting 1, this deposit is cut by a foundation trench for a later medieval structure – indicating phasing in the buildings here.

Thirteenth-/fourteenth-century structures

Two masonry structures have been recorded at the site which may date to the thirteenth and fourteenth centuries. They contain a total of six surviving walls, all of which have been extensively quarried since the medieval period (see chs 4, 9). For ease of description these structures are referred to as Structure A and Structure B (Figures 5.13–5.15). Their walls follow this naming convention – SA1 is the first-described wall of Structure A.

Structure A (Figure 5.13)

Structure A is composed of three identified walls, with the western extent still not located. The southernmost wall (SA1) is located directly on the interior of the bank and measures 6.2m long by 70cm wide by 70cm high in surviving extent; it is orientated broadly east–west. The wall survives to a height of four courses and sits on an occasional footing of a single course of flat stones on the wall's north extent and a rubble-like foundation on its southern extent. The south side of the wall is abutted by

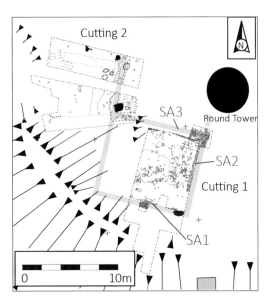

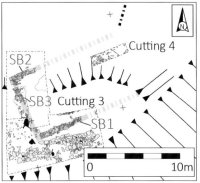

5.13 (*left*) Projected limits of Structure A, overlaid on planned masonry. Showing three walls SA1, SA2 and SA3, as well as the robber trench in Cutting 2

5.15 (*above*) Projected limits of Structure B, overlaid on planned masonry, showing three walls – SB1, SB2 and SB3 – as well as the curtain wall, at the lower limits of the image

5.14 Junction of walls SA2 (F1010) and SA3 (F1011), which are keyed into each other

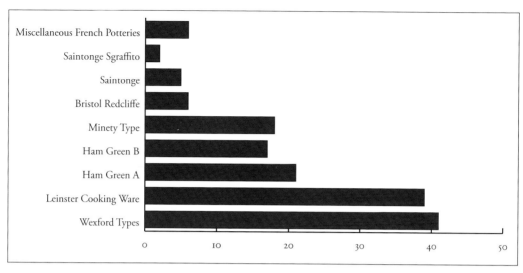

5.16 Classification of medieval potteries recovered from the 2018 season, by type

redeposited boulder clay that forms part of the bank. SA2 is perpendicular to SA1 and measures 8.7m long by 94cm wide by 30cm high in exposed extent. SA2 generally survives to only a single course, beneath which is a thin rubble foundation. SA3 joins with SA2 in north-east corner of Cutting 1 and measures 5.2m long by 1.17m wide by 53cm high in exposed extent; it is parallel to SA1. Wall SA3 survives to a total of six courses, five of which are in the wall foundation. SA3 is the only wall with an evident foundation cut. This cut is through a mixed rubble deposit, indicating previous construction or demolition phases. SA3 is entirely quarried out at its western extent in Cutting 1 but continues in the form of an L-shaped 'robber trench' in Cutting 2; this trench was excavated in the 1980s, when it was found to continue across the width of Cutting 2, a distance of *c.*6.4m.

All the walls appear to from a single structure, with SA2 and SA3 keyed into each other. Each is of notably different construction, however, and contains different stone types/percentages (see geology section, below), inferring phasing or rebuilding over time. Clarification of the form, function and construction method of the 'building' may come with further excavation. Current knowledge indicates a structure with a possible maximum length of 15m and width of 9.5m, oriented broadly north–south. The function of the building is currently unknown; however, it is worth noting that the castle of Carrick-on-Slaney is first recorded at the time of William Marshal II's death in 1231 (Colfer 2002, 124; Orpen 1968, vol. iii, 59). An inquisition of 1324 lists the 'Castle of Carryk' as ruinous and valued at nothing; this inquisition also records a ruinous hall and chapel within an 'enclosure' (or *classum*) at the Carrick ringwork (Bradley and King 1990, 66; Hore 1900–11, vol. v, 33). The stone remains on site could relate to either of these structures/phases.

Structure B

Structure B is also composed of three walls with the eastern extent still unexcavated. The southernmost wall – SB1 – measures 4.9m long by 1m wide by 35cm high as exposed (Figure 5.15); just a single course survives, and no foundation cut is evident. It overlies the earliest phase of bank material identified in 2018 and appears to be aligned with SB3 to form a rectilinear structure – both walls being parallel and oriented broadly east–west. Wall SB3 (measuring 3m long by 1.1m wide by 43cm high) at the north end of the cutting is parallel to SB1. This wall was heavily robbed out and a single random course of stone is all that remains. No foundation cut was evident for the wall; however, a sondage at the wall's northern face established that it was constructed on top of a mortar pad, which itself lay on a rubble deposit.

SB1 and SB3 are both perpendicular to SB2, and are assumed to have originally been joined by it. This wall has been extensively robbed out with only a few stones surviving (Figure 5.11); originally this would have been 5.4m in length, presumably being of similar width to the other walls. Structure B, like Structure A, is of unknown function. Unlike Structure A, Structure B's walls are more consistent in their geological composition. The structure is located at a curious direct east–west axis, an unnatural angle to either the curtain wall, ringwork bank or cliff face, and one that makes poor use of the already limited internal space. One can only deduce that the orientation was both deliberate and important to the original builders and, as chapels are typically oriented east–west, it is tempting to associate the structure with the chapel recorded in 1324. Clarification of this association requires additional excavation, in particular at the structure's eastern extent.

Overlying deposits

Both structures, and the site in general, are overlaid by a series of deposits. These include post-medieval rubble, which relates to the construction of the round tower in the mid-nineteenth century and previous quarrying activity on the site (see ch. 4). Beneath these, but still overlying the structures, are a series of deposits from which the only artefacts recovered were medieval. These deposits were excavated in the 1980s and their exact form and function remain elusive until further excavation.

Artefacts

From the first season(s) of the current excavation a total of 236 artefacts and 121 ecofacts were recovered. The ecofacts consist primarily of animal bone and shell, which will be fully analysed by project zoo-archaeologist Fiona Beglane once cuttings are closed. Other samples included soil, brick, metal slag, mortar, stone, possible plaster and plant macrofossil (for a full description, see Shine and Mandal 2018). The finds assemblage consisted predominantly of medieval pottery, although ferrous items (including 48 nails), stone, flint, miscellaneous metal and worked wood were also encountered (see Shine and Mandal 2018). The non-ceramic finds included a 1790s

5.17 Medieval ceramic 'antlers' from an aquamanile recovered during the 2018 season

Condor token, which may have been lost during subsequent quarrying of the building stones (see ch. 4), and a copper clasp/buckle. All finds have been conserved at Cardiff University or University College Dublin.

The most instructive collection was certainly the medieval pottery, which has been identified by project medieval ceramic specialist, Clare McCutcheon (see Figure 5.16, Table 5.3). As expected, the dominant potteries are local Wexford types and Leinster Cooking Ware. A good range of imported potteries were also in the collection, including Ham Green A and B, Minety Type, Bristol Redcliffe, Saintonge, Saintonge Sgraffito and other miscellaneous French potteries.

Table 5.3 Types and numbers of medieval pottery sherds, identified by the project's medieval ceramic specialist, Clare McCutcheon

Type	Number
Wexford Types	41
Leinster Cooking Ware	39
Ham Green A	21
Ham Green B	17
Minety Type	18
Bristol Redcliffe	6
Saintonge	5
Saintonge Sgraffito	2
Miscellaneous French Potteries	6

While it is outside the scope of this essay to describe the artefacts in detail, the find of the season, a set of ceramic antlers, merits some elaboration (Figure 5.17). The antlers, which are consistent in shape with those of a fallow stag, are from an aquamanile (from *aqua + manus* = 'water' + 'hand') – a medieval water jug, typically in the form of one or more animal or human figures. An aquamanile usually contained water for the washing of hands over a basin, either as part of high-status feasts or as part of the Eucharist. Most surviving examples are in metal, but more rarely ceramic examples are known, including from Ireland (Clare McCutcheon, pers. comm.). The significance of the find is partly that the jug is associated with higher-status sites, but more so that it speaks to Carrick's deer park. Deer parks are thought to date predominantly from 1250 to 1300, with the park at Carrick likely to be one of the first in the country, and certainly one of the earliest where fallow deer, an Anglo-Norman introduction, are recorded (see Beglane 2012; 2015; ch. 7, below, for a full discussion of Carrick deer park).

In the 2018 season, three lithics were recovered and these have been identified by Dermot Moore as dating to the later Neolithic/Early Bronze Age. These are significant as they offer further evidence of human activity at Carrick well before the Anglo-Normans arrived. A collared urn burial (RMP WX037–029) was uncovered on Carrick hill in 1984, *c.*200m south-east of the ringwork; while a flint implement was also uncovered in previous excavations (Bennett 1984, 16; 1985, 41; ch. 4, above). These (together with the bank's radiocarbon date) are all tantalising suggestions that the promontory at Carrick – such a prominent and strategic point in the landscape – held importance long before the arrival of Robert Fitz Stephen; of course, any such theorising can only be confirmed through continued archaeological excavation and research.

NON-INVASIVE SURVEYS

The aim of the inaugural season of IAFS excavations was to maximise the return of archaeological information, while undertaking as little 'new' excavation as possible. To this end, several surveys were undertaken in tandem with the summer dig season. Lidar surveys at Carrick are described elsewhere (see ch. 8) with the results of the geological assessment and geophysical surveys contained herein.

Geological assessment

At the close of the 2018 excavation season in August the remains of the lower levels of seven walls had been uncovered. At that stage, a systematic visual inspection of each of the stones in the remaining walls was undertaken; stone by stone, course by course. In total, 127 stones were identified, though it was not possible to identify two, due to weathering and their position in the ground; the results of the assessment are shown in Figure 5.18.

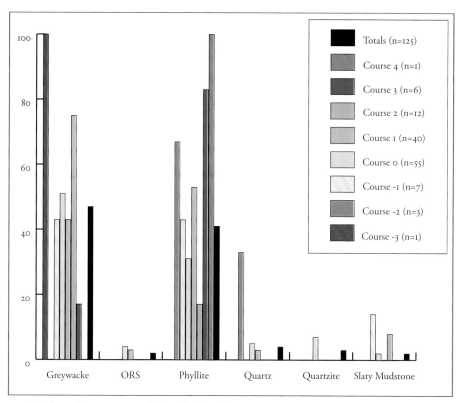

Legend:
- Totals (n=125)
- Course 4 (n=1)
- Course 3 (n=6)
- Course 2 (n=12)
- Course 1 (n=40)
- Course 0 (n=55)
- Course -1 (n=7)
- Course -2 (n=3)
- Course -3 (n=1)

5.18 Geological composition of the walls from Structure A, Structure B and the curtain wall (CW)

Six different rock types were identified in the assessment. Of these, two (greywacke and phyllite) are readily available as they occur in the local bedrock, which is overlain by only a thin layer of glacial till and soil. Shale occurs very widely in the tills to the south, north and east, and it is also possible that these are slaty mudstones, which occur in the bedrock at the site. The remaining two rock types used are ORS (Old Red Sandstone – a coarse conglomerate) and quartz (large blocks of vein quartz). Geologically, these rocks are probably derived from the Duncormick Formation to the east. It is most likely that they come from tills in the lower slopes of the hill where alluvial deposits relating to the retreat of the ice sheets of the last glaciation are present. The quartzite is probably derived from the Shelmalier Formation (SH), which occurs to the south and south-east, and notably immediately to the north across the river.

Bedrock is very close to the surface on the hill itself, so it is likely that the excavation of the ditch of the ringwork was into bedrock and produced a significant quantity of stone. The remaining ditch is *c.*8om in length and has an average depth of *c.*2m. Taking into consideration the substantial bank, which is composed of soil cast up from the ditch, it is likely that more than 375m³ or 750 to 1,000 tonnes of stone was quarried and therefore available for use in building. While this is not an insubstantial volume of stone, it is clearly not enough to build a castle, even to build the currently known walls to a significant height. It appears the stone may still have been sourced locally, however, as a field survey of the surrounding hills revealed large areas on the north-western cliff face that appear to have been quarried away – although the dense tree cover makes closer inspection difficult.

While the sample sizes are relatively small, the results show some interesting patterns. All of the walls, with the exception of the curtain wall (CW), predominantly contain a mixture of greywacke and phyllite. It is interesting, however, that walls SA1, SA3, SB1 and SB3 contain a higher percentage of greywacke than phyllite, whereas the walls SA2 and SB2 contain a higher percentage of phyllite than greywacke. It is not possible at this juncture to state definitively whether this varying composition and/or the using of phyllite over greywacke and vice versa represents phasing, with different walls being constructed at different times, in different seasons, or by different masons.

While it is not possible at this time to confirm or date this quarrying, or to estimate its extent, it is highly likely that the majority of the stone used in the building of the castle was sourced on the hill itself. Further research will be undertaken as the excavation proceeds and hopefully more extensive walls will be uncovered.

It may be significant that the curtain wall contains a high percentage of quartzite, which is not used at all in the other walls. This is particularly interesting given that this rock most likely was sourced in the cliffs at the opposite side of the River Slaney, where the bedrock is of a different formation. Interestingly, the majority of the medieval buildings in Wexford town contain quartzite and a medieval quarry in the middle of the town was excavated by Stafford and McLoughlin (2009). It is plausible that quartzite came by river from Wexford town at some stage in the construction of the castle.

The majority of the stones in walls on the site show no evidence of having been carefully cut or dressed. They vary greatly in size and shape, their shape principally determined by the natural breaking properties of the stone being used; coarser-grained sediments and meta sediments being blockier, whereas finer-grained laminated shales are thinner. Future research will examine the potential differential use of stone sizes and proportions and the geotechnical properties of the rock types used, with a view to determining how selective (or not) were the people who built these walls.

Geophysical survey

The geophysical survey was undertaken in July 2018 by Ashely Green of Bournemouth University (licence 18R0099). Two techniques, electromagnetic induction (EMI) and ground-penetrating radar (GPR), were employed.

EMI

EMI measures the magnetic susceptibility (in-phase component) and apparent electrical conductivity (quadrature component) of subsurface materials. It can reach up to 1.8m in depth in a best-case scenario and is suitable to delineate large earth

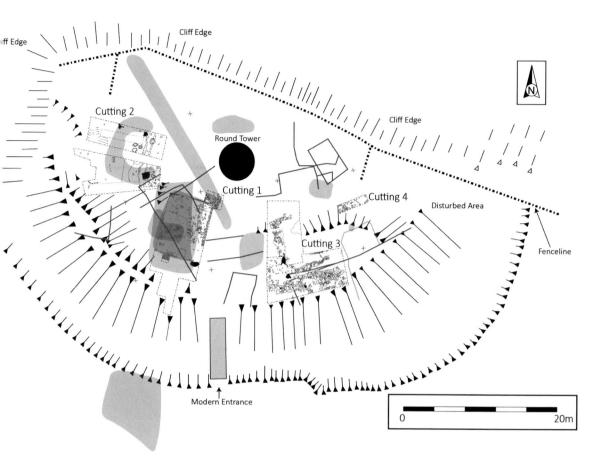

5.19 Site plan showing all geophysical anomalies (EMI and GPR)

features (remnants of mounds, backfilled ditches etc.), settlement activity (houses, storage or industrial activity etc.) and modern anthropogenic activity/disturbance (pipes etc.). EMI was preferred for Carrick as the survey area was quite small and the equipment was portable enough to survey within the cuttings as well as the surrounding unexcavated areas (for a full description of the survey and survey method, see Green 2018).

GPR

Ground-penetrating radar (GPR) detects slight variations in the subsurface conditions (for example, geological variations, anthropogenic activity, services) by emitting electromagnetic pulses through the ground from a transmitting antenna. When the emitted signal interacts with changes in the subsurface material, it is reflected to the ground surface to the receiving antenna and converted to wavelets presented on a monitor held by the surveyor. As such, GPR detects changes in the subsurface matrix, whether they are significant archaeological features or variations in geology.

Under optimal conditions, GPR (which can penetrate up to 20m under certain conditions) can detect a large range of features including large voids, stratigraphic changes, interments (modern and archaeological), geomorphological changes, structures (or their foundations), large stones, pits and ditches.

The GPR survey at Carrick served to complement the EMI survey, as GPR would not be affected by modern lighting and conductor works around the round tower and allowed for a much higher-resolution data-acquisition strategy.

Processing and results

The data was processed and written up off-site (Green 2018), with both techniques integrated to form a single geophysical map of the site (Figure 5.19). As the purpose of the survey was to inform future excavations, and as all anomalies remain to be 'ground-truthed' at the time of writing, it is difficult to comment on the results of the survey. In total, twelve trends were recorded that were considered of low to medium archaeological potential. These are best viewed in graphic form, with the sub-circular response in Cutting 2 and a rectangular response north of Cutting 4 selected as the most urgent for excavation.

CONCLUSION

The inaugural season at Carrick was a great success, with over ninety students from the United States of America, Canada, Australia, South Africa, South Korea and Ireland participating in a variety of teaching and research programmes ranging from one to four weeks. Specialists in disciplines as diverse as geology, geophysics, 3D Lidar scanning, ceramic analysis and conservation came together to contribute to the excavation and the wider research project. Results exceeded expectations, as we now have a clearer image of the point at which the 1980s excavations ceased and, more importantly, tantalising evidence of the archaeological features that remain to be investigated.

This season is best considered as a snapshot in time, as much more detailed results will be forthcoming from what is an on-going major research, teaching and excavation project with an anticipated lifespan of over ten years. In time, this project will allow students, the local community, the wider Irish public and international visitors a chance to understand in a deeper and experiential way what happened at Carrick eight-hundred-and-fifty years ago, shortly after the very first Anglo-Normans arrived in the country.

BIBLIOGRAPHY

Arbuthnot, E. 2011. 'The ringwork castles of medieval Leinster and Meath'. PhD, TCD.

Beglane, F. 2012. 'Parks and deer hunting: evidence from medieval Ireland'. PhD, NUI, Galway.

Beglane, F. 2015. *Anglo-Norman parks in medieval Ireland.* Dublin.

Bennett, I. 1984. 'Archaeological excavations at Newtown td, Co. Wexford'. Unpublished archaeological report.

Bennett, I. 1985. 'Preliminary archaeological excavations at Ferrycarrig ringwork, Newtown td, Co. Wexford'. *Journal of the Wexford Historical Society,* 10, 25–43.

Bradley, J. and King, H. [1990]. 'Urban Archaeology Survey, part 11: County Wexford'. Unpublished report prepared for the OPW, Dublin.

Bronk Ramsey, C. 2009. 'Bayesian analysis of radiocarbon dates'. *Radiocarbon,* 51:1, 337–60.

Colfer, B. 2002. *Arrogant trespass: Anglo-Norman Wexford, 1169–1400.* Wexford.

Cotter, C. 1987. 'Ferrycarrig, Newtown, ringwork'. In Cotter, C. (ed.), *Excavations 1986: summary accounts of archaeological excavations in Ireland,* p. 37, no. 79. Dublin.

Cotter, C. 1988. 'Ferrycarrig, Newtown, ringwork'. In Bennett, I. (ed.), *Excavations 1987: summary accounts of archaeological excavations in Ireland,* p. 30, no. 56. Dublin.

Green, A. 2018. 'Newtown, Ferrycarrig, Wexford: geophysical report (consent no./detection licence 18R0099)'. Unpublished technical report issued to IAFS.

Hore, P. 1900–11. *History of the town and county of Wexford.* 6 vols. London.

Orpen, G. (ed.). 1892. *The song of Dermot and the earl.* Oxford.

Orpen, G. 1968. *Ireland under the Normans.* 4 vols. Reprint. Oxford.

Reimer, P., Baillie, M., Bard, E., Bayliss, A., Beck, J., Blackwell, P., Bronk Ramsey, C., Buck, C., Burr, G., Edwards, R., Friedrich, M., Grootes, P., Guilderson, T., Hajdas, I., Heaton, T., Hogg, A., Hughen, K., Kaiser, K., Kromer, B., McCormac, F., Manning, S., Reimer, R., Richards, D., Southon, J., Talamo, S., Turney, C., van der Plicht, J. and Weyhenmeyer, C. 2009. 'IntCal09 and Marine09 radiocarbon age calibration curves, 0–50,000 years cal BP'. *Radiocarbon,* 51:4, 1111–50.

Scott, A. and Martin, F.X. (eds). 1978. *Expugnatio Hibernica by Giraldus Cambrensis.* Dublin.

Shine, D. and Mandal, S. 2018. 'Digging the lost town of Carrig: archaeological report 2018'. Unpublished technical report for the NMS.

Shine, D., Mandal, S., Hayes, C. and Harris, M. 2018. 'Finding Carrig'. *Archaeology Ireland,* 32:2, 35–40.

Stafford, E. 2015. 'Report on works at the Crimean War memorial, Newtown, Co. Wexford'. Unpublished report prepared for WCC.

Stafford, E. and McLoughlin, C. 2009. 'Archaeological excavation report: Wexford Opera House, High Street, Wexford (licence no. 06E0049)'. Unpublished report submitted to NMS.

Tietzsch-Tyler, D. and Sleeman, A. 1994. 'Geology of south Wexford: a geological description of south Wexford and adjoining parts of Waterford, Kilkenny and Carlow to accompany the Bedrock Geology 1:100,000 scale Map Series, Sheet 23, south Wexford'. Enniscrone.

CHAPTER SIX

Carrick town and manor: archaeological, geophysical and landscape assessment

CATHERINE McLOUGHLIN & ASHELY GREEN

INTRODUCTION

Prior to the inception of the *Digging the Lost Town of Carrig Project*, archaeological investigation of the Carrick site was primarily confined to the immediate vicinity of the ringwork itself (see ch. 5). One exception was an archaeological assessment of an area approximately 250m to the south-east of the site of the ringwork. The assessment, which was undertaken in 2005, uncovered medieval features during the excavation of test trenches (Figure 6.1). In 2018, in collaboration with the Irish Archaeology Field School (IAFS), Ashely Green undertook geophysical survey of the field in which the medieval features were uncovered and additional potential archaeological features were identified. The results of the combined investigations can be used to assist in the interpretation of the extent of the medieval borough that is known to have developed around the Carrick ringwork in the thirteenth century. In addition, inferences can be made on the use of the landscape prior to, and after, the founding of the town.

ARCHAEOLOGICAL ASSESSMENT

The field in which the archaeological assessment was undertaken is located to the west of the findspot of a prehistoric pit burial, which was unearthed during the construction of a bungalow in 1984 (RMP WX037–029). It was proposed in 2005 to build a private dwelling in the field and, due to the proximity of the proposed development site to the findspot of the pit burial, the National Monuments Service requested that archaeological assessment be carried out to inform the planning process. As a result, a desk-based archaeological assessment was undertaken in November 2005, and this was followed by archaeological test-trenching of the proposed development site in January 2006 (McLoughlin 2006; licence 05E1405). Test-trenching of the site was undertaken using a mechanical excavator fitted with a toothless bucket. The driver of the excavator was directed by the archaeologist to excavate test trenches at specifically chosen locations, and trenches were excavated to the depth of naturally occurring subsoil or archaeological features. The subsoil occurred at a depth of approximately 30–40cm in the area tested.

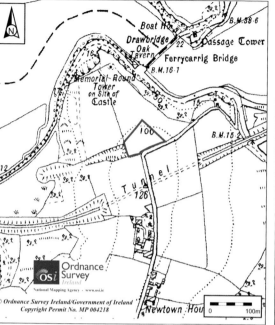

6.1 Location of archaeological assessment
and geophysical survey

6.2 Location of archaeological test trenches
and features uncovered

A series of five test-trenches was excavated within the footprint of the proposed new dwelling, and archaeological features or potential archaeological features were uncovered in all of them. These features can be seen in Figure 6.2 and are briefly described in Table 6.1. The term 'context number' refers to the identification number of archaeological features or potential archaeological features uncovered during the testing.

The archaeological test-trenching confirmed the presence of extensive features of definite archaeological significance dating to the medieval period. The location of these features at such a remove from the ringwork is not surprising given the description of the historic borough of Carrick in the various medieval inquisitions (see ch. 4). The town was known to be relatively large and contained a stone castle, a chapel, a hall and two watermills, among other buildings; a deer park is also known to have been associated with the borough, and such parks generally are located on higher-status sites only (see ch. 7).

No definite prehistoric features were uncovered during the archaeological assessment in the field. Unless accompanied by prehistoric artefacts, however, it is sometimes difficult to interpret features in test-trenches as prehistoric, especially if they have been truncated or ploughed through by later features.

Table 6.1 Archaeological features ('contexts') found in the excavated trenches

Trench	Context number and description
1	C2 Possible ditch or large pit that contained medieval pottery C3 Possible pit that contained medieval pottery C4 Gully or pit terminal C5 Possible pit C6 Possible pit
2	C7 Possible pit C8 Possible pit C9 Wide shallow gully with frequent charcoal inclusions
3	C9 Continuation of this feature from Trench 2 C10 Shallow soil, possibly related to C3 C11 Pit or post-hole C12 Gully or ditch that contained medieval pottery
4	C12 Gully or ditch also uncovered in Trench 3 C13 Ditch or pit that contained medieval pottery C14 Slot or pit that contained medieval pottery C15 Possible pit
5	C16 Possible pit C17 Possible pit C18 Possible pit C19 Possible pit

GEOPHYSICAL SURVEY

Due to the significance of the findings of the 2005 assessment, this area was chosen for geophysical survey in 2018 as part of the *Digging the Lost Town of Carrig Project*. The survey was carried out by archaeologist Ashely Green, of Bournemouth University, using electromagnetic induction (EMI) and ground-penetrating radar (GPR) (see Green 2018; licence 18R0099; see also ch. 5 for detailed description of geophysics methodologies). EMI was used because it allowed for large-area coverage and multi-depth data acquisition of potential archaeological deposits. Targeted GPR survey was used to complement the EMI survey to relocate the previously excavated test trenches and to determine the extent of features recorded during the earlier assessment.

The EMI survey was conducted using continuous GPS tracking with data collected at 0.1s and GPS messages sent at 1.0s. The instrument was operated in vertical coplanar orientation, allowing data to be collected at 25cm, 50cm and 90cm below

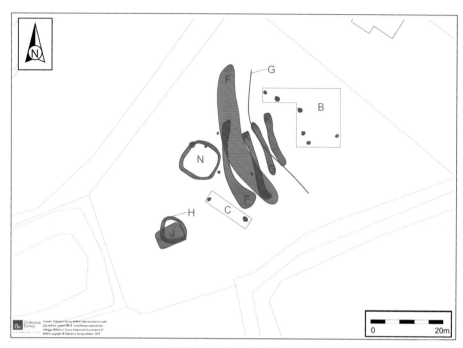

6.3 Location of possible features identified through geophysical survey

ground level. Conductivity (quadrature) and magnetic susceptibility (in-phase) data were logged simultaneously. GPR survey at the site was conducted with a MALÅ RAMAC X3M system using a cart-mounted 500MHz central frequency antenna. The geophysical survey relocated the archaeological test-trenches excavated in January 2006. The EMI survey was conducted over the entirety of the field and the GPR survey was centred over the area of the archaeological testing. The results show a correlation between the geophysical survey data and the test-trenching data in that the archaeological features uncovered in the testing were picked up in the EMI and GPR surveys.

The ditches uncovered in the archaeological testing were identified in the geophysical survey data and a series of probable archaeological pits were also uncovered at the eastern extent of the field. Interestingly, a circular feature was picked up by the survey in the area of archaeological testing and a second possible circular feature was noted a short distance to the west. The results of the geophysical survey are shown on Figure 6.3 and are described briefly in Table 6.2.

In addition to the features identified in the archaeological testing of the site, two potential circular features were uncovered by the geophysical survey. These anomalies, shown as H and N on Figure 6.3, may represent prehistoric features such as ring-ditches, but the data suggests that H is modern and so this interpretation must be used with caution, and requires ground-truthing to ascertain the true nature of the anomalies. Interestingly, a similar sub-circular trend was also identified in the geophysical survey of the ringwork, 250m to the north-west (ch. 5).

Table 6.2 Geophysical anomalies identified during the survey in 2018

Reference	Description
B	Cluster of positive conductive, low magnetic susceptibility responses
C	Cluster of non-conductive responses
F	North–south aligned linear conductive, high-amplitude response that aligns with a shallow ditch with charcoal inclusions recorded in Trenches 2 and 3 (C9)
G	North–south aligned linear conductive, high-amplitude response that aligns with a shallow ditch containing medieval pottery recorded in Trenches 3 and 4 (C12)
H	Circular low-amplitude response in the south-west sector of the survey area, *c.*7m diameter
J	Rectangular low-amplitude response
K	Two linear high-amplitude responses
N	Sub-rectangular high-amplitude response, *c.*11m diameter

HISTORIC LANDSCAPE ASSESSMENT

Carrick was founded as both a town and a manor and was located in the medieval parish of the same name. Manors were established as a territorial unit and settlement type following the Anglo-Norman conquest and were created in a process during which land was distributed between knights and their retainers in return for military service (Murphy 2015, 70; ch. 2, above). The manor is often equated in size with the medieval parish (Keegan 2004, 21) and one of its most important elements was its centre of administration, or *caput*, which in the case of Carrick was located around the ringwork and later stone castle. Manorial tenants worked the land and may have been located in dispersed settlements throughout the manor, away from the manorial centre itself (Murphy and Stout 2015, xxiv). In the case of Carrick, although the centre was the ringwork and surrounding town, there may have been dispersed settlement around the parish church of St Nicholas as well as at the watermills and bridges.

While there are good documentary sources relating to Carrick (see ch. 4), we must attempt to reconstruct the geographical bounds and organisation of the manor using archaeological and cartographic sources, with no definitive records surviving.

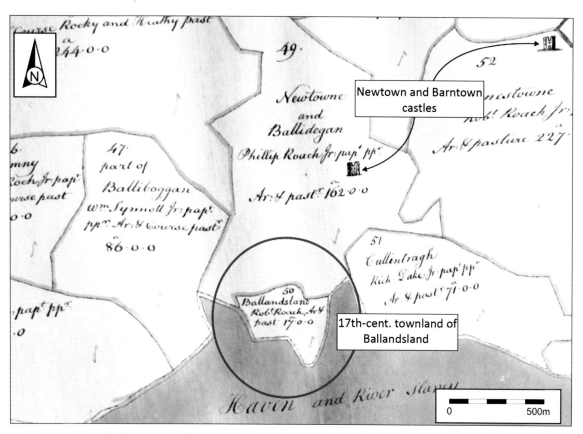

6.4 Extract from the Down Survey map (© National Library of Ireland MS 725)

The earliest informative cartographic source for the area is the Down Survey map of 1656–8 (Figure 6.4). The Down Survey was so-called because a chain was laid down and a scale created, which made this the first systematic mapping of a large-scale area. Teams of surveyors were sent out under the direction of William Petty to measure every townland in Ireland, which was to be forfeited to soldiers and adventurers after the 1652 Act of Settlement. The maps record the townland boundaries of the time as well as notable features such as towns, castles, churches, mills and roads.

The Down Survey map shows the known location of the ringwork and town at Carrick to be within a small parcel of land known as Ballandsland. There is no evidence, however, on this seventeenth-century map for either the ringwork or the settlement. The accompanying terrier, which is a written description of the boundaries and notable features of the parish, makes no mention of the ringwork or settlement either but does mention 'a castle in repaire' at Newtowne (Newtown) and at Barnestown (Barntown). Although the mentioned castle at Newtown is no longer extant, the castle at Barntown is still a visible feature in the landscape today. Newtown Castle is depicted on the Down Survey map close to, or possibly at, what would become the now-demolished Belmont House, close to the parish church of Carrick (St Nicholas').

The historic townland name Ballandsland, in which the ringwork is located, presumably refers to a personal name. Many such geographical names are recorded on

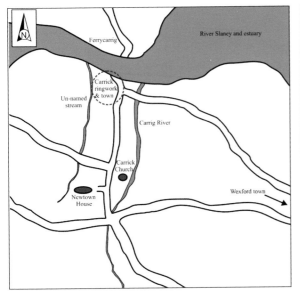

6.5 Location of principal roads and Newtown House
from Taylor and Skinner's 1777 road map

6.6 Postulated extent of the town of Carrick
and later medieval settlement to the south

the Down Survey map for Co. Wexford and many are still evident in townland names such as Sinnottstown and Rochestown. The name Ballandsland has disappeared, however, and the ringwork is now in the townland of Newtown. This townland name is of relatively recent English origin and appears to have superseded another English place-name, 'Churchtowne', which is recorded in the area in 1565 (Ó Crualaoich and Mac Giolla Chomhghaill 2016, 1375). The older name reflects the location of the parish church of Carrick.

The Down Survey map also records an interesting boundary. Ballandsland is a small area with an extent that appears to correspond with a series of joined boundaries recorded on the first-edition Ordnance Survey (OS) map. That roughly east–west-oriented field boundary effectively cut off the promontory of Carrick from the terrain to the south of the historic town. A portion of the boundary survives as a small country road. This road follows a north–south alignment before taking an abrupt eastern turn, respecting the line of the townland boundary depicted on the Down Survey map.

The small country road that respects the Ballandsland boundary is depicted on George Taylor and Andrew Skinner's 1777 map of the principal roads of Ireland (Figure 6.5). The road came from the south Wexford hinterland to the important ferry crossing shown as 'Ferry Carrick' on the map. Taylor and Skinner's map also depicts a 'Newtown House' in the approximate location of the now-demolished Belmont House.

Analysis of the historic maps shows the location of the ringwork to be on a promontory flanked to the east and west by small rivers flowing into the Slaney. The promontory location has been somewhat obscured by the construction of the modern N11 road. Construction of the road in the 1980s required the excavation of a very wide cut into the landscape. This road cutting has severed the ringwork from its surrounding landscape and given it the appearance of a stand-alone feature. The flanking of the promontory by two rivers is significant; all the historic documentation refers to the two watermills that were associated with the town and were obviously located on one or both of these rivers. While their location can be postulated, no remains of the mills has yet been found. It is interesting to note the depiction of historic mills along the River Carrig on the first- and second-edition OS maps. The River Carrig clearly remained a focus of milling into the twentieth century.

Although the Down Survey map (1656–8) does not record any castle at the location of the ringwork, the mid-nineteenth-century first-edition OS map does. The ringwork is shown on that map as a semi-circular feature hugging the promontory cliff-top, containing a faint rectangular structure within it, shown as a dotted line. The Ballandsland boundary indicated on the Down Survey map appears to be depicted as a field boundary on the first-edition OS map, which also includes the road shown on Taylor and Skinner's map (1777). As mentioned above, this quiet country road takes an abrupt eastern turn along the surviving field boundary, which appears to be consistent with the boundary of the seventeenth-century townland. The reason for the sudden shift in the road line may be that its builders wanted to avoid this field boundary, which may once have formed the southern boundary of the town of Carrick. The cartographic and landscape evidence show that by the seventeenth century the focus of the settlement within the parish of Carrick may have shifted permanently to the south, centred on Newtown Castle and the parish church of St Nicholas.

DISCUSSION

The different types of evidence – archaeological, geophysical and landscape assessment – present us with a range of information that can be used to infer the size of the medieval town of Carrick and the distribution of settlement within the associated manor (Figure 6.6). Taking the Down Survey map as a guide, the area of Ballandsland (which is suggested to be the immediate area of the medieval town) on the promontory at Carrick is shown as seventeen acres (6.9 hectares) in the seventeenth century. This area is confirmed at the turn of the twentieth century when the second-edition OS map shows the area of the promontory to be roughly eighteen acres (7.3 hectares). This area is bounded to the south by the field boundary and road depicted on Taylor and Skinner's eighteenth-century map and contains both the ringwork and the field in which the 2005 archaeological assessment and 2018 geophysical survey were undertaken.

When viewed in relation to the size of known medieval towns, the area of the promontory defined by these boundaries is similar to Clonmines, which had an estimated enclosed area of around twenty acres (8.1 hectares) (Thomas 1992, vol. i, 30). Other smaller medieval towns in Co. Wexford such as Bannow and Fethard appear, based on cartographic evidence, to be a similar size, while the major port towns of Wexford and New Ross are considerably larger (ch. 2).

The second-edition OS map (1897–1913) records an interesting boundary detail at the southern extent of the promontory. This feature is shown as a substantial escarpment or embankment on the map. It is not recorded on the mid-nineteenth-century first-edition OS map. The feature appears large and is close to the late nineteenth-century railway line. Unfortunately, much of this feature was removed during the construction of the modern road network and its purpose and function remain unclear.

In addition to the features discussed above, wider manorial settlement and organisation is likely to have been undertaken throughout the medieval parish of Carrick. The church dedicated to St Nicholas was situated roughly in the centre of the parish and, by the seventeenth century, the Down Survey records the presence of a castle in repair at Newtown. A house referred to as 'Newtown' is shown on Taylor and Skinner's roads map in proximity to St Nicholas' Church and, as mentioned above, this appears to be the location of the now-demolished Belmont House. The historic sources indicate that by the seventeenth century the castle and town of Carrick were deserted. The church of St Nicholas is recorded in possession of Henry Wallop in 1615 (Hore 1900–11, vol. v, 268), however, and a castle is recorded at Newtown at that time. It is probable that the focus of settlement on the manor shifted southwards as the town itself fell into terminal decline by the sixteenth century.

By at least the eighteenth century a mill complex at Glenville on the River Carrig was in existence (McLoughlin 2018a) and it is likely that at least one of Carrick's medieval mills was also located along this significant river. The historic mapping shows both Glenville and another mill complex in proximity to St Nicholas' Church. Both streams flanking the promontory are shown on Taylor and Skinner's map, so they were still significant features in the landscape up until the late eighteenth century at least. Bridges were therefore required, and these were probably located close to the mill sites.

Promontories such as the one on which the Carrick ringwork was located were often the focus of earlier settlement and activity. The siting of the ringwork at this particular location was a strategic decision relating to the control of the valuable River Slaney and the inland territory in the heart of the county. Another similarly located defensive site is the impressive ringwork at Dunanore on a high point on a bend of the River Boro, a tributary of the Slaney (RMP WX026–012001).

The well-attested medieval use of the Carrick site does not preclude earlier activity there. The defensive Anglo-Norman earthworks at Baginbun Head, for example (Moore 1996, 26 (no. 226), 94 (no. 962)), were erected in 1170 by Raymond le Gros and his men on the site of an earlier promontory fort. Similarly, the village of Duncormick in south Co. Wexford contains an important cluster of monuments that includes an inland promontory fort on which a later medieval tower house was built as well as a motte-and-bailey and an early ecclesiastical site that continued in use as the location of the medieval parish church (McLoughlin 2004).

Coastal, promontory and riverine sites are known for their multi-period use all over Ireland and the Carrick site may well prove to be unexceptional in this regard. Very close to Carrick ringwork is the findspot of a Bronze Age urn burial (RMP WX037–029), and prehistoric flint artefacts were recovered from recent excavations at the Carrick site, suggesting earlier use of the area (see ch. 5). In addition, the geophysical survey discussed above shows two features that may be interpreted as prehistoric funerary ring-ditches – with a similar feature recorded at the site of the ringwork.

Ring-ditches similar to the potential features identified at Carrick have been excavated at Kerloge (*c.*5km south-east of Carrick). At that site Neolithic pits, Bronze Age and Iron Age ring-ditches, as well as early medieval activity were located in proximity to the site of a medieval church, which is no longer extant (McLoughlin 2012, 161). The Down Survey map records the Kerloge church close to a mill on a river and a large house showing the continued importance of this settlement cluster in the local landscape in the seventeenth century.

Similar co-locations of medieval and prehistoric archaeology have been identified elsewhere in Co. Wexford. Although the medieval church there is no longer extant, recent investigations at Ballymore in Screen have found remains of medieval settlement in the adjacent field as well as prehistoric archaeological material that included worked-flint artefacts and burnt-mound deposits (McLoughlin 2017; 2018b). Similarly, at Churchtown in the village of Kilrane, a complex of prehistoric ring-ditches and other features was uncovered during archaeological assessment in 2005 (McLoughlin 2005). These features were located 100m to the north of the medieval parish church of Churchtown.

CONCLUSION

An analysis of the available sources shows that the extent of the medieval town of Carrick could be the same as the seventeen-acre (6.9 hectare) land division of Ballandsland shown on the seventeenth-century Down Survey map. Dispersed manorial settlement associated with the medieval town of Carrick can also be suggested around the nearby St Nicholas' Church and, in the case of mills and possible bridge crossings, along the rivers that flank the Carrick promontory. The location of Newtown Castle, which was standing in the seventeenth century, can also be postulated, as can the high potential of the area for prehistoric funerary and settlement activity. When researching archaeological landscapes, there are sometimes more questions than answers. Happily, in the case of the Carrick, landscape assessment as well as recent and ongoing investigations are closing the gap between speculation and knowledge.

BIBLIOGRAPHY

Green, A. 2018. 'Newtown, Ferrycarrig, Wexford: geophysical report (consent no./detection licence 18R0099)'. Unpublished technical report issued to IAFS.

Hore, P. 1900–11. *History of the town and county of Wexford*. 6 vols. London.

Keegan, M. 2004. 'The archaeology of manorial settlement in west County Limerick in the thirteenth century'. In Lyttleton, J. and O'Keeffe, T. (eds), *The manor in medieval and early modern Ireland*, 17–39. Dublin.

McLoughlin, C. 2004. 'Archaeological assessment, Duncormick, Co. Wexford'. Archaeological licence 04E1335. Unpublished technical report.

McLoughlin, C. 2005. 'Archaeological assessment, Churchtown, Co. Wexford'. Archaeological licence 05E1303. Unpublished technical report.

McLoughlin, C. 2006. 'Archaeological testing report, Newtown, Co. Wexford (archaeological licence 05E1405'. Unpublished technical report issued to James and Rita Codd.

McLoughlin, C. 2012. 'Excavation of an Iron Age ring-ditch and associated features at Kerloge, Co. Wexford'. In Corlett, C. and Potterton, M. (eds), *Life and death in Iron Age Ireland in the light of recent archaeological excavations*, 161–74. Dublin.

McLoughlin, C. 2017. 'Archaeological assessment report, Ballymore, Screen, Co. Wexford'. Archaeological licence 16E0616. Unpublished technical report.

McLoughlin, C. 2018a. 'Built heritage assessment report, Glenville House, Coolcots, Wexford'. Unpublished technical report.

McLoughlin, C. 2018b. 'Archaeological assessment report, Ballymore, Screen, Co. Wexford'. Archaeological licence 18E0011. Unpublished technical report.

Moore, M. 1996. *Archaeological survey of Co. Wexford*. Dublin.

Murphy, M. 2015. 'Manor centres, settlement and agricultural systems in medieval Ireland, 1250–1350'. In Murphy, M. and Stout, M. (eds), *Agriculture and settlement in Ireland*, 69–100. Dublin.

Murphy, M. and Stout, M. 2015. 'Farming and settlement: an introduction'. In Murphy, M. and Stout, M. (eds), *Agriculture and settlement in Ireland*, xvi–xxx. Dublin.

Ó Crualaoich, C. and Mac Giolla Chomhghaill, A. 2016. *Townland names of Co. Wexford*. Dublin.

Thomas, A. 1992. *The walled towns of Ireland*. 2 vols. Dublin.

CHAPTER SEVEN

The medieval park at Carrick

FIONA BEGLANE

INTRODUCTION

At least forty-six parks are known to have existed in high medieval Ireland (Beglane 2015a, 15), but very few have been studied in any detail. Documentary sources and archaeological evidence show that Irish parks had a range of uses and varied between four acres (1.6 hectares) and 913 acres (369.5 hectares), with the majority being between twenty (8.1 hectares) and two hundred acres (80.9 hectares) (Beglane 2015a, 92–3). These areas of enclosed land were used to confine cattle and horses and some, but not all, elite parks were also used to hold fallow deer for hunting and for venison. Medieval parks were also used to grow trees for timber and firewood and sometimes had areas of arable agriculture within them. They could be surrounded by a pale created from wooden palings, a hedge or, in some cases, a stone wall (Beglane 2014; 2015c). Parks were also symbolically important in the way that they demarcated landholding and prevented access to land by the lower orders (Beglane 2015a, 88–9, 122–60).

Carrick ringwork was probably constructed by Robert Fitz Stephen as part of the initial conquest of the area (Bennett 1985, 28; Scott and Martin 1978, 53; Orpen 1892, lines 1775–9, 1395–9; see ch. 4, above). By 1231 a stone castle was in place (Sweetman 1875–86, vol. i, pp 278–9, no. 1872) and while land may have been set aside for the park during the initial layout of the manor, it is probable that the park boundaries would have been constructed around the time that the stone castle was built. The modern townland of Park lies just across the River Carrig from the ringwork and represents the majority of the land previously enclosed within the medieval park. Fieldwork demonstrates that the medieval park enclosed approximately 308 statute acres (124.6 hectares); however, Park townland encompasses only 249 statute acres (100.8 hectares). With the River Carrig on the west, the Slaney to the north and an unnamed stream running into the Slaney to the east, the park had water on three sides (Figure 7.1). The southern pale ran further south than the modern townland boundary. This was within what is today Ballyboggan, where a relict ditch and road-bed can still be followed for over 1km. Although it will not be discussed in any detail, it is important to note that there was also a 60-acre (24.3 hectares) park that belonged to Wexford Castle (Crooks, PR 1 Rich. II, no. 11). It is likely that this second park was close to the castle, in the area now known as The Faythe (Beglane 2015a, 29–30).

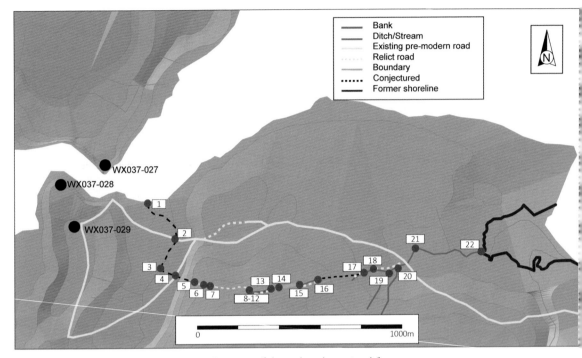

7.1 Location of the park and associated features

Given the proximity of the two, the park at Wexford Castle may have originally served as a 'little park', functioning more as an extensive garden, while the larger park at Carrick was more suited to keeping herds of deer and cattle.

DOCUMENTARY EVIDENCE

The first mention of a park at Carrick comes sometime between 1231 and 1234 in the charter of disafforestation of the forests of Ross and Taghmon, by which time it had clearly been established for some time. In this document Richard Marshal stated:

> Now of the forest around Tauchmune [Taghmon] I have deforested outside the metes and bounds hereunder-written, that is to say, from the place where the river which flows between the castle of Karrich [and] the park [into] the Slaney, and by that river ascending to my mill on that river (Orpen 1934, 56).

After the death of the last of the male members of the Marshal family in 1245 Leinster was partitioned into five inheritances. Wexford became the caput of the portion allotted to William Marshal's second daughter Johanna and, as a result, Wexford and

Carrick passed through the de Munchensy family and then to the de Valences. This led to a level of absenteeism, and the park seems to have fallen out of its primary use during that period, instead being used as agricultural land. On the death of Joan de Valence in 1307 no park is mentioned but it is noted that

> In Carrick there is a castle with two carucates and 20 acres of appurtenant land in demesne worth 60s. a year (Dryburgh and Smith 2007, no. 156).

A carucate is calculated as approximately 120 modern statute acres (48.6 hectares), giving an area of between 260 and 290 statute acres (105.2–117.4 hectares), depending on the size of a local acre, which could vary (Bennett 1985, 30; MacCotter 2008, 25). A later inquisition in 1324 on the death of Aymer de Valence included a value of £2 for 'two carucates arable and pasture in demesne' (Dryburgh and Smith 2007, no. 228), presumably the same lands. Neither inquisition specifically mentions a park, which at an area of *c.*308 statute acres (124.6 hectares) should be significant in the possessions of a manor, and no further references to the park at Carrick before the mid-sixteenth century have come to light. This supports the notion that it was no longer serving its primary function but that instead it was being used as demesne agricultural land. At some point between 1537 and 1540, there was a grant to William Seyntlo (Synnott) of Roscarlon of

> 60a of land in the parish of le Parke, parcel of the manor of Carge, with the ferry or passage of the town of Wexford; which were parcel of the possessions of the late George earl of Shrewsbury, in the county of Wexford, and since granted to the king by authority of parliament (Morrin 1861, 49).

Furthermore, in 1567 Richard Devereux is recorded as having a twenty-one-year lease that included the same lands and ferry (Morrin 1861, 517). In 1575 (enrolled 1582) Lancelot Allford sold rights to this same land to Richard Synnott of Ballybrenan (cited by Hore 1900–11, vol. v, 34, 186). Hore (1900–11, vol. v, 180) cited a crown rental of 1582 that stated that the lands and ferry were granted to George Bourchier, with the rent for the ferry being 5s. a year. Another undated manuscript cited by Hore (1900–11, vol. v, 182) has Walter Synnott as the tenant of 'Park or enclosure near Wexford town' at a rent of 6s. 8d. and William Synnott and Nicholas Turner as joint tenants of the 'Ferry of the town' at a rent of £2 7s. 8d. This sixty acres (24.3 hectares) 'in the parish of le Parke' could be confused with the park at Wexford Castle, but these are in separate manors and so should not be conflated.

In 1635 Sir William Brereton noted that travelling from Carrick to Wexford,

> about a mile hence lies a farm called the Park, which is now leased unto one Mr Hardye, an Englishman, who lives upon it and hath an estate in it about thirteen years. The landlord is one Mr William Synode of the Lough, a man that needs

money. This land is [worth] about £16 per annum. He saith it contains about
300 acres, others say 200 (cited by Hore 1900–11, vol. v, 246).

This confirms that the Synnott family held the area of Park; it also supports the idea
that this is the high medieval park associated with Carrick, and that it is of the order
of 300 statute or English acres (121.4 hectares) as measured by Hardye, which was
equivalent to 185 plantation (Irish) acres, as measured by the 'others'.

The *Books of Survey and Distribution* (Simington 1949–67) and Petty's (1655) map
of the 'parrish of Carrigge' shed light on the seventeenth-century land divisions, which
differed considerably from the modern townland boundaries mapped on the first-
edition Ordnance Survey (OS) maps. Nevertheless, if they are overlain on each other
the majority of the land divisions could still be traced in the later field systems (Figure
7.2). William Synnott held 144 plantation acres (94.5 hectares) in the 'The Parke' and
two portions of 'Balliboggan', which had areas of 38 and 86 plantation acres (24.9–
56.4 hectares), resulting in a total landholding of 433 statute acres (175.2 hectares).
The 53-plantation-acre (34.8 hectares) area between these two portions of Ballyboggan
was held by Robert Roch[e] and was known as Fortumny. The modern townlands of
Stonybatter and Carricklawn did not exist. Stonybatter was split between Park and
Ballyboggan while Carricklawn was split between Ballyboggan and Fortumny. The
extreme western extent of the modern Park townland was also part of Ballyboggan.

Pender's census of 1659 shows that 'Parke' had only three households: two English
and one Irish, while Ballyboggan was occupied by twenty-two Irish and two English
households. Landholdings within 'Parke' were therefore relatively large, since on Petty's
(1655) map 'The Parke' had an area of 144 plantation acres (94.5 hectares). This would
fit with its history as a land block formerly held in demesne, which would have been
more likely to be leased to substantial tenants than to have been greatly subdivided.

Another century passed before the area was mapped again. Scalé and Richards'
maritime map of 1764 shows little of interest, however, apart from a building between
Wexford and Carrick that is likely to be a predecessor to Slaneyhill House, which was
built in 1832 (NIAH number 15607026). Slaneyhill House stands just inside the
likely boundary of the medieval park, at its highest point. Other eighteenth- and
nineteenth-century maps have even less detail, however Vallancey's (1776) and Taylor
and Skinner's (1778) maps both show a road running directly from Wexford to
Carrick and separating Ballyboggan and Park townlands. This road, part of which is
Old Hospital Road, was described by Hadden (1969, 13) as a 'Tudor engineered road'.
He provided no evidence to support this, but it runs along the boundaries shown on
Petty's map and so is likely to pre-date the mid-seventeenth century. The Mail-Coach
Road (R730) was constructed in the early nineteenth century as part of the
development of the bridge connecting Carrick to Ferrycarrig (Lewis 1837, 279–80,
701) and so this particular road need not be further discussed.

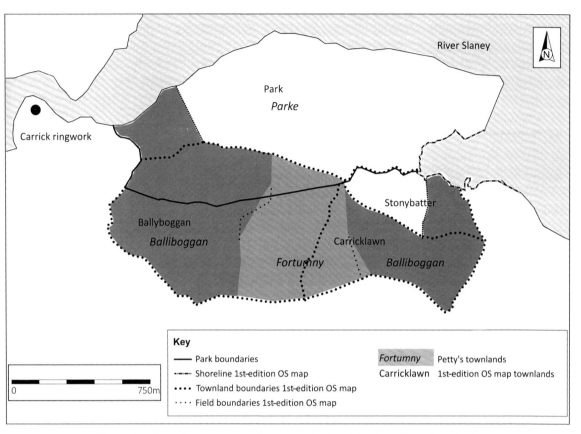

7.2 William Petty's parish map transposed onto townland and field boundaries from the first-edition OS map with the proposed Carrick park boundary also shown

LANDSCAPE EVIDENCE

Combining cartographic and satellite imagery with fieldwork has shown that the present southern boundary of Park townland, running along Hadden's 'Tudor engineered road', is not the boundary of the medieval park. The first-edition OS map shows that in several places this road bisects pre-existing fields, so that these fields must be earlier than the road. Since there is no reason for field boundaries to exist within a newly constructed park, these suggest that the road, and hence the townland boundary, is more recent than at least part of the field system, which fits with the notion that it is Tudor or later and not Anglo-Norman in origin. Furthermore, at the western end, the road runs through an east–west valley, with rising ground to the north and, more steeply, to the south. Evidence from other parks in both Ireland and England, as well as common sense, suggest that a deer park boundary should be close to the top of a slope to maximise the difficulty for a deer seeking to escape and to minimise the height of the palings needed to retain stock within the park (Beglane 2015a, 119; Moorehouse 2007, 106).

From this east–west road the land to the south rises steadily with a gentle break of slope at around 50m OD. At 45m OD the first-edition OS map shows a curving line of field boundaries, with two places where short stretches of road or track run alongside this. This relict road also has a short length running southwards, parallel to the river, towards the probable former site of the mill and St Nicholas', Carrick's parish church. This curving line is a much more likely southern pale for the park, and so was selected for field survey in 2011.

The survey began at the River Carrig (shown as 1 on Figure 7.1), which meets the River Slaney just downstream of Carrick ringwork, in a treacherous area of marshy reeds that would have constituted an effective barrier for deer and poachers. This is presently crossed by a bridge (2), but cartographic evidence suggests that in the medieval period the river was crossed further upstream, close to St Nicholas' Church or to the present Newtown Bridge. A curvilinear feature, which appeared as a field boundary on the first-edition OS map, is still visible on some satellite images (www.googlemaps.com, 16 December 2010, 5 May 2011). It begins at the river (3) and runs eastwards across the reed beds to the modern Park-to-Newtown road (4). On the eastern side of this road there is a series of modern one-off houses, but the site boundaries of two of these respect the line of the continuing curvilinear feature. This boundary travels up an extremely steep, almost cliff-like, section of ground and beyond this continues as a field boundary separating pasture fields to the north and the recently built Ard na Sláine housing development to the south (5–8). On the first-edition and second-edition OS (25-inch) maps a short section of road is shown running along the northern side of part of this boundary (6–8); however, even at the time this appeared to be a relict section, serving little function. It is no longer visible, and comparison of satellite imagery with the 25-inch map suggests that the line of the boundary has been straightened.

At this point the line approaches Slaneyhill House and enters a copse of trees (8–9). From here on, relict features survive more clearly. The boundary first continues as a line of substantial, mature sycamore trees growing on a denuded bank, which runs eastwards along the line of the relict road. Immediately to the north of these trees is a ditch, which becomes more substantial as it continues eastward. Most field boundaries in the area have been constructed from banks without ditches, and it is only at major property and townland boundaries that ditches seem to have been used to demarcate the landscape. In this regard, this ditch is unusual and worthy of note since this is not a townland boundary. A fence and disused gateway separate the copse from a small, grassed enclosure (Figure 7.3) (10). Beyond this, the line of the relict road is visible as a surface feature. To the immediate north of this roadbed is the line of a ditch with a

7.3 Line of the relict road marked by a disused gateway, 10

further bank 3m wide and 30cm high on the north side. To the immediate south of the relict road is a revetted bank that forms the boundary to the fields to the south. Passing into the next field the ditch reappears as a substantial steep-sided feature up to 1.8m deep and 3m wide (11–13). This has a bank on the northern side that contains substantial mature trees, but no bank is visible on the southern side. This bank and ditch separate the yard and garden at Slaneyhill House from the agricultural land to the south. The ditch segment extends over a length of 40m. Continuing eastwards, the line of the ditch is retained as a modern boundary fence and when viewed along the length of the fence it is apparent that a raised area runs parallel to the fence, suggesting that the relict road continues under this area (14–15).

Beyond this the boundary line has been bisected by the gardens of a series of large houses constructed in the eighteenth and nineteenth centuries (15–18). While they essentially follow the line of the boundary, they have been squared off, and within those portions that were accessible, there was evidence for the continuation of the ditch and of a stony base that is likely to be the relict roadbed. Eventually (19) the ditch feeds into a larger stream (20) that travels north, meeting another larger stream that forms the townland boundary separating Ballyboggan from Carricklawn and that continues northwards, separating Park from Stonybatter. Immediately to the north of the confluence the combined flow passes under Hadden's (1969) 'Tudor engineered road', re-emerging on the opposite side. At the time of the fieldwork in 2011 this field had recently been topsoil-stripped, but the satellite image still showed the undisturbed field, with a thick line of bushes fringing the external side of the stream. On the first-edition OS map this stream continued northwards (21) and eastwards, to meet the Slaney River in an area that was subsequently drained by the time of the 25-inch map (22), and modern aerial photographs show that it is now relatively dry land to the south-east of the St John's Volunteers GAA club.

DISCUSSION

The site of the park was carefully chosen to minimise the complexity of construction while maximising the visual impact of the park. Locating it on a peninsula, bounded to the north, east and west by water, meant that only a southern boundary needed to be constructed. A curving boundary was identified cartographically, and survey strongly supports this being the boundary of the park.

This presently consists of a relict road with a ditch and bank, or in some cases a revetment to either side. By comparison, the majority of field boundaries in the area consist only of hedges or of banks and hedges without ditches. While the form of the boundary is unusual for field systems in the area, it does not immediately stand out as a feature of archaeological importance. It should be considered in the context of the apparently short lifespan of the park, however, which means that the park pale would soon have become obsolete. The cartographic evidence is more convincing than the physical remains, clearly demonstrating a constructed boundary running across a distance of approximately 1.2km and enclosing an area of 308 statute acres (124.6 hectares).

In order to access the park from the ringwork, or indeed to travel to Wexford, it would have been necessary to cross the River Carrig. It is likely that a bridge spanned the river some distance to the south and that the relict road extended south to meet this. The current, more direct, crossing is much wider and flanked by reed beds so that while there may have been a ford or a causeway at this point for foot traffic and horses, heavy carts, used for example to transport timber, would have been more likely to cross the river further to the south and then access the park through a gate either in the south-west corner or at Slaneyhill House, which is the highest point within the park.

Many English and European parks, as well as the example at Earlspark, Co. Galway (Beglane 2014), had a number of gates, and a gate on the Wexford side is also extremely likely, since the two manors were adjacent and were both within a single lordship. This would probably have been sited at the modern townland boundary intersection of Park, Ballyboggan, Stonybatter and Carricklawn, where the present road crosses the unnamed stream. While the evidence from the field boundaries suggests that the modern road through the park is a later, maybe Tudor, feature, it is quite likely that a path or track wound from there through the east–west valley bottom, essentially following the same line. This would have provided access to the park from Wexford and easy removal of timber along flat ground to Wexford.

Parks in Ireland were constructed primarily for political and economic purposes, rather than as pure hunting parks, but the most elite examples did contain fallow deer (Beglane 2015b, 155, 166). The park at Carrick was already present in 1231–4, and so was created early in the Anglo-Norman occupation of the area. As such it was an essential part of the Anglo-Norman elite 'package' of castle, park, mill, church, demesne lands and borough (Bailey 2002, 2–5; Liddiard 2005, 100–19; O'Conor 1998, 26–38) – all of which are documented at Carrick (see ch. 4).

The high status of the park is demonstrated by the fallow deer remains found during excavation of early thirteenth-century contexts at the ringwork (McCormick n.d.). Artefacts recovered from excavations in 2018 also included a set of ceramic fallow antlers from a medieval *aquamanile* (water-jug) (see ch. 5 for discussion). Fallow deer were imported from England in the early thirteenth century, specifically to stock parks (Beglane 2015d, 14). In England, fallow deer numbers increased and they became more accessible to the gentry classes. By contrast, in Ireland only thirteen later medieval sites have produced fallow deer remains to date, all either at the highest level of society or urban sites (Beglane et al. 2018, table 2). There is documentary evidence that in 1225 William Marshal II received twenty does to be brought to Ireland (Sweetman 1875–86, vol. i, p. 200, no. 1323), demonstrating that by that time at least one of the Marshal parks in Ireland was ready to be stocked with fallow deer.

The park was positioned for maximum visibility. It could be clearly seen from the Carrick ringwork as well as from the northern shore of the River Slaney (Figure 7.4). Similarly, any travellers on the river would have had to pass by the park en route to Carrick or further upstream. The park is also visible from Wexford town. Anyone travelling between Carrick and Wexford by land would have had to either pass through the park, if they were permitted to do so, or skirt it to the south using the relict road, in which case the view northwards would be dominated by the park boundary. This visibility was important because parks were created as much for their value as status symbols as for their practical uses. Any residents or visitors to the area would have been aware of the park and of its symbolism. The park represented potentially useful land that was inaccessible to the non-elite. It was not designed to be cultivated or primarily used for pasture, but instead was designed to hold deer and timber that were for the exclusive use of the lords. This park was not constructed on marginal land; even today some of the land within it is used for arable agriculture, while the remaining open ground is good-quality pasture.

7.4 The high medieval park from the later Roches' Castle (Recorded Monument Number WX037–027) on the north bank of the River Slaney, with the probable park boundary as it may have looked (modified from Beglane 2015a, fig. 54)

At 308 statute acres (124.6 hectares), the park was typical of the size of those surveyed in Ireland (Beglane 2015b, fig. 9.1). By comparison with some parks in England, however, it was modest. In an Irish context, extensive timber stocks and the more prestigious red deer hunting were freely available to the magnates within their liberties, and parks were relatively uncommon. For these reasons, and given the relative scarcity of parks and of fallow deer in later medieval Ireland, it was the possession of a park at Carrick, rather than its absolute size, that was of significance. The presence of the park, and the act of stocking it with fallow deer, meant that the Marshals could show their power and prestige both by displaying this landscape feature and by having the ability to provide venison for feasting and for gifts to their peers and subordinates.

The park at Carrick was initially a success; it was situated on an important manor of a major lord and was stocked with fallow deer. But the partition of Leinster led to a significant downturn in the fortunes of the area. The castles at Carrick and Wexford were administered by seneschals throughout their history (Colfer 1991, 21; ch. 4, above) and were rarely occupied by the lord, culminating in the mid-sixteenth century in the confiscation of the land by the king (Bennett 1985, 31). This lack of focus on

the two manors was reflected in the level of maintenance afforded to the fabric of the castles, which in 1324 were both in a very poor condition (Dryburgh and Smith 2007, no. 228). With no elite inhabitants or guests, the park was superfluous and was soon turned over to mundane agricultural use. Later it was rented out, albeit to substantial tenants. The physical remains are ephemeral and, while the evidence suggests that the park was used for deer for a maximum of one hundred years, the place-name has endured for some eight centuries. This is testament to the longevity of place-names in the landscape and their importance in understanding the past.

BIBLIOGRAPHY

Bailey, M. 2002. *The English manor, c.1200–1500*. Manchester.

Beglane, F. 2014. 'Theatre of power: the Anglo-Norman park at Earlspark, Co. Galway, Ireland'. *Medieval Archaeology*, 58, 307–17.

Beglane, F. 2015a. *Anglo-Norman parks in medieval Ireland*. Dublin.

Beglane, F. 2015b. 'Deer parks: lost medieval monuments of the Irish countryside'. In McAlister, V. and Barry, T. (eds), *Space and settlement in the Middle Ages*, 151–66. Dublin.

Beglane, F. 2015c. 'The medieval park of Maynooth'. *Journal of the Kildare Archaeological Society*, 20:5, 56–70.

Beglane, F. 2015d. 'The social significance of game in the diet of later medieval Ireland'. *Proceedings of the Royal Irish Academy*, 115C, 167–96.

Beglane, F., Baker, K., Carden, R., Hoelzel, A., Lamb, A., Mhig Fhionnghaile, R., Miller, H. and Sykes, N. 2018. 'Ireland's fallow deer: their historical, archaeological and biomolecular records'. *Proceedings of the Royal Irish Academy*, 118C, 1–25.

Bennett, I. 1985. 'Preliminary archaeological excavations at Ferrycarrig ringwork, Newtown td, Co. Wexford'. *Journal of the Wexford Historical Society*, 10, 25–43.

Colfer, B. 1991. 'Medieval Wexford'. *Journal of the Wexford Historical Society*, 13, 5–29.

Crooks, P. (ed.). *CIRCLE: a calendar of Irish chancery letters* (http://chancery.tcd.ie).

Dryburgh, P. and Smith, B. (eds). 2007. *Inquisitions and extents of medieval Ireland*. London.

Hadden, G. 1969. 'The origin and development of Wexford town, pt 3: the Norman period'. *Journal of the Old Wexford Society*, 2, 3–12.

Hore, P. 1900–11. *History of the town and county of Wexford*. 6 vols. London.

Lewis, S. 1837. *A topographical dictionary of Ireland*. 2 vols. London.

Liddiard, R. 2005. *Castles in context: power symbolism and landscape*. Bollington.

MacCotter, P. 2008. *Medieval Ireland: territorial, political and economic divisions*. Dublin.

McCormick, F. n.d. 'The mammal bones from Ferrycarrig, Co. Wexford'. Unpublished report.

Moorehouse, S. 2007. 'The medieval parks of Yorkshire: function, contents and chronology'. In Liddiard, R. (ed.), *The medieval park: new perspectives,* 99–127. Macclesfield.

Morrin, J. (ed.). 1861. *Calendar of the patent and close rolls of chancery in Ireland of the reigns of Henry VIII, Edward VI, Mary and Elizabeth*. Dublin.

NIAH. *National Inventory of Architectural Heritage* (www.buildingsofireland.ie; accessed 3 March 2018).

O'Conor, K. 1998. *The archaeology of medieval rural settlement in Ireland*. Dublin.

Orpen, G. (ed.). 1892. *The song of Dermot and the earl*. Oxford.

Orpen, G. (ed.). 1934. 'Charters of Earl Richard Marshal of the forests of Ross and Taghmon'. *Journal of the Royal Society of Antiquaries of Ireland*, 64, 54–63.

OSI. *Ordnance Survey of Ireland mapviewer* (http://maps.osi.ie/publicviewer/#V1,702786, 622867,0,0).

Petty, W. 1655. 'Down Survey parish map of Carrick, Co. Wexford, copied 1786'. NLI microfilm.

Scott, A. and Martin, F.X. (eds). 1978. *Expugnatio Hibernica by Giraldus Cambrensis*. Dublin.

Simington, R. (ed.). 1949–67. *The Books of Survey and Distribution*. 4 vols. Dublin.

Sweetman, H. (ed.). 1875–86. *Calendar of documents relating to Ireland, 1171–1307*. 5 vols. London.

Taylor, G. and Skinner, A. 1778. *Maps of the roads of Ireland*. London.

Vallancey, C. 1776. *Military itinerary to the south of Ireland*. London.

CHAPTER EIGHT

Capturing Carrick: a digital approach to constructing and deconstructing the modern and relict landscape

MICHAEL 'BODHI' ROGERS, RYAN BOURICIUS, DENIS SHINE & STEPHEN MANDAL

INTRODUCTION

Carrick is a broad archaeological landscape, the medieval history of which, for the most part, is preserved below the ground. The medieval landscape is also frequently hidden, or at least hard to decipher, due to modern roads, pathways, tree growth and the construction of early modern and modern buildings. The most radical alteration of this landscape has been the construction of the N11 Rosslare road (completed in 1988; see ch. 4) which separated, and presumably removed, a large portion of the borough of Carrick from the ringwork and later masonry castle (ibid.). Other notable alterations to the landscape include: the construction, and subsequent revisions, of Ferrycarrig bridge(s) in 1795 (ch. 5); nineteenth-century quarrying of the ruined remains of the castle and the construction of the round tower in 1857 (ibid.); the opening of the Wexford train line from Dublin to Carcur in 1870 (Jenkins 2001, 97); the launch of the Irish National Heritage Park (INHP) in 1987 (ch. 10); and the innumerable other modern changes to the landscape, such as the construction of one-off houses, installation of services, and changes to field boundaries and roadways. These alterations to the landscape mean that only the ringwork ditch and bank were defined and recognisable prior to the commencement of the 2018 excavation. Even the form of this monument was less than obvious due to the growth of scrub and woodland over the site since 1987. The rest of the story of Carrick was much subtler and difficult to ascertain, except to the most educated and informed eyes. It was hoped that this programme of scanning would not only capture a detailed record of the site at a 'moment in time', but also assist in education and outreach efforts, providing a more nuanced and decipherable explanation of this historically significant landscape.

At historic sites such as Carrick, 3D laser scanning can document every small detail of the archaeological landscape (see Figure 8.1). Laser scanning not only records every detail down to the millimetre level, it allows us to look at the site from different perspectives by virtually removing trees and/or modern features and taking slices or

8.1 The Leica P40 3D laser scanner positioned to digitally record the round tower by taking positional readings every 5mm

8.2 The laser scanner positioned to record Roches' Castle. The undulating terrain made positioning the scanner challenging

profile cuts in areas of interest without having to physically alter the landscape (O'Sullivan et al. 2018, 40). In other words, it is possible to digitally reconstruct and deconstruct both the modern and relict landscapes, allowing a more layered examination of space through time (Rogers et al. 2018, 59). This application can prove particularly useful at sites like Carrick, which have been altered to the point where their original historical importance is completely belied to the human eye. A programme of digitally preserving Carrick began in June 2018 initiated by a team from Ithaca College in Ithaca, New York. The 2018 fieldwork focused on laser scanning the Carrick ringwork and its immediate surrounds – including Ferrycarrig bridge, Roches' Castle (see Figure 8.2), the site of Carrick borough and the River Slaney with its associated banks/escarpment. This was this first stage towards producing a comprehensive digital model of the entire medieval settlement of Carrick, which will be used to examine future research questions as the project progresses and/or added to with more scans in future seasons.

HOW LASER SCANNING WORKS

The basic principle of 3D laser scanners is that they send out pulses of laser light that travel from the scanner, reflect from the object being scanned, and return to the scanner. The scanner records the time it takes each laser pulse to travel out and back. This two-way travel time is converted to a distance and the scanner's precise horizontal and vertical angular measuring tools facilitate the conversion of each pulse to an X, Y and Z location in space for each spot from which the laser reflects. Modern laser scanners pulse the laser 50,000 to 1,000,000 times per second. While pulsing this fast, they spin the laser in the vertical and horizontal directions to cover 360 degrees horizontal and 270 degrees vertical. The scanners cannot 'see' 360 degrees in the vertical because they cannot image beneath them where they sit upon a tripod. Most scanners also have a digital camera onboard, which is used to take a full dome of photographs. These photographs are used to map an RGB (red-green-blue) colour to each point recorded using the laser. Photographs can also be taken with a standalone camera and registered to the laser scan post-acquisition. The Historic England (2018) volume on 3D laser scanning for heritage is an excellent source for the various scanning methods, and 3D-Icons Ireland has fantastic examples of other scanning efforts in Ireland.

A single Leica 3D laser scanner, the P40, was used at Carrick. A local surveying grid system was established by creating a number of site datums – these site datums were placed at permanent locations, for example on a fixing on the modern bridge to the Carrick Archaeological Centre and on a readily identifiable point on the concrete bridge to the site. This grid was also transferred by total station north-east across the River Slaney to Roches' Castle and south-east across the N11 to the site of Carrick

8.3 Plan view map showing scanner locations. Some locations are used as a waypoint to get to the desired place to conduct a scan

borough. The scanner always worked in this grid system to facilitate all the data merging easily once back in the laboratory (see Figure 8.3). The scanner is programmable on site to take the desired resolution laser data and accompanying photographs. With the scanner set up over the site datum it was programmed to take position readings every 5mm by 5mm at a distance of 10m to 20m to record the features of interest at a high resolution. Data are recorded beyond the distance setting, out to approximately 120m, with resolution decreasing with distance from the scanner. At the high-resolution setting the laser scanner takes approximately five to fifteen minutes and an additional ten minutes to record a 360-degree by 270-degree dome of photographs. With scanning complete at the first point, the next scanner location is established using the laser scanner. The location is selected to fill in areas that could not be scanned from the previous location and the position of this new scan location in the local grid system is recorded by the scanner and the operators. The scanner is then moved to the new location and once oriented on the local grid system, by back-sighting to the previous point, a new scan is initiated. Occasionally, a waypoint is needed to get from the current scanner location to the next desired location. Typically, this waypoint is used only to get to the desired location without conducting a laser scan. It took a total of fifty-two scan locations to fill in all of the details of the desired scan area at Carrick.

PUTTING IT ALL TOGETHER

The data from each scan location are loaded into the Leica programme Cyclone. Because each scan location has coordinates within the local grid system the data from different locations automatically come together to form a three-dimensional data set called a point cloud (see Figures 8.4, 8.5). The photographs are adjusted to ensure uniform exposure and colour vibrancy, and then extraneous data are removed from the point cloud. The point cloud can now be manipulated to look at features of interest.

But how might the data be manipulated, and to what end? The 3D scanning at Carrick has generated a detailed model composed of billions of data points that can be used in a host of innovative ways relating to heritage management, archaeological research, outreach and education, remote touring, virtual reality modelling and so on. As with more traditional archaeological work, in practice the data will be most effectively used in a holistic fashion, drawing from a range of disciplines and expertise.

As the point cloud from Carrick continues in post-processing, the full functionality of the data will become clearer and in fact may not be used in its entirety for some time as additional research resources and finance are secured. It was a key aim of the *Digging the Lost Town of Carrig Project*, however, as part of its conservation and management strategy, to capture a mm-scale 'snap-shot' of the site at the point the 1980s excavations concluded, before additional cuttings were excavated (see Figure 8.6). The data from the scan will be made available to the site owners and all relevant regulatory authorities, ensuring (in theory) that the scan can be used in perpetuity to monitor the Carrick site. While work on the point cloud continues, the applications of the scan, and its contribution to the project's wider research, are already evident.

The most obvious application is to allow monitoring of the site, giving a mechanism to accurately observe and record any substantive changes, damage or decay. The scan would allow reconstruction of any damage on a stone-by-stone basis. The history of Carrick in the last two decades (ch. 4) reinforces the need for a detailed and impartial record, or digital preservation, of sites such as Carrick. Although the site has been in decline since the fourteenth century, the first-edition Ordnance Survey map infers that a structure was still standing in the mid-nineteenth century. Most of that structure appears to have been quarried at the site for the construction of the round

8.4 The point cloud of Roches' Castle

8.5 A close-up of the point cloud of Roches' Castle showing the level of detail recorded by the laser scanner and how the photographs can be used to colour the point cloud

tower by 1857 (chs 5, 9). The systematic removal of the medieval site in the early modern period highlights the need to have a detailed record to help ensure the continued long-term preservation of the monument. This is especially true in the case of an ongoing research excavation where the scan might be used more effectively than

8.6 View of the point cloud at the 2018 excavation site looking towards the round tower. This image highlights the ability of the laser scanner to preserve a snap-shot of the site that can then be used to monitor change. This image also highlights the challenges of laser scanning at a busy excavation site

photographs or other archaeological surveys (such as line drawings) to monitor and mitigate against any degradation of masonry or other features as they are exposed through digging. The need for a management strategy – and the desire to publish this eight-hundred-and-fiftieth-anniversary volume – were highlighted as the two initial aims of the project when it commenced; the scan was the first significant practical step in the management strategy for the site.

The 3D model will allow archaeologists, academics from other disciplines or the general public for that matter to assess the landscape on a layered and more nuanced level (see Figures 8.7–8.11). A whole host of questions can be assessed – from the more basic level of taking accurate measurements or generating sections, profiles or drawings, to a holistic landscape assessment in which the landscape is pulled apart layer by layer (period by period). All modern growth, modern intrusive features or recent housing can be easily removed, old views can be reconstructed, and relict landscapes can be virtually recreated. The practical applications of this at Carrick are obvious – for example, the nineteenth-century tower and railway or 1980s road can be removed, allowing glimpses of the site through time. More practically, where foliage is not too dense (where the scanner can penetrate with reasonable regularity to the ground surface), the site can be displayed without covering vegetation, giving a much better impression of how the landscape looked without its recent heavy vegetation.

On a virtual landscape, data can be inserted as easily as removed. The 3D scan can be used as a template on which reconstructions are added to give an impression of the

8.7 The point cloud looking from the excavation site and round tower towards Roches' Castle. Because the point cloud is composed of three-dimensional data, Leica Cyclone allows the user to pick any viewpoint to include aerial views

8.8 The same point cloud as shown in Figure 8.7 but manipulated to remove some of the modern features. The area where the N11 Rosslare road near Roches' Castle was deleted was filled in by copying a portion of the point cloud containing only grass and moving it into the location where the road used to be. An X, Y and Z coordinate icon can be seen where the road used to be north of Roches' Castle. The location of this origin can be moved to facilitate aligning the copied portion of point cloud (see Rogers et al. (2018) for an illustration of how this was done to replace the missing tower at Trim Castle, Co. Meath)

8.9 The point cloud can also be cut into thin slices (called cut planes) in any direction to gain a new perspective of the site. This image is a thin slice creating a profile view of the area south-west of the River Slaney. Because the point cloud is a three-dimensional photograph, Leica Cyclone can be used to take measurements, area calculations and volume calculations. The point cloud can also be transferred into a programme such as Autodesk Revit for conversion to an architectural drawing

site through the centuries. As the model is accurately geo-referenced, it would be possible to create models that can be viewed in real space on the site. For example, a smart phone could be rotated around Carrick allowing reconstructions to pop up from the ground in various locations, such as a twelfth-century palisade, gatehouse and wooden structures, thirteenth-century stone castle or fourteenth-century hall and chapel (ch. 5). A project of landscape modelling could involve partnership between heritage professionals and programmers to make more interactive simulations of the past, opening up new ways to explore Carrick's history. For example, the combination of 3D modelling and simulation software has already been used to good effect by RealSim, a simulation company based in Galway, to explain sites such as Clonmacnoise (RealSim 2018).

All the above has obvious applications to education and outreach, particularly to younger generations. One possible benefit is remote touring, whereby people can virtually tour the site, without the need to visit. Carrick ringwork is positioned at the top of a steep hill, which is not accessible for all members of the community. The medieval borough is located to the east of the N11, in private ownership, and so cannot be visited at all. As stated, were the town ever to be made publicly accessible, no traces survive above the ground – meaning a virtual or actual model is likely to be of greater interest to much of the general public. While remote or virtual touring cannot replace bodily experience of a place, it does allow a new way to interact with the history of a site or examine certain facets of it. Certainly, in the case of Carrick where only the twelfth-century ditch and bank remain permanently visible (augmented by archaeological features in the cuttings while excavations continue), new approaches must be sought to explain the history of this complex settlement. The scan

8.10 View of the point cloud looking south-west of the River Slaney towards the earthen cut created during the N11 Rosslare road construction

8.11 The same view as Figure 8.10 with most of the modern features removed and the landscape 'restored' to its condition prior to the road construction. Although the round tower is a modern feature that can easily be removed from the point cloud, it was intentionally left in this image to help orient the view

from Carrick and its suitability to 3D modelling, virtual reality and simulated experiences could be an important component of this educative process.

Figure 8.11 illustrates only the beginning of what is possible. Ongoing efforts are leading to the creation of a WebGL platform where the point cloud can be displayed on a website. This platform will allow the user to pan, rotate and zoom around Carrick as it appeared when the digital snap-shot was taken. The magnitude of the data poses a challenge for displaying the point cloud on a website. The Ithaca College 3D visualisation laboratory has specially built computers with enhanced memory and video-processing capabilities. The point cloud will need to be reduced in size without losing details of the site. Another tool being explored is the ESRI's CityEngine, which uses layers of topographic data, aerial imagery and digital reconstructions to create a virtual space for exploration. Features of interest, such as Roches' Castle, can be converted from a point cloud to a 3D architectural rendering, which can then be imported in CityEngine (for an example of efforts to make a 3D map of the Ithaca College campus in CityEngine, see https://tinyurl.com/y9ucmhol).

The 3D visualisations may also include time-slider bars similar to Google Earth's feature that lets one look backwards in time at increasingly older aerial photographs. It is even possible to include virtual tour guides or historic figures who can help bring the site further to life. All of these features can be accessed by a 'visitor' sitting at home or in a classroom, at the site through a display kiosk, or on mobile technology such as tablets and smart phones. With mobile technology we hope to make the 3D visualisation dynamic to the point where a visitor can walk 'inside' buildings, which is referred to as a portal (Ballarte 2017). The 3D laser-scanning data create the foundation for developing these new and exciting visualisations while also providing a foundation for the conservation and management strategy.

BIBLIOGRAPHY

3D-Icons Ireland (www.3dicons.ie; accessed 8 October 2018).

Ballarte, C. 2017. 'Augmented reality lets you step through Museum of Flight's portal and onto NASA's historic 737 jet' (https://tinyurl.com/y9xzzdhg; accessed 8 October 2018).

Historic England. 2018. *3D laser scanning for heritage: advice and guidance on the use of laser scanning in archaeology and architecture*. London.

Jenkins, J. 2001. *The port and quays of Wexford, 800–2000AD: an industrial, commercial and social history*. Wexford.

O'Sullivan, M., Rogers, M., Shine, D. and Mandal, S. 2018. 'Seir Kieran: place, pilgrimage and tradition in the monastic midlands'. *Offaly Heritage*, 10, 21–42.

RealSim. 2018. *RealSim history* (https://realsim.ie/realsim-history/; accessed 28 August 2018).

Rogers, M., Bouricius, R., Shine, D., Mandal, S. and Stull, S. 2018. 'Laser-scanning Trim Castle'. *Archaeology Ireland*, 32:3, 34–9.

CHAPTER NINE

The Crimean monument at Carrick: one tower, several stories

DEREK O'BRIEN, STEPHEN MANDAL & ISABEL BENNETT

INTRODUCTION

The round tower at Carrick has long been a landmark on the approach to Wexford from the north, standing proud on top of the hill on the right-hand side as one crosses Ferrycarrig Bridge over the River Slaney. Some readers will remember it being even more of a feature before the road that now leads to the Wexford bypass was cut through the landscape, changing it utterly. It is synonymous today not only with the

---

THE CRIMEAN WAR

The Crimean War was fought between 1854 and 1856, between Russia on one side and Britain, France, Turkey (the Ottoman Empire) and Sardinia-Piedmont on the other. It followed decades of political friction after the Napoleonic Wars and the declining fortunes of the Ottoman Empire, with Britain and France concerned that Russia was gaining power and territory at the expense of the Ottoman Empire. In addition, Russia promoted the rights of the Eastern Orthodox Church in the Holy Land, while the French promoted those of the church of Rome.

Russian troops occupied the Turkish principalities of Moldovia and Wallachia in July 1854, and by October British and French fleets were anchored in the Dardanelles. Hostilities involving all parties did not begin until the following year. The war was ended by the Treaty of Paris, signed on 30 March 1856 (Murphy 2014, 1–3). The war had cost the lives of over half a million people (Huddie 2017, 25).

An industrial war, it was also the first conflict in which eyewitness reports from the front were available to the public, reported by the first war correspondents. Public opinion in Britain, on the reading of eyewitness reports, became critical of the war. These were relayed by reporters such as William Howard Russell, a Dublin man and journalist for the *Times*, and one of the first journalists to write as a war correspondent using the telegraph to send back reports.

The Crimean War was infamous for its lack of planning and command coherence; generals and politicians often hesitated and made very poor decisions, which cost thousands upon thousands of lives on both sides.

9.1 The Crimean round tower, during archaeological excavations at the site in 2018

Irish National Heritage Park (INHP), but also with the ringwork at Carrick, in the townland of Newtown – overlooking this important pinch-point on the river, just as the twelfth- and thirteenth-century castles did before it.

This volume marks the eight-hundred-and-fiftieth anniversary of the construction of Fitz Stephen's fortification (chs 4, 5), but 2019 is also the eight-hundredth anniversary of the death of William Marshal, first earl of Pembroke, and the one-hundred-and-sixty-fifth anniversary of the beginning of the Crimean War. The round tower, more than other monuments, speaks to each of these periods but in very different ways, being particularly relevant to the Crimean associations of the site, although also having relevance, in a backward-facing sort of way, to its medieval history. It is a fascinating monument and one that reflects many stories (Figure 9.1).

THE IRISH IN THE CRIMEAN WAR

The round tower at Carrick is primarily a monument to the Wexford men who fought and died in the Crimean War; it is a giant memorial remembering their sacrifice. The

Irish contribution to this war was immense; at the beginning of the Crimean War approximately one-third of the British Army was made up of Irish troops, many having left Ireland at the time of the Great Famine. The British Army was a source of employment and, above all else, a source of food and clothing for many Irish. Newspaper accounts at the outbreak of the war show that young men rushed to enlist in an almost unseemly haste, with near hysterical scenes in towns and cities across Ireland, as was the case in Britain (Murphy 2014, 7). There was a strong military presence in Ireland at this time, with large numbers of British military barracks, or garrison towns, in numbers that exceeded even their density in Britain (Smyth 2017, 7).

A significant number of Irishmen served as battalion commanders in the British Army. In command of the 50th Foot (infantry) was Wexford native Lieutenant-Colonel Richard Waddy. In February 1854, the 50th were the first regiment of the British Army to leave for the Crimea (Murphy 2014, 187). Irish soldiers were joined in the Crimea by navvies, civilian workers, chaplains and indeed Irish women, who travelled as camp-followers; among the Irish women were eleven Sisters of Mercy nuns, recruited from houses in Ireland (ibid., 125, 228).

This war followed in a long tradition of Irishmen serving in 'foreign armies', among them the French army, where officers of Irish extraction remained in the 1850s, despite the disbandment of Napoleon's Irish Legion in 1815 (although it has been estimated that up to 40 per cent of the men fighting for Britain in the Peninsular Wars were Irish (McGreevy 2015)). Among the Irish officers was General Marie Edmé Patrice Maurice de MacMahon, who later served as governor of Algeria and as president of France (1873–9). Perhaps one of the last Irish-born generals in the French army was Charles Richard Sutton, comte de Clonard, born in Co. Wexford in 1807. He was promoted to brigadier-general in 1857. Irishmen also served in the Russian army throughout the eighteenth and nineteenth centuries, including a Count John O'Rourke, whose son Count Joseph attained the rank of general. The O'Rourkes still had descendants serving in the Russian army at the outbreak of the Crimean War (Murphy 2014, 23–5). On the opposing side, Irish officers in the British Army who were sent to the Crimea were mainly attached to Turkish contingents during the conflict, including one of the more famous, General Coleman, known as 'Fehti Bey'.

The total number of casualties suffered by the British was approximately 22,000; therefore, it is possible to deduce that about seven thousand Irish were killed, assuming a broadly equal fatality rate among different nationalities (Huddie 2017, 25). In the conflict, later immortalised by Alfred, Lord Tennyson, in the poem *The charge of the light brigade*, of the 114 Irishmen who took part, twenty-one lost their lives, sixteen were wounded, seven were taken prisoner and two were reported as missing (Murphy 2014, 73–4; Russell 1999, 163–4).

THE ROUND TOWER: A MEMORIAL TO THE CRIMEAN WAR

There are at least sixteen Crimean memorials in Ireland, many of which were erected while the war still raged on (Huddie 2015, 83), including four in Dublin, three in Wexford and one each in Kerry, Monaghan, Armagh, Clare, Limerick, Mayo, Offaly, Waterford and Galway. The majority of the memorials are in memory of individuals, typically in the form of plaques in Church of Ireland structures dedicated to serving officers. In Wexford and Kerry, public committees were set up to collect subscriptions and to organise and oversee the erection or placing of memorials dedicated to all the men who served from their respective counties. The Wexford memorial at Ferrycarrig was built between October 1857 and July 1858 and, standing at a height of 24.5m, is the largest monument to the Crimean War in Ireland (Figure 9.2).

The public committee charged with funding, designing and building the memorial comprised Lord Carew, Sir Thomas Esmonde MP, a number of civic and military officers and the high sheriff of the county. It was built during a difficult period in Irish history, amid high tensions following the Famine and the growth of the Fenian movement of the 1860s (Moody 2011). Contributions of £1 were sought from 'those who could afford it'. This was difficult for the less well-off, and it proved controversial in Wexford that the poor were approached to contribute in the first instance.

The construction of the tower was documented by the newspapers at the time, and a photographer from the *Illustrated London News* was present on the day the foundation stone was laid. A total of £300 was collected, including subscriptions such as that documented in the *Wexford Independent* of 7 October 1857 from a Mr John Bolton who donated £3 towards the construction; £1 for himself, £1 for the first soldier killed and £1 for the last hero who fell at Sevastopol (Huddie 2015, 84–5). The idea for the design of the memorial had originated from Major Boyd, a veteran himself, with the assistance of a Mr Nunn and a Mr Talbot, during his time as sheriff.

A public meeting was called by the then sheriff, Percy L. Harvey, of all freeholders of Wexford, to discuss the building of the tower and the laying of the foundation stone, and to organise for the arrival of the lord lieutenant of Ireland, the seventh earl of Carlisle. The plans and design of the tower were drawn up by the county surveyor, Mr Farrell, and Edwin Thomas Willis was appointed to design the tower. He designed the memorial as a replica of an early medieval round tower, by far the tallest and most prominent relics of the ancient Irish church. While some people expressed enthusiasm for the monument, others expressed opposition towards both the design and the amount of money collected. Although no evidence or illustrations have ever been discovered of its design, it was proposed that a canon, preferably one which had been used in the war itself, be placed on top of the completed monument (Bennett 1989, 59).

A full description of the event entitled 'The laying of the first stone of the Wexford Crimean Heroes' Monument' was presented in the *Wexford Independent* on 10 October 1857, two days after the occasion. The newspaper recorded that a ceremony took place 'on Thursday last under very auspicious and gratifying circumstances'. The earl of Carlisle had been staying at Johnstown Castle the night before and left from there on the morning of the event. Colours flew from the ships in the port and crowds gathered all along the quay cheered as the procession, including 'his excellency and suite', passed through several triumphal arches erected along the way. A twenty-one-gun salute was fired from the HM cutter *Gipsy*, a custom ship moored in Wexford Harbour. The earl was greeted at the courthouse by the mayor of Wexford, John Coghlan, the vice lieutenant, Charles A. Walker, the high sheriff, Percy Harvey, the lieutenant of the county, Lord Carew, and a great host of other dignitaries. The fashion and beauty of the ladies of Wexford who occupied the gallery were reported to be unrivalled at the time. The courthouse was crowded with all classes of the Wexford community. Lord Carew addressed those in attendance: 'We mourn over our young heroes who perished in their prime and left desolation in many a heart and home among us … from the best blood of our people … for the liberties of Europe'. Lord Carew added that it was with 'deep-felt satisfaction' that the earl was present, 'one who has never failed to appreciate Irish worth, and to sympathise with Irish suffering'. The earl replied that it was pleasing for him to find in Wexford, which had been a 'scene of civil discord and conflict', that these 'turbulent and sorrowful effects seem banished from the land' or at least 'relegated to far distant districts' and that all classes of the Wexford community had joined together in honouring this great occasion and 'the glory of the fallen'. It is likely that his mention of civil discord/conflict is a reference to the 1798 rebellion, or perhaps the Great Famine. The mayor then addressed the crowd, not only by welcoming the earl, but also by referring to other business matters of the day – referencing trade and commerce, the improvement of the harbour, and the railroad that would be brought to Wexford.

From Wexford the procession moved to Ferrycarrig, or 'John's Court' as it was known, for the laying of the foundation stone. On arrival, Vice-Lieutenant Walker, chairman of the committee, addressed the assembled crowd on the hilltop of Carrick, where thanks were again given to the earl of Carlisle for his kind patronage and for being a 'kind friend to Ireland', who had encouraged Irish art, literature and industrial pursuits. Mr Walker spoke of the gallant conduct of the departed heroes in the war and mentioned that the 'Irish portion of them bore their full share, being surpassed by none, in devoted loyalty, patient endurance and deeds of daring on the battlefield'. He also talked on the hilltop's history, informing the crowd (incorrectly) that Strongbow was responsible for the original structure, and proposing that Fitz Stephen built his castle at the opposite side of the River Slaney (the site of the sixteenth-century Roches' Castle); he further suggested that King John built the first stone castle at Carrick, leading to the name 'John's Court'. Thanks were also given to the earl of Donoughmore (who had donated the land for the memorial) and John Codde, his tenant, who apparently was a descendant of the Anglo-Norman settlers.

9.2 The plaque at the Crimean round tower, which reads 'In memory of the officers, non-commissioned officers and men of the County Wexford who lost their lives in the Crimea during the war with Russia 1854, '55–'56'

It had been raining that morning, but the sun came out in the afternoon, which led it to be reported that 'heaven itself looked propitiously on the solemn and deeply affecting' ceremony. As the earl of Carlisle arrived on site, he was greeted with a loud roar from the gathered crowd, while the Wexford regimental band played *God save the queen*, with an apparent 'pleasing and delightful effect'. The dedication of the monument was read out in Latin, and afterwards translated into English 'for the satisfaction of the female portion of the assemblage'. The earl entered the excavation to lay the first stone and described the memorial, and the site on which it stood, as incorporating all the topographical, geographical and historical features of Wexford (Bennett 1989, 32; Huddie 2017, 23). The foundation stone was a block of granite with a leaden case in the centre; this may be one of the earliest purposely located time capsules in Ireland (Bennett 1989). Placed in the capsule were a parchment on which the dedication, delivered by the earl and written by a Mr M. Saunders Greene, was inscribed; a list of those who donated money; a copy of a newspaper reporting the arrival of the lord lieutenant for the ceremony; and coins of the period (Huddie 2015, 86). While the time capsule was placed in the ground the band played *The heights of Alma*.

The stone was then lowered into place, the case was welded shut with molten lead, and mortar was spread on top to seal it, declaring the 'foundation stone well and truly laid'. A special trowel had been fashioned for the day – forged in silver, with an oak handle and decorated with shamrocks. The blade of the trowel was engraved with a round tower and an inscription in Latin commemorating the event, written by Sir Bernard Burke. When it ended, the earl went on to Woodstock House in Inistioge, Co. Kilkenny, and the townsfolk dispersed in an 'effective manner' under the command of the police. There would be no further ceremonies – at least no reference to any has been found – and the tower was complete by July 1858.

Shortly after its construction, the tower was well documented by Thomas Lacy in 1863, in his travel writings on Wexford. He describes the tower as

> another highly important adjunct, which, whether looked upon as an object suggestive of sympathy for the loss of the young and brave, whose memory it has been erected to commemorate, and the recollection of whose gallant and heroic deeds it is well calculated to perpetuate, or as a faithful representation of the old pillar temples of the country, must, in a pictorial point of view, be considered of the most unquestionable advantage to those who delight in sketching scenes of natural and artificial beauty.

The author records both the relevance of the site to the Crimean War, and the laying of the foundation stone. Surprisingly, he notes the site's association with an early Fitz Stephen castle, but still incorrectly associates his first foundation with the adjacent Roches' Castle. A good description of the finished tower is provided, which is documented as having a diameter of fourteen feet six inches (14.4m) with a height to the apex of its conical roof of eighty-five feet (25.9m). The tower is described as 'plainly built' with 'poor materials' with a number of lighting 'slits', a door '9 feet from the ground' and projecting internal corbels, 'so as to serve as supports for floors' (Lacy 1863, 463–4).

A SIMILAR, ALMOST CONTEMPORARY, MONUMENT

This was not the first 'replica' round tower to have been built as a memorial in mid-nineteenth-century Ireland. A similar (but taller) tower was built of granite in Prospect Cemetery, Glasnevin, to commemorate Daniel O'Connell (1775–1847) but, unlike the tower at Carrick, one can actually enter this one. It was built between 1851 and 1855, but not opened until 1869. It was designed by Patrick Byrne (1782/3–1864). Perhaps it was this tower that provided the immediate inspiration for the construction of the Wexford example. It is interesting to note that there are no 'true' early medieval round towers known from Co. Wexford.

THE ROUND TOWER: A WINDOW TO THE STONE CASTLE

The construction of the tower as a Crimean War monument is a fascinating story, but its relevance to the medieval archaeology at the site is no less interesting. Undoubtedly, the medieval structures were irrevocably damaged by the memorial tower; for example, in digging through the site to construct foundations (Shine et al. 2018; Shine and Mandal 2018). One of the most intriguing aspects of the tower, however, is the stone from which it is made and where that stone was sourced. What insight does the tower give to the thirteenth-century stone castle and/or later fourteenth-century structures that once stood at this site, of which there are now almost no above-ground remains surviving? The decline of the castle and its fall into ruin is documented in detail in Chapter 4. It is speculated that much of the above-ground remains of the stone walls of the castle were quarried between 1840 and 1866 (as well as in the previous century), broadly coinciding with the construction of the memorial tower. A historical fictional novel, published in 1866, refers to the fortification that stood 'on the high cliffs on the right bank' of which no 'trace now remains' (Hanrahan 1866, 90).

The quarrying and reuse of medieval architectural stone and other building materials is well recorded throughout Ireland. Medieval building stone was reused in the construction of residences and associated structures, especially from the seventeenth to the nineteenth century (O'Brien 2017, 126–33; Moss 2012, 115–17). There are several contemporary references to the Carrick site being used as a quarry during the eighteenth and nineteenth centuries.

9.3 Ruins associated with Belmont House outbuildings (the insert shows close-up of stones used)

Built in approximately 1800, Belmont House stood less than 2km south of Carrick and cut stone from the castle was apparently used in its construction (Hore 1900–11, vol. v, 34). Jeffrey (1979, 103), citing *The People* newspaper from 1889, stated that no trace of a castle existed for it had been demolished more than 160 years previously and the materials were used in the construction of Belmont House. No trace of Belmont House survives, but several stables and other farm buildings associated with it are still extant. These buildings are situated west of the house site, and north of castle site (Bennett 1985, 33). It is also recorded that in the early twentieth century stone from the demolished mills at Carrick (of which two are recorded) was also used in the building of Belmont House (Jeffrey 1979, 102–3; Bennett 1985, 30–3). An inspection of the extant remains was undertaken in January 2019. The stones are consistent with those identified in the tower and in the remaining walls uncovered during the archaeological excavations (see Figure 9.3 and below).

9.4 (*right*) IAFS excavations resuming on the site in January 2018, overlooked by the Crimean tower

9.5 (*below*) Geological assessment of the tower fabric in progress in August 2018

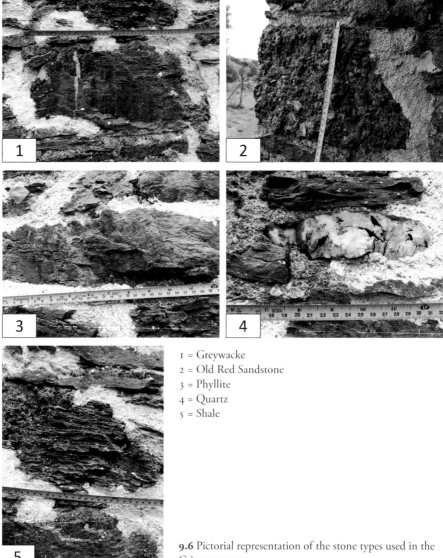

1 = Greywacke
2 = Old Red Sandstone
3 = Phyllite
4 = Quartz
5 = Shale

9.6 Pictorial representation of the stone types used in the Crimean tower

It is possible that other estate houses close to Carrick drew stone from the medieval castle (see ch. 4; Lewis 1837), which is last referred to as standing, albeit as a ruin, in 1587 (Holinshed 1587, 11). The Ordnance Survey letters of 1840 (O'Donovan 1840, 357) state that stone was taken from the site of the castle to build the 'stone part' of Wexford Bridge in 1795. Lemuel Cox designed both Wexford and Ferrycarrig bridges. It is more credible that stone was used in the building of any stone part of Ferrycarrig Bridge as it sits directly below the site of the castle. Stone may also have been brought

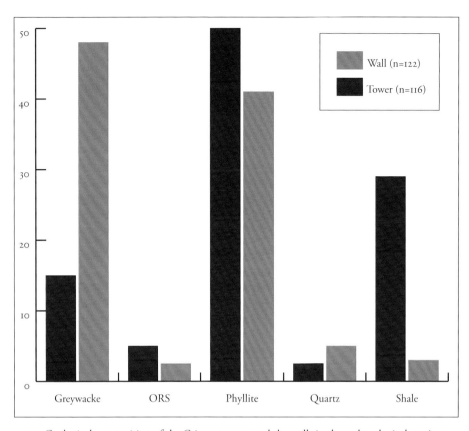

9.7 Geological composition of the Crimean tower and the walls in the archaeological cuttings

the 3.5km into the town of Wexford for the construction of the bridge there, especially as the adjacent River Slaney may have provided a cost-effective transport option.

It is intuitive to assume that the stone used in the building of the memorial was taken from what remained of the stone castle at that time. The reopening of the 1980s archaeological excavation cuttings of Bennett (1985) and Cotter (1987; 1988) during investigations in 2018 by the Irish Archaeology Field School (IAFS) provided an opportunity to systematically assess this assumption (Figure 9.4). The results of the assessment of the stone walls is given in Chapter 4 and summarised here in the context of the stone used in the memorial tower.

A visual assessment of the stone types used in the tower was undertaken in August 2018 (Figure 9.5). Using a ladder to view the exposed stone above the limewashed base, five representative 1m x 1m grids were chosen and the stones were measured and identified geologically. In total, 116 stones were identified, and these were compared to the available close-up drone survey footage provided by the INHP and deemed to be representative.

The same five rock types identified in the remaining walls exposed during the 2018 excavations (see Figures 9.6, 9.7; geology section of ch. 5) occur in the tower. It is notable, however, that the percentage distribution of the stone is different. In particular, there is significantly more shale and less greywacke used in the tower than is evident in the site's walls. There are a number of possible explanations for this disparity. It is important to note that the currently exposed remains of the castle walls appear to be the base or foundation courses, and it is possible that the stone used in the higher courses contained more shale. This makes sense in the context of the coarser-grained and more massive (containing fewer internal structures) greywackes and phyllites being better at load bearing than shale, which has inherent weaknesses due to the built-in lamination. Conversely, shale naturally breaks into flat units and makes a good building material. It is also possible that shale was discarded during the earlier phases of quarrying at the site and was therefore in abundance at the time of the building of the tower. Further examination of walls as they are discovered and exposed may shed further light on these questions. Based on the historical evidence and the results of this assessment, however, it is beyond reasonable doubt that the tower was constructed using the remaining stone from the then remnants of upstanding walls of the thirteenth- and fourteenth-century stone structures at Carrick.

CONSERVATION OF THE MONUMENT

In 2014, a programme of conservation was undertaken at the tower as the conical cap had been struck by lightning and the masonry was in need of re-pointing with lime mortar. The entire structure was scaffolded and this allowed an inspection of all the stonework to the top of the tower. In places it was noted that there was existing lime plaster on some of the stones, showing that some of the stone had clearly been reused (Catherine McLoughlin, pers. comm.). These works also saw the construction of a new conical cap, which was made of stone from the grounds of Ardcandrisk House, 2km west of the site, an interesting return of building materials from a nineteenth-century estate house.

CONCLUSION

The Crimean tower is an instantly recognisable and much-loved landmark in the Wexford landscape. The affection for the tower and its location appears to be something that has endured for generations if the writings of Lacy (1863) are accurate. The construction of the tower was not without its controversy, however, and it offers a fascinating insight into the socio-political context of mid-nineteenth-century Wexford and Ireland. Importantly, the tower also offers intriguing glimpses into the final days of the medieval buildings on the site, which themselves had their antecedents in the first ever Anglo-Norman fortification in the country.

That the site has undergone many transformations over the decades is obvious – another seminal moment in its history being the establishment of the INHP in 1987 (ch. 10) – but it continues to stand as a beacon for those travelling southward across the Slaney. The continued existence of the tower was secured in 2014 following conservation, and these works should ensure that the Crimean War memorial, and the historically crucial site from which it rises, should sit proudly in the landscape for generations to come.

BIBLIOGRAPHY

Anon. 1857. 'The laying of the first stone of the Wexford Crimean heroes' monument'. *The Wexford Independent*, *c.*10 October.

Bennett, I. 1985. 'Preliminary archaeological excavations at Ferrycarrig ringwork, Newtown td, Co. Wexford'. *Journal of the Wexford Historical Society*, 10, 25–43.

Bennett, I. 1989. 'The Crimean War memorial, Ferrycarrig, Co. Wexford: a precisely dated round tower'. *Archaeology Ireland*, 3:2, 58–60.

Cotter, C. 1987. 'Ferrycarrig, Newtown, ringwork'. In Cotter, C. (ed.), *Excavations 1986: summary accounts of archaeological excavations in Ireland*, p. 37, no. 79. Dublin.

Cotter, C. 1988. 'Ferrycarrig, Newtown, ringwork'. In Bennett, I. (ed.), *Excavations 1987: summary accounts of archaeological excavations in Ireland*, p. 30, no. 56. Dublin.

Hanrahan, R. 1866. *Eva or the buried city of Bannow*. Wexford.

Holinshed, R. 1587. *The first and second volumes of chronicles … now newly augmented … to the year 1856 by John Hooker alias Vowell gent and others*. 3 vols. London.

Hore, P. 1900–11. *History of the town and county of Wexford*. 6 vols. London.

Huddie, P. 2015. *The Crimean War and Irish society*. Oxford.

Huddie, P. 2017. '"What round tower?": the restoration of the Crimean War monument at Ferrycarrig, Wexford'. *Journal of the Wexford Historical Society*, 26, 23–30.

Jeffrey, W. 1979. 'The castles of Co. Wexford'. Notes presented to Wexford County Library by Old Wexford Society. Unpublished.

Lacy, T. 1863. *Sights and scenes in our fatherland*. London.

Lewis, S. 1837. *A topographical dictionary of Ireland*. 2 vols. London.

McGreevy, R. 2015. 'Just how many Irish fought at the Battle of Waterloo' (www.irishtimes.com/culture/heritage/just-how-many-irish-fought-at-the-battle-of-waterloo-1.2254271, accessed 17 February 2019).

Moody, T. 2011. 'Fenianism, Home Rule and the Land War, 1850–91'. In Moody, T. and Martin, F.X., *The course of Irish history*, 240–56. Cork.

Moss, R. 2012. 'Reduce, reuse, recycle: Irish monastic architecture, *c.*1540–*c.*1640'. In Stalley, R. (ed.), *Irish Gothic architecture: construction, decay and reinvention*, 115–59. Dublin.

Murphy, D. 2014. *Ireland and the Crimean War*. Dublin.

O'Brien, D. 2017. 'The evidence for the importation and use of foreign limestone in Cork city and county during the later medieval period'. *Journal of the Cork Historical and Archaeological Society*, 122, 123–37.

O'Donovan, J. 1840. *Ordnance Survey letters.* Dublin.

Russell, W. 1999. 'The charge of the light brigade'. In Lewis, J. (ed.), *True war stories*, 153–64. New York.

Shine, D. and Mandal, S. 2018. 'Digging the lost town of Carrig: archaeological excavation report'. Unpublished technical report for the NMS.

Shine, D., Mandal, S., Hayes, C. and Harris, M. 2018. 'Finding Carrig'. *Archaeology Ireland*, 32:2, 35–40.

Smyth, W. 2017. 'Nineteenth-century Ireland: transformed contexts and class structures'. In Crowley, J., Ó Drisceoil, D. and Murphy, M. (eds), *Atlas of the Irish Revolution*, 4–20, Cork.

CHAPTER TEN

The Irish National Heritage Park, home to Carrick: a personal reflection

CHRISTOPHER HAYES

INTRODUCTION

Upon its opening in 1987 the Irish National Heritage Park (INHP) declared its mission statement loud and clear to the public: 'come to us to learn 9,000 years of Irish history, from the arrival of the first humans to the Norman invasion of 1169'.

On paper that is quite a boast, but for thirty-one years the park has been doing just that, telling the story of human settlement in Ireland – in the process inspiring many of its visitors with a lifelong passion for history and archaeology. Over the years we have heard many anecdotal stories, such as from teachers who were brought on school tours as children and still recall eating meat from the *fulacht fiadh* – being amazed that four thousand years ago this was how we cooked for the family reunion! It is a mark of our enduring success that these teachers are now bringing their own history class in for that same experience. Indeed, some of the contributors to this volume have fallen victim to the charm of the park's winding paths; there is early photographic proof of Denis Shine having his ninth birthday party here, while Niall Colfer's first paid employment was as a tour guide in the INHP. They are just two of the tens of thousands of tourists to have passed through our gates – all of whom leave with their own individual experience, as evident in the early visitor books and letters sent to the park, or the more recent instant reviews on social media and travel blogs.

THE PARK ORIGINS

The purpose of this essay is to set out the origins of the INHP, the changes to the park over the last thirty-one years and how its story of human settlement evolved to the establishment of the *Digging the Lost Town of Carrig Project* in 2018. This essay is not a definitive history of the park's origins, to do that would require detailed documentation on a wide range of areas from financing to administration to staffing. Instead, the focus is on information garnered through a programme of interviews carried out during the thirtieth-anniversary celebrations of the park in 2017. These interviews have been supplemented by a collection of documents that were put together by Edward Culleton (now held in the INHP archive) as well as through conversations with the current general manager, Maura Bell, who has been at the helm of the park for the last eighteen years. It is a series of personal accounts of this unique outdoor museum.

In March 1983, Culleton wrote an article called 'Field monuments: a neglected resource. An outline proposal for development', which was presented to various tourist interests within Wexford and across the country. In this article he argued that the visual remains of our ancestors, which are dotted throughout the country, should be treated as an important national resource that needed to be sensitively exploited; specifically that these monuments should be revealed to an international audience, resulting in benefits for local communities in the form of employment and an increased sense of local importance of heritage in its own right (Culleton 1983; see also Culleton 1994). As summarised by Johnson (1999, 195), the park was developed with 'the twin aims of attracting tourists to south-eastern Ireland and educating the public in field monuments'.

Culleton maintained that a site needed to be found in south Co. Wexford where a selection of field monuments – dolmens, raths, motte-and-baileys, stone castles etc. – could be reconstructed and open for public viewing; this location would serve to whet the appetite of the visitor to further explore the Irish landscape and its cultural treasures. When first developing this vision, Culleton floated the idea of acquiring these sites in different parts of the south of the county, but it soon became apparent that it would be easier to execute the vision if the monuments could all be reconstructed at a single site.

His reasoning for strategically focusing on this part of Wexford was in part informed by the presence of Rosslare Port, a gateway into Ireland from mainland Europe and the United Kingdom. At that time air travel remained prohibitively expensive and the sea ports were often the more accessible way for visitors to move between continental Europe, the UK and Ireland. If the thousands of visitors travelling through the port could stop somewhere and get a sense of the depth of history imbued in the Irish landscape, then they would be better motivated to explore and find the 'real thing' in other parts of the country.

Culleton's article, which was circulated widely, expanded on the practicalities of how such a project could be delivered; he proposed using back-to-work schemes to deliver some of the building work, spelled out the multiplier effect that such an attraction would have via spin-offs from the tourism spend locally, and highlighted the positive effect it would have on youths visiting such an attraction. He went as far as to include a section on the different guidebooks that would be needed and the authors who were available to work on these; for example, Jim Hurley for 'Fishing and Wildlife' and John Maguire for 'Industrial Archaeology' (Culleton 1983).

The early 1980s in Ireland was a bleak time economically for the country, where a succession of unstable governments were trying to handle high levels of government debt and huge unemployment. The proposal to build a national heritage park was a hard sell at the time, but the idea was clearly well thought out and so caught the attention of others in the county who came together to form the Heritage Committee of the Wexford Tourism Council. This committee met formally for the first time on 13 April 1983 and was constituted as follows:

- Edward Culleton, chairman
- William Colfer, secretary
- Gerard Forde, county engineer
- Rosaleen Nixon, county planning officer
- William Ringwood, county development officer
- John Walsh, South-East Regional Tourism Organisation
- Austin O'Sullivan, independent
- Fr Seamus Wall, parish priest of Oulart
- Richard Roche, independent
- Nicholas Furlong, independent
- John Small, independent

Apologies were sent to the meeting by Noel Dillon, county manager, and Rory Murphy, chairman of the Wexford Tourism Council.

At the time of the meeting all the above would have been aware of various responses to the idea of establishing the park. The Office of Public Works (OPW) sent a three-line response that promised 'careful consideration' (OPW 1983). Bord Fáilte's (the predecessor to Fáilte Ireland, the National Tourism Development Authority of Ireland) response was a little longer and remarked that the proposals were interesting, heavily supporting a self-contained park rather than a series of monuments spread over the south of Wexford (Bord Fáilte 1983). The more detailed response came from the Wexford county manager Noel Dillon (WCC 1983), and was followed by an enthusiastic letter from Rory Murphy, chairman of the Wexford Tourism Council. The ball was now rolling that would set up the Heritage Committee.

While the early 1980s were depressed economically, Ireland's road infrastructure was being improved by structural funds from Europe. One of the first roads to be upgraded was the N11 from Rosslare Port to Dublin. This upgrade necessitated a series of compulsory purchase orders of land to enable the building of a bypass around Wexford town, which would cut through agricultural land and re-join the old Dublin road at Ferrycarrig. The purchase of land associated with the bypass resulted in an isolated strip of land, running from the hill at Carrig down to the lowlands below, remaining in the possession of Wexford County Council to the west of the bypass. This plot covered almost forty acres (16.2 hectares) and, although much of it was covered in water, the potential of the site was clear to those who were working to make the concept of the park a reality.

10.1 Opening day tour for President Patrick Hillery in June 1987

10.2 The 'completed' crannog in 1989

It took a lot of time, energy, expertise and finance to get the INHP ready for its launch on 12 June 1987 by then president of Ireland, Patrick Hillery (Figure 10.1). On the morning of the opening the workers on site were still spreading fine stone around the reception area, transforming the worksite into a well-presented tourist attraction, even as the president's car made its way down the N11!

Following from the mission statement for the INHP, the design of the park was based on a chronological walk through nine thousand years of human settlement (see O'Brien and Channing 1988 for a good early review). The first site would focus on the Mesolithic and from there the story of our ancestors was woven into a meandering path that comes to an end at the top of the rock of Carrick where Fitz Stephen established the first Anglo-Norman castle in Ireland. The path through the park was carefully planned and landscaped so that the visitor got a real sense of walking away from the modern world. Arthur Murphy, a Wexford County Council engineer at the time, was responsible for engineering the path layout, as well as the installation of the millpond and associated works (Interviews 2017a). His expertise was to prove vital in delivering an accessible attraction, in a challenging landscape topographically, to people of all abilities. While he was working to a timeline worked out by the Heritage Committee, he also knew it was crucial that visitors experience the full range of environments on the site – woodlands, streams, ponds, riverside and open meadow. His clever design extended to the millpond weir, which has stood the test of time, maintains the correct water level for demonstrations at the horizontal mill, and remains easy to clean when sediment builds up at the weir.

Once the park was opened to the public it was the responsibility of the tour guides to tell the story of Irish history. John Ormonde was one of the first guides to lead groups around the park (Interview 2017b). Having interviewed for the post, he was invited to attend a one-day training course at the old Whites Hotel in Wexford town. John was anxious about the task of learning nine thousand years of history, as presumably were the other guides, and so was looking forward to the training. The day provided only minimal training on the layout of the park, however, and Irish prehistory and history in general. John remembers going home and putting together a series of flash cards that he then shared with the other tour guides (Interview 2017b). At the time, the guides wore a uniform of black shoes and trousers, with a white shirt, green tie and a name tag. This gave them a formal look and an 'air of authority' that, at the time, was considered the best approach to guiding and teaching history. Many of the recreated sites in the park were roped off, allowing visitors to view from a distance as part of a somewhat controlled and formalised experience.

THE PARK TODAY

Fast forward thirty-two years and those early tours would be virtually unrecognisable from what the park offers today. Our understanding and delivery of heritage experiences to visitors has changed radically over the years and continues to evolve today. Maura Bell became general manager of the park in 2000 and initiated a policy of removing the gates and hurdles that kept the public at arm's length from the exhibits; she also encouraged the lighting of real fires in parts of the park. Our tour guides are now dressed in period costume – as Vikings, Gaels and Anglo-Normans – and all of our buildings are open to the public to move around in and to get a sense of history up close, which engages all the senses. Visitors often remark on the smell of burning fires – a simple but important way to transport people back in time by playing on their sense of smell. In the twenty-first century, when much of the world's population live in urban areas, the opportunity to provide people with a sense of the basic elements that have shaped our development in society is an important tool in our storytelling kit.

There was an awareness when the park opened of the importance of living history experiments in helping visitors and students comprehend our past. The *fulacht fiadh* demonstration possibly best exemplifies this and is now one of the oldest continually running experimental archaeology sites in the world! Schoolchildren and presidents have eaten there – with the children's frequent initial inhibitions at the idea of eating from a pit always lost once they have had a taste (and a smell). School visits to the park have always formed an integral part of our visitor base – indeed, it was a part of the INHP's original core ethos that we make history accessible to schoolchildren of all ages to enhance their understanding of our past.

Building on this ethos and appealing to the natural curiosity of children was one of the key drivers in the 2010–13 redevelopment work in the park. Ronan O'Flaherty was instrumental in this phase of the park's history, after he approached the park with a proposal to apply to Fáilte Ireland (the National Tourism Development Authority of Ireland) for funding to rebuild several replicas, as well as to install new activities. It is commendable to be earnest in wanting to teach history to children, but if they cannot have fun and be trusted to discover the world on their own terms then we lose their interest immediately. During this phase of the redevelopment, the *Trials of Tuan*, a series of interactive events focused on children, were introduced to the park; taking coracles on the millpond became a part of the summer camps while archery and spear-throwing in the Anglo-Norman castle were introduced. The ringfort was repurposed so that families or groups of friends could book a night there, having the whole park to themselves long after the gates were closed to the public. One of the main aims of this redevelopment was to immerse visitors in our history and landscape, permitting them the chance to experience history through all their senses. There is a deep appreciation within the park that people learn differently, and our challenge is to appeal to every 'learning quirk' so that our story is clearly understood – hopefully whetting the appetite so the visitor leaves wanting to discover more.

The park and the philosophy that guides it have grown and adapted well over its short history, just as our broader understanding of history has changed over the years. Shifting sands of knowledge are one thing that keeps us on our toes, as is the reworking of history as it is revisited anew. This is especially so when it comes to dealing with the Anglo-Norman invasion of Ireland, which resulted in such profound consequences for our island. There are of course meticulous lines drawn around certain events in our history that serve to inform our understanding of those times. We can talk about the 'first wave' of Anglo-Norman invasions and the shared religion of both sides, the technology that arrived with those Anglo-Normans and the positive influence it had (ch. 1). There were then the later waves of invasion when religious, linguistic and social persecution became part of our nation's story. Revolt and rebellions and the different reasons behind them are blended into the one struggle against a 'foreign invader' and all these stories become entangled and conflated into an

10.3 The mock Anglo-Norman motte-and-bailey during its construction, also showing Fitz Stephen's ringwork under excavation in the 1980s and the new N11 road shortly before opening

10.4 Aerial photograph of the new N11 road during construction (courtesy of INHP)

'eight hundred years of occupation' refrain (see ch. 12 for an extended discussion). Once established, it can be difficult and time-consuming to dismantle national histographies and re-tell our national story in all its complexities – but it is always worth making that effort.

The portrayal of Anglo-Norman history was at the forefront of the park's original intent (see ch. 12). As established, their remit was to tell the story of human settlement through fifteen carefully reconstructed sites, and one original site. The one original site is Fitz Stephen's ringwork, the site of the first Anglo-Norman castle in Ireland. Indeed, the location of the castle, and its surrounding medieval landscape, was one of the main motivations in creating the park at Ferrycarrig to begin with (for a discussion, see ch. 12).

During the early construction phase of the N11, Isabel Bennett carried out an archaeological survey of the ringwork in 1985 (Bennett 1985). She was followed by Claire Cotter, who continued the archaeological work in tandem with the park construction in 1986/7 (see chs 4, 5 for full details). The 1980s excavation resulted in significant findings and the ringwork, stone castle and associated settlement were brought back into the public sphere. A sign was erected identifying the site when the park opened – but then the site was left to return to nature and soon became overgrown. Guided tours would stop at the Viking site and the story of the most important site in the INHP was allowed to go cold.

Why was this site not given the attention and detail that it deserved? From a story-telling point of view, it is the 'once-upon-a-time a castle was built …' opening that would captivate an audience. Is it because it is the beginning of the infrastructure of colonisation? Perhaps this story was too hard to approach in an Ireland where violence was still dominating the narrative around colony. A discussion of this intriguing question is, unfortunately, beyond the scope of this essay, but it is considered in chapter 12, below. Certainly, when the park invited the Irish Archaeology Field School to begin the *Digging the Lost Town of Carrig Project* with us we felt that the time was right to start unearthing this past, to delve into the story of that first wave of the Anglo-Norman invasion.

This live archaeological project has brought new life and energy to a corner of the park that was for too long hiding in the shadows. The aims of the project are many – to educate, to inform, to bring forensic analysis and eager students together, to introduce children to source material in a fun way and to add more chapters to our story. But it is also about shedding new light on those first Anglo-Normans that set foot on this rocky outcrop at the edge of the River Slaney. Ultimately, it is a project that fittingly exhibits all that is good about the INHP – its adaptability, its ingenuity and, most of all, its deep commitment to tell the story of Irish history.

BIBLIOGRAPHY

Bennett, I. 1985. 'Preliminary archaeological excavations at Ferrycarrig ringwork, Newtown td, Co. Wexford'. *Journal of the Wexford Historical Society*, 10, 25–43.

Bord Fáilte. 1983. 'A response to "Field monuments: a neglected resource. An outline proposal for development. A submission to the tourist interests in County Wexford"'. INHP archive.

Culleton, E. 1983. 'Field monuments: a neglected resource. An outline proposal for development. A submission to the tourist interests in County Wexford'. INHP archive.

Culleton, E. 1994. 'Address to the World Archaeological Congress, Delhi, India, December 1994'. INHP archive.

Interview. 2017a. 'Interview with Arthur Murphy (former park engineer) by Christopher Hayes in September 2017'. INHP archive.

Interview. 2017b. 'Interview with John Ormonde (former tour guide) by Christopher Hayes in August 2017'. INHP archive.

Johnson, N. 1999. 'Framing the past: time, space and the politics of heritage tourism in Ireland'. *Political Geography*, 18, 187–207.

O'Brien B. and Channing, J. 1988. 'Wexford Heritage Park'. *Archaeology Ireland*, 2:3, 112–14.

OPW. 1983. 'A response to "Field monuments: a neglected resource. An outline proposal for development. A submission to the tourist interests in County Wexford"'. INHP archive.

WCC. 1983. 'A response to "Field monuments: a neglected resource. An outline proposal for development. A submission to the tourist interests in County Wexford"'. INHP archive.

CHAPTER ELEVEN

The Carrig field school: a model for the benefits of field-school education

STEPHEN MANDAL, RAN BOYTNER, DENIS SHINE, DANNY ZBOROVER & MADELEINE HARRIS

INTRODUCTION

On 7 January 2018 a group of international students arrived at Ferrycarrig to commence excavations at the Hill of Carrick as part of a field school led by the Irish Archaeology Field School (IAFS; see Figure 11.1). This excavation is the central pillar of a major collaborative project – *Digging the Lost Town of Carrig Project* – founded by the IAFS and the Irish National Heritage Park (INHP). The main aim of the project is to draw the archaeological site into the park in a creative and sustainable manner, thus providing added economic, educational and amenity value to the local community. Unusually, although the site is of national significance, at the commencement of this project it did not feature highly in the public consciousness. Thus, the project is intended to increase awareness of Carrick and its role in Irish history. In short, the partnership between the IAFS and the INHP is a commitment to explain in a deeper and more meaningful way, to visitors and locals alike, what happened at Ferrycarrig eight-hundred-and-fifty years ago when the first Anglo-Norman castle in the country was constructed.

The cornerstone of the project has been the establishment of a leading archaeological research and teaching dig on the site, facilitated through key partnerships such as with the Institute for Field Research (IFR). The IAFS and the IFR have partnered on a range of programmes since 2013, focused on diverse fields of heritage-related study including bio-archaeology, medieval history, environmental science, public archaeology and landscape archaeology. These programmes have taken place in several locations in Ireland including the east coast, the midlands, the west and Ferrycarrig. The core ethos of each programme is that they must deliver excellence in research and education. Field-school programmes, such as at Carrick, ensure students are not restricted to their home campus but instead enjoy the multitude of benefits of experiential learning in an outdoor classroom – frequently at lower tuition costs than they pay in their home country. While the students excavate and learn they are generating a more vivid picture of the past for their host community – it is a partnership model with many benefits and no discernible shortcomings.

11.1 IAFS and INHP staff with the inaugural group of IFR students in January 2018

A BACKGROUND TO ARCHAEOLOGICAL FIELD SCHOOLS

Field schools have been a mainstay of archaeology for over 130 years. They are a rite of passage for aspiring academic archaeologists and a locus where generations of young students learn as much about themselves as about cultures vastly different to their own. Challenging body and mind, archaeology field schools involve intensive research schedules, intellectual rigour and physical work at sites across the world. Nobody returns unchanged. For some, field schools are the first step in academic careers. For others, it is the entry point to commercial archaeology (also known as Cultural Resource Management (CRM) in the US). For most, field schools are transformative experiences that instil lifelong relationships with archaeology.

All participants develop a deep understanding of the past, its important role for our understanding of the present and its ability to help make informed decisions about the future – as individuals and as communities. Archaeology field schools provide experiential learning where all senses are engaged and where lives are changed. They also ensure the discipline continues to hold a central place in the public consciousness and imagination. Archaeology is a public good; it cannot and will not survive without public support.

It is unclear when or where the first archaeology field school took place. In Europe, and especially in the Anglo-Saxon world, avocational archaeology has been a mainstay of culture for a long time (see Mytum 2012b, 9). The genesis of its formalisation and integration into proper academic training endeavour is unclear. We know much more about the formulation of archaeology field schools in the US. The first such programme likely took place in 1878, when Lewis Morgan of Columbia University took students for an exploration of Pueblo ruins in New Mexico (Beauregard et al. 1911; Gifford and Morris 1985; Springer 1913). In the summer of 1919, the University of Arizona offered the first formal field course that allowed eager students to partake in the investigation of important sites (Brace 1986; Haury 1989; Nesbitt 1931; Thompson and Longacre 1966). Since then, many universities and scholars began offering programmes to train students, both within and outside the US (see Joiner 1992; McManamon 1991; Mytum 2012a; Perry 2006). In more recent years, field schools have become an important economic engine, both to fund archaeological research and to support local communities (Boytner 2012; 2014).

The spirit of adventure and discovery continues to inspire participants, but modern-day field schools are further motivated by specialised training, experiential learning and rigorous research agendas. Across diverse geographic areas, time periods and cultural horizons, students learn how to conduct archaeological research through hands-on, intensive training. From survey and excavation through conservation and ethnographic work, participants glean knowledge from a broad range of research activities. Throughout the last century, numerous important discoveries were made, and generations of scholars trained in field schools around the world. Today, ground-breaking student research is an indispensable component of the design and the outcome of many such programmes.

As economic, political and social changes are shifting global perspectives and priorities, funding for basic research – including archaeology – has become scarce. Governments, foundations and individuals are seeking 'impact' where funding can show measurable, rapid impact on employability and income. Archaeology has never been a well-paying field and its findings are only indirectly impacting technological or economic improvements, if at all. There is nothing rapid about the discipline – quite the opposite; it is slow and becoming slower. Modern archaeology uses a range of scientific methods and techniques that produce nuanced, deliberate, controlled and slow excavation processes. As costs to pay for these scientific tools increase and funding decreases, archaeologists find themselves in tight spots.

Many archaeologists found the solution to the funding crunch by turning to the North American model of field schools. In return for training and transferable academic units, North American students are willing to pay field schools significant sums, as well as provide free labour. Since the turn of this century, the number of archaeology field schools has flourished, as can be seen on the field school listing on

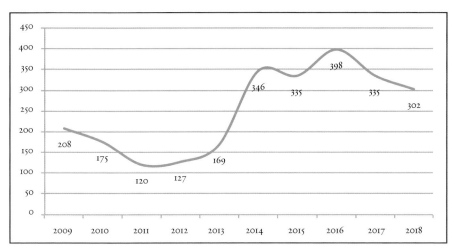

11.2 Number of field schools offered as listed on the AIA website, 2009–18

the Archaeological Institute of America (AIA) website (see Figure 11.2).[1] Not all field schools are listed on the AIA website – some are run by colleges and universities for their own students only – and not all field schools listed on the AIA site get enough students to go ahead. Yet anecdotal evidence suggests that about 80 per cent of all field schools listed on the AIA site proceed each year and that approximately fifty more archaeology programmes take place that are not listed.

Beyond the AIA website, verifiable, hard data about archaeology field schools is not collected and none is available – at least to the best of our knowledge. The following analysis, therefore, is based on conjectures and interpolations of the limited data available. We will clearly indicate what hard data is available and what our interpretations of that data are.

We assume that each field school accommodates – on average – ten students. Some may be larger, others smaller. We further assume that each student contributes – again, on average – €2,175 ($2,500) to the project in which they participate. This is certainly not the cost of the average field-school tuition. Universities and organisations take overhead charges to support the cost of credit units, insurance, liability and general funds. Only a portion of tuition is paid directly to programme directors to support actual field work.

Tabulating the AIA data with our conservative estimates yields some interesting insights. Between 2016 and 2018, an annual average of 3,500 students attended archaeology field schools, producing €7.6 ($8.75) million annually to support

---

1 The data suggest a dramatic decrease in field school offerings for 2011 and 2012. The impact of the 2008 economic crisis took a while to hit both scholars and students. The US economic stimulus packages provided significant sums to support all types of research immediately after the crisis. But these resources dried up by the end of 2010 with a pronounced impact on the number of field schools offered to, and likely attended by, US students.

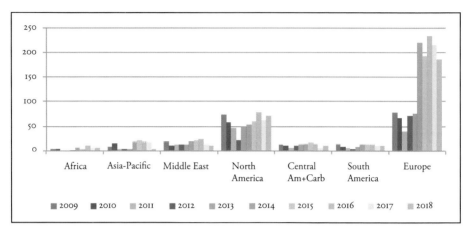

11.3 Archaeological field school locations by continent, as listed on the AIA website, 2009–18

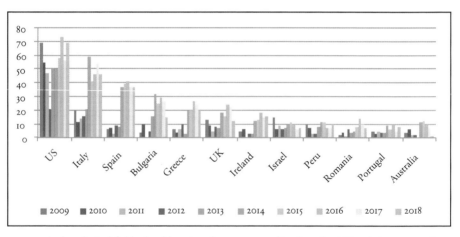

11.4 Archaeological field school locations by country, as listed on the AIA website, 2009–18

archaeological research. To provide context, the US National Science Foundation awarded about $7 (*c.*€6.1) million annually for archaeology research in each of these years (Boytner et al. 2017).[2]

Although North American students make up the vast majority of those attending – and paying for – field schools listed on the AIA site, their preferred destination is Europe (see Figure 11.3). As funding declined in Europe, many local archaeologists jumped on the North American field-school wagon and since 2014 the number of archaeology field schools offered there almost tripled. According to the AIA, 186 field schools were offered in Europe for North American students in 2018. Based on the

---

2 These numbers include funding for senior archaeologists and archaeometry but exclude funding for dissertation improvement grants.

above averages, this represents €4.05 ($4.65) million in research funds, or 53 per cent of all available field-school funding. This is not a small sum.

Europe is a large place with diverse cultural heritage. Funding is not equally distributed across the continent. When mapping the number of field schools in each country – both within and outside Europe – some surprising results emerged (Figure 11.4). Due to cost and security concerns, increasing numbers of US students stay at home and train in domestic programmes. Italy is a leading destination, while the number of programmes in Spain and Bulgaria also far supersedes those in traditionally favourite US destinations – Greece, the UK and Ireland. Two separate but mutually related forces combine to yield such results: the force of markets and the force of fear.

As the post-First World War bi-polar world order came to a close in the 1990s, a single ideology emerged to dominate world affairs – capitalism and the power of markets (recent writers suggest this era is now coming to an end – a discussion that is beyond the subject of this chapter (but see Ferguson 2018; Harari 2018)). Within archaeology, this process resulted in the creation of specialised and independent organisations that run field schools outside universities. Sanisera in Spain and the Balkan Heritage Foundation in Bulgaria are among the best known in Europe, each having created a niche market and attracting hundreds of students. Similar entities, such as the IAFS, the Achill Field School and Archaeotek, offer similar programmes but are more limited in scope and number of programme offerings – partly as they concentrate on undertaking research, rather than simply supporting it.

At the same time, many US universities became risk averse. As government funding declined and cost of liability increased, universities were seeking ways to reduce exposure and spread risk. For archaeology field schools, with their potential for illness and injury, universities began 'offloading' students to independent operators and allowing these organisations to carry the burden of liability and exposure. Combined, both forces dramatically increased the number of offered field schools. Effective marketing by the independent operators further increased the number of students attending such programmes.

Looking at the AIA data in isolation, it seems that the market has matured and that top capacity for field schools has been reached. At its peak in 2016, 398 field schools were listed on the AIA website. By 2018, that number had declined substantially and only 302 programmes were listed. While this may be due to market correction, looking at the AIA data alone may be misleading. Other data points may suggest this is a temporary pause and the number of field schools and students attending them is bound to grow again in coming years.

Each year, the Institute of International Education publishes the Open Doors Report. This report aggregates data about foreign students studying in US universities.

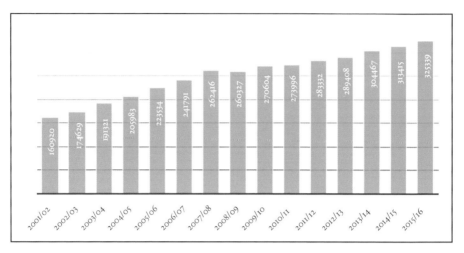

11.5 Number of US students studying abroad each year

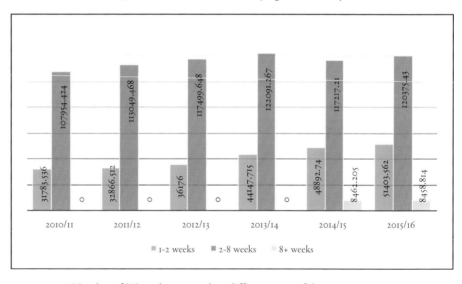

11.6 Number of US students attending different types of short-term programmes

More important here, the report also provides data about US students studying abroad (Figure 11.5; at the time of writing, data was available up to the 2015–16 academic year only). Since the turn of this century, the number of US students seeking educational experiences outside the US had increased considerably, with average growth of 5 per cent each year. The demand to study abroad is so resilient that even during the 2008 economic crisis, the numbers decreased only slightly (just 1 per cent) and then immediately recovered. As the economy in the US improves, these numbers will likely continue to robustly grow.

The cost for US students to study abroad is quite high and can easily reach $15,000 (€13,045) per semester.[3] As the overall number of US students studying abroad increases, the economic reality dictates that students will seek to reduce costs where possible. Many do so by forgoing traditional semester- or year-abroad options and, instead, join short-term programmes – defined as eight weeks or less. In the academic year 2001–2, 48 per cent of all US students studying abroad attended short-term programmes. By 2015–16, that portion increased to 63 per cent.

Not all short-term programmes have been created equal. Between 2010 and 2015, the number of US students attending snap programmes (one to two weeks in length) increased by 62 per cent (Figure 11.6). For the same period, the number of US students attending traditional short-term programmes (two to eight weeks) increased by only 12 per cent. Not surprisingly, most independent field-school operators' basic unit of operation is the two-week block.

As more US students seek study-abroad experience and as their choices shift to shorter programmes, great opportunities await. Archaeology field schools offer immersive and intensive education experiences that combine exposure to the social and hard sciences. Archaeology field schools provide training that is relevant far beyond the discipline: they teach students self-discipline, leadership skills and team work and provide exposure to technologies that are relevant to many professions; for example, Geographical Information System software is now used in almost every profession, drones and photogrammetry have broad applications and everyone needs to know and practise statistics.

In 2006, Brian Fagan wrote that the golden age of archaeology is coming to a close (Fagan 2006, 59). Far from it – archaeology field schools are thriving and training growing audiences for the discipline. Archaeology is a public good and can survive only with public support. There is no better way of gaining strong, committed and long-lasting support than through field schools. Archaeology's Golden Age is ahead of and not behind us!

CARRIG AND THE IAFS: A MODEL OF FIELD-SCHOOL EDUCATION IN IRELAND

Ireland has a long history of archaeology field schools and there are approximately six currently operating in various locations on the island. Some are run by universities as training schools, others are private enterprises. Most target overseas students as well as Irish students, and most have some sort of community participation element (see Baker et al. 2019).

---

3 Many UK, and increasingly Irish, universities are trying to capture this market and bring these high-paying students to their midst. Once again, this trend is out of the scope of this chapter.

The IAFS is a professional year-round field school that has partnered with the IFR since 2013. Founded in 2005, the IAFS has developed as Ireland's leading provider of accredited, field-based archaeological research and training programmes. The ethos of the school is to provide opportunities for students of archaeology and anthropology to experience at first hand the excitement of archaeological excavation in a well-supported teaching environment. IAFS archaeological and heritage programmes include research projects at several locations throughout the country (see, for example, Mandal et al. 2015; Shine et al. 2016; Rodgers et al. 2018; O'Sullivan et al. 2018). Since January 2018, the core focus of IAFS' work has been the excavation and associated research at Carrick ringwork and borough (Shine et al. 2018; ch. 5, above).

The Carrig project focuses on live archaeological survey, excavation and research – all facilitated by third-level students and academic partnerships. Excavations, while the most important part of the project, are but one component, with the initial project scope including three main pillars – *Excavation*, *Education* and *Experience*.

Collectively, these pillars provide a new and unique experience for students, locals and visitors at Carrick, lending each an exceptional insight into the process of archaeology in an engaging, up-close manner. 'Experiences' include archaeological training, archaeological tours, open-air museums, lectures, community excavations, children's events, simulated digs and interpretive displays varying in length from a casual 'walkabout' of the site to months-long in-depth participative involvement in the excavation.

Each pillar complements the strategic direction of the INHP to develop interactive experiences, which already include: guides in costume/character; overnight stays or demonstrations in replica buildings; birds-of-prey experiences; *fulacht fiadh* cooking demonstrations; and an extensive range of traditional craft courses. Students on the *Digging the Lost Town of Carrig Project* bring an enthusiasm and love of learning that is infectious, providing a sense of discovery, authenticity and excitement that is palpable for visitors to the INHP. Equally, student experience is greatly augmented through their placement within what is effectively a large interactive outdoor classroom, focused on immersive learning. A core component of this field school is dealing with visitors to the park, communicating the site's story and explaining the process of archaeology. All students are provided with training on how to interact with the public as part of the programme, and actively taught that the communication of archaeology is a vital element of the discipline. As part of this, every student is encouraged to hone her/his skills in communicating heritage to a diverse audience through rotations as a site tour guide (Figure 11.7). This teaching ethos follows much contemporary thinking in archaeology that its relevance is contingent on public engagement, where circumstances allow (see, for example, Berliner and Nassaney 2015; Wernecke and Williams 2017).

11.7 Students Sloane (left) and Wade preparing for project ambassador duty

11.8 Students working on the site in summer 2018

Student placement within the park means a unique holistic experience, where students are immersed in Irish heritage and the multitude of ways this can be communicated. This is complemented by student accommodation, with each student placed in homestay (staying with families in the local area). Homestay provides the students with a more authentic experience of family life in rural Ireland, frequently lending itself to unique student experiences that would not occur at other field schools. As important as the economic benefit of placing students with local families is the fact that students act as ambassadors for the site and project, disseminating the excavation findings to the homestays and their extended networks – thus engendering an increased awareness of the importance of Carrick.

The IAFS strives to unify and solidify the strengths of each component of the *Digging the Lost Town of Carrig Project* – the site, the academic research, the park, the homestay and the experience of Ireland in general. Collectively, these come together to provide a one-of-a-kind learning and cultural opportunity. In 2018, the first two groups of IFR students availed of this opportunity across two four-week dig seasons in January and July (Figure 11.8). Each of these students was interviewed while on site, and it is perhaps their feedback that best summarises the opportunities and strengths of the partnership approach being employed by the IAFS, the INHP and the IFR in this project. The interviews have been condensed into a workable narrative, augmented by the students' own words, describing the core components of their experience.

Student experience

For students, the project is viewed as more than simply a place to learn medieval history, improve archaeological skills or build their CV. They view it equally as a cultural and social experience – a place to step outside their comfort zone, build relationships and create lasting memories. Although the education garnered from attending a teaching-focused project is arguably the most important incentive to attend, the homestay accommodation and the site's location within Ireland (in general) and the INHP (in particular) are all features that not only attracted students to Carrick, but ultimately contributed to a more rewarding learning experience.

The 2018 students were drawn to Carrick for various academic reasons, predominantly due to their interest in the history of the site and/or their goal of gaining practical archaeological experience. Many pointed to the lack of opportunities in their home institutions to gain field experience, where archaeology or anthropology degrees were mainly theory-based. In the absence of hands-on opportunities at home, several students wanted to participate in a field school to decide if archaeology was a career path they wished to pursue – regardless of whether it was required to complete their degree (Figures 11.9, 11.10).

The students also identified the homestay experience as a core attraction that sets the programme apart. Several students noted that the opportunity to live with a local

11.10 Carrick in a word

"Denis and Richard put their trust in us and allowed us to make mistakes and to learn from them ourselves. I really enjoyed just having two mentors that weren't overbearing but were also very knowledgeable that would allow us to really get what we needed out of the experience."

"I'm really excited about all the new technical skills because I've done a dig before and it was just digging…"

"I just liked digging… playing in the dirt is a dream come true."

"…It's just really cool to see how the whole site operates, and seeing how professional archaeologists run a site"

"I learned that I do really enjoy doing this."

"I hoped to gain a certain level of hands-on, practical experience by working in the field and learn about whether this is the kind of thing I'd be interested in doing long-term"

"Obviously excavating and finding things is exciting, but also using the machinery, such as the levels, and doing documentation is all exciting."

"I liked being able to work in all different parts of archaeology, not necessarily just digging all the time."

"I really wanted to see if archaeology was something that I enjoyed"

"I just wanted to learn how to be a better archaeologist."

11.9 Student perceptions of the learning experience at Carrick

11.11 Student perceptions of the homestay experience at Carrick

I've met most of the locals… [my homestay family] knows everyone. I went to a wedding and I knew people there… I've been going to peoples' houses and talking to people and it's been really great.

In my homestay, I immediately felt like part of the family, and that was really cool.

This really allowed us to delve into Irish culture- living with families in a town that maybe isn't talked about much outside of Ireland.

The homestay was a big draw for doing this field school.

Instructors, staff, and the homestay families were all so warm and welcoming, not just to me, but to everybody.

It's like getting another family.

I was able to experience Irish culture, live in an Irish household and connect with a local family.

Carrick, to me, was a home away from home.

11.13 Ireland in a word

I wanted to learn more about what archaeology, in terms of interacting with the public, was like… So now we get to talk to people and we get to make other people who are coming on site get excited about archaeology, and I think that's really awesome.

"You have this site that's just, incidentally, in the middle of this park and it's really cool that people will be able to come and actually see it and experience it."

"One cool thing [is] the contact with the local people visiting the site. It's an amazing opportunity to engage with people from all over the world."

"They make you feel welcome and make you want to be there."

"Ferrycarrig and the Irish National Heritage Park showed me some wonderfully kind people who were overwhelmingly welcoming of students from all over the world."

"There's a sense of community here, especially with the park - it's homey."

"Though it was very cold, the warmth we students received from our host families and the staff at the [Irish National] Heritage Park more than made up for it."

11.12 Student perceptions of working within the INHP

Irish family was a significant factor that influenced their decision to attend this programme; all agree it ended up being one of the best aspects of the field school. The benefits of homestay were several, including: getting to see an authentic, hidden Ireland; having an active family support structure; gaining unique insight to Irish society; adopting an immediate social network; building enduring connections that will last long past the end of the programme (Figure 11.11).

Students perceive the IAFS partnership with the INHP as creating a unique learning setting for the students, where they were literally surrounded by Irish heritage (Figure 11.12). Several benefits of working within the park were identified, not least the friendliness and support provided by the park staff, which was seen as contributing to a community, family-like, atmosphere on the dig. A more obvious advantage of the park was the access to its amenities including: an indoor archaeological skills centre that was particularly useful in bad weather; an on-site office, canteen, lecture hall and post-excavation space; and a restaurant in the visitor centre. Students perceived these as rare, if not impossible, to find at another field school. Of more relevance to the students' education and professional development is the public nature of the INHP. The park receives *c.*70,000 visitors per annum and these visitors directly influence student experience each day. Every day, two students were scheduled as IAFS ambassadors to answer any questions visitors may have had. From the students' perspective, this ensured that they had to be knowledgeable on the site history and archaeological method and, more crucially, to learn how to communicate with people from greatly varying cultural backgrounds and demographic groups. The opportunity to interact with visitors to the park and enthuse them on history and archaeology was viewed as one of the most satisfying components of the programme.

Students also identified Ireland, as a host country, as a key attraction in coming to Carrick (Figure 11.13). Almost 75 per cent of students listed this as a main, or initial, reason to choose this programme. There were several reasons students wanted to visit Ireland, including its culture, landscape, people and ancestral connections. Whatever the reason, all students availed of free time to explore the country and were pleased the programme allowed for weekends off to facilitate independent travel time. Some used this to spend time with their host family, exploring Wexford and the surrounding area. Others took the opportunity to travel further afield to places such as Kilkenny, Waterford, Dublin, Galway and the Aran Islands. While international travel did not frequently occur during the programme, several students saw the position of Ireland, as a launch-pad into north-west Europe before or after the programme, as another key advantage of visiting Ireland.

CONCLUSION

It is clear that the *Digging the Lost Town of Carrig Project* meant more to students than simply a place of learning or a chance to obtain college credit. Without exception, the students complimented the teaching strengths of the project and the academic rigour and commitment invested in the research. Ultimately, however, what makes the Carrick experience so affirming is the people they encounter while on the project and the sense of friendship and community they engender. This includes park staff, IAFS instructors, fellow students, visitors to the site and individuals met while travelling. Carrick is much more than an archaeological dig or an outdoor classroom – it is a community that brings people from diverse backgrounds together, allowing them to grow as individuals, learn from one another, and forge lasting relationships. This is what all field school experiences should aspire to and it shows the strengths and tremendous potential of field-based experiential learning. Academic credit and new skills may be essential, but so too are life-long memories – it is in the creation of these that field schools in general, and the project at Carrick in particular, really excel.

BIBLIOGRAPHY

Baker, C., O'Carroll, F., Duffy, P., Shine, D., Mandal, S. and Mongey, M. 2019. 'Creating opportunities and managing expectations: evaluating community archaeology in Ireland'. In Jameson, J. and Musteață, S. (eds), *Transforming heritage practice in the 21st century: contributions from community archaeology*. New York.

Beauregard, D., Fletcher, A., Hewett, E., Judd, N., Freire-Marreco, B., Morley, S., Munk, J. and Numbaum, J. 1911. 'Rito de los Frijoles Gazette'. *Archaeological Institute of America and the School of American Archaeology*, 1910–11, vols 1–2.

Berliner, K. and Nassaney, M. 2015. 'The role of the public in public archaeology: ten years of outreach and collaboration at Fort St Joseph'. *Journal of Community Archaeology and Heritage*, 21, 3–21.

Boytner, R. 2012. 'The changing nature of archaeological field schools'. *The SAA Archaeological Record*, 121, 29–32.

Boytner, R. 2014. 'Do good, do research: the impact of archaeological field schools on local economies'. *Public Archaeology*, 131:3, 262–77.

Boytner, R., Zborover, D. and Chan, A. 2017. 'Historical perspectives on funding for archaeology'. Paper presented at the Society for American Archaeology, 82nd annual meeting. Vancouver.

Brace, M. 1986. 'On the road and in the field in 1919: the University of Arizona summer archaeological field season'. *The Kiva*, 51:3, 189–200.

Fagan, B. 2006. 'So you want to be an archaeologist?' *Archaeology Magazine*, 59:3, 59–64.

Ferguson, N. 2018. *The square and the tower: networks, hierarchies and the struggle for global power*. New York.

Gifford, A. and Morris, E. 1985. 'Digging for credit: early archaeological field schools in the American Southwest'. *American Antiquity*, 502, 395–411.

Harari, Y. 2018. *21 Lessons for the 21st century*. New York.

Haury, E. 1989. *Point of Pines, Arizona: a history of the University of Arizona Archaeological Field School*. Tucson.

Joiner, C. 1992. 'The boys and girls of summer: the University of New Mexico archaeological field school in Chaco Canyon'. *Journal of Anthropological Research*, 481, 49–66.

Mandal, S., O'Carroll, F. and Shine, D. 2015. 'The Black Friary, Trim'. *Archaeology Ireland*, 29:1, 34–8.

McManamon, F. 1991. 'The many publics for archaeology'. *American Antiquity*, 561, 121–30.

Mytum, H. (ed.). 2012a. *Archaeological field schools: constructing knowledge and experience*. New York.

Mytum, H. 2012b. 'The pedagogic value of field schools: some frameworks'. In Mytum, H. (ed.), *Archaeological field schools: constructing knowledge and experience*, 9–24. New York.

Nesbitt, P. 1931. *The ancient Mimbreños*. Beloit.

O'Sullivan, M., Rogers, M., Shine, D. and Mandal, S. 2018. 'Seir Kieran: place, pilgrimage and tradition in the monastic midlands'. *Offaly Heritage*, 10, 21–42.

Perry, E. 2006. 'From students to professionals: archaeological field schools as authentic research communities'. *The SAA Archaeological Record,* 61, 20–9.

Rogers, M., Bouricius, R., Shine, D., Mandal, S. and Stull, S. 2018. 'Laser-scanning Trim Castle'. *Archaeology Ireland*, 32:3, 34–9.

Shine, D., Green, A., O'Carroll, F., Mandal, S. and Mullee, B. 2016. 'What lies beneath: chasing the Trim town wall circuit'. *Archaeology Ireland*, 30:1, 34–8.

Shine, D., Mandal, S., Hayes, C. and Harris, M. 2018. 'Finding Carrig'. *Archaeology Ireland*, 32:2, 35–40.

Springer, F. 1913. 'The summer school'. *El Palacio*, 11, 4.

Thompson, R.H. and Longacre, William A. 1966. 'The University of Arizona archaeological field school at Grasshopper, East-Central Arizona'. *The Kiva*, 31:4, 255–75.

Wernecke, D. and Williams, T. 2017. 'From Maya pyramids to Paleoindian projectile points: the importance of public outreach in archaeology'. *Journal of Archaeology and Education*, 1, 1–34.

CHAPTER TWELVE

Remembering the Anglo-Normans in Wexford: 1969 and now

DENIS SHINE, RONAN O'FLAHERTY, IAN W. DOYLE & STEPHEN MANDAL

INTRODUCTION

When this publication was originally conceived of in early 2018 it was understood to be an extremely ambitious venture to produce a volume within a year of commencing a new excavation and research project. Nonetheless, it was agreed that the impending eight-hundred-and-fiftieth anniversary of the Anglo-Norman landing in 1169, and indeed the construction of the ringwork and subsequent stone castle at the Carrick site, was too important an occasion to go without commemoration and so a unanimous decision was taken to pursue this volume as part of a range of commemorative events, culminating in a major conference in October 2019.

More so than anywhere else in Ireland, the Anglo-Norman conquest left an indelible mark in the built and social landscape of Wexford, as well as on the population itself (Colfer 2002, 248). The decision to proceed with a commemoration of the Anglo-Norman arrival still raised inevitable discussions on the need or appropriateness of 'celebrating' such a conquest and the legacy of the eight hundred years that followed. On balance, it was agreed that the landing event – which was so pivotal in Irish, English and European history – and the Anglo-Norman contribution to shaping modern Wexford that followed should be readily recalled and commemorated on such a significant anniversary. A desire to celebrate Anglo-Norman Wexford in 2019 represents a radical shift from the public mindset on the last major anniversary of the Anglo-Norman landing in 1969. In this chapter, we explore the contestation of Anglo-Norman 'memory and landscape' in Wexford and how this has shifted in the fifty years between the anniversaries of the landing.

ANGLO-NORMAN WEXFORD: A CONTESTED PLACE?

Since at least the 1980s the archaeological profession has recognised that place, history and landscape are imbued with social, as well as ecological, dimensions (see, for example, Thomas 1981; David and Barker 2006). Landscape was re-envisaged as a collection of places, inscribed with memories of the past (Casey 2008; Van Dyke 2008). Place was in turn understood to be a social construct that, following from Schama (1995, 6–7), is built as much 'from strata of memory as from layers of rock'. It follows that memory consists of 'the selective preservation, construction and obliteration of ideas about the past' (Van Dyke 2008, 277). Memories, and by association places, that hold continued importance will be continually recalled but can variously be contested, defended, maintained or discarded, depending on their importance to contemporary populations.

For example, in examining Irish prehistoric landscapes, Cooney (1994; 2000) observed early modern images of the land as timeless, remote and pastoral, largely derived from attempts to write a new national identity from the nineteenth-century Gaelic revival onward; what Foster (1983, 173) eloquently refers to as the 'heyday of patriotic historiography'. These perceptions of the Irish landscape, although a construct, remain important to Irish self-identification today. The creation of the national image, outlined by Cooney (2000), is derived from the entanglement of place and the immediate socio-political background at that time, with such entanglements frequently most complex and contested in colonial and/or post-colonial contexts (see, for example, Croucher 2010; Meskell 2010; Lydon and Rizvi 2010a; 2010b; Strang 2008; Tilley 2008).

Specifically, in discussing the arrival of the Anglo-Normans, Cosgrove (1990, 99) argues that we are still struggling to escape a nationalist histography established, and eloquently promoted, in the early decades of the twentieth century by leading Irish nationalists. He cites a failure to develop a popular alternative to the simplistically conflated '800 years of English occupation', meaning our nationalist histography remains persuasive today. As the writings of historians (and archaeologists) is both a hermeneutic exercise (Johnson 1999) and positioned according to our own backgrounds, upbringings and world views (Hall 2006, 202), what does this 'national histography' mean for the recollection and portrayal of the Anglo-Normans today? Have 'older landscapes and identities', such as that of the Anglo-Norman period, been re-written? Alternatively, as both place and identity are constantly created, renewed, manipulated and discarded (Tamisari and Wallace 2006, 205), does a nationalist histography still prevail? Specifically in Wexford, a place synonymous with the Anglo-Norman landing and colony, how persuasive has nationalist sentiment been in our writing of an 'Anglo-Norman Space', and how has this impacted recollections of the Anglo-Normans in 1969 and today?

WRITING ANGLO-NORMAN WEXFORD

More so than many other parts of Ireland, Co. Wexford has been well served by historians of the Anglo-Norman period. During the late nineteenth and early twentieth centuries Wexford was fortunate to have Philip H. Hore and Goddard H. Orpen as historians. Hore, writing from Pole Hore, outside Wexford town, and later from London, compiled a six-volume *History of the town and county of Wexford* (Hore 1900–11). As a historian, his sympathies lay with the land-owning Anglo-Irish and he took a particular view of Irish history that saw the Anglo-Norman invasion as the arrival of a superior culture. Hore was clearly uncomfortable watching the development of Irish nationalism and in particular how this interpreted historic events. In the final pages of volume 5 dealing with Wexford town there is an extraordinary tirade:

> How is it that our countrymen cannot be brought to see that the best interests of their country are indissolubly connected with those of England, or cannot write or think with a fair and equal mind when a matter of national sentiment arises? ... they will only damage themselves and drive away capital and prosperity from their shores (Hore 1900–11, vol. v, 407).

Orpen shared this view of Ireland as an integral part of the British Empire and his four-volume history *Ireland under the Normans* remains, in the words of Seán Duffy, controversial to this day, but also 'a work of quite the most stupendous scholarship' (Duffy 2000, 246, 259; Orpen 1968). Much of it was written at Monksgrange in north Co. Wexford, where his archive remains. Orpen offered a detailed but restrained account of the initial Anglo-Norman landing at Bannow of 1169, simply commenting 'such was the small beginning of a movement of peoples destined in a brief period to have big results for Ireland' (Orpen 1968, vol. i, 145).

Leaving aside any such political or ideological bias, these early twentieth-century narratives identified places in the landscape with events of historical import and created a view that the Wexford landscape, in all its forms, was very much a medieval creation where traces of this period dominated. In an address from 1930 marking an excursion of the Royal Society of Antiquaries of Ireland to Wexford, R.A.S. Macalister remarked that 'for although the remains of earlier periods are present, those of the medieval centuries are here the more important' (1930, 79–80). In many ways this characterisation is difficult to argue with, although traces of preceding and indeed subsequent influences or narratives in the landscape are equally apparent (Doyle 2016; Colfer 2004).

By the time the eighth centenary of the Anglo-Norman invasion had come around in 1969–70 a new generation of historians were readying themselves to write a new narrative, but would their work alter establishment sentiments still held then?

THE 1969 COMMEMORATION

While far beyond the scope of this paper, it is worth briefly recalling the socio-political climate at the last major anniversary of the Anglo-Norman landing in 1969. The year 1969 opened (1–5 January) with Loyalist attacks on Civil Rights marchers, culminating in the Royal Ulster Constabulary (RUC) entering the Bogside area of Derry and the creation of the Free Derry movement and area (Coogan 1995, 549). The preceding years had seen an escalation of violence, discontent, marching and civil rights protests in Northern Ireland. Coogan (1995, 548–9) lists the first bombings of the contemporary Troubles as occurring in 1969 (when Loyalists destroyed utilities infrastructure). The year 1969 also witnessed, among other events: the 'Battle of the Bogside'; the deployment of British troops on the streets of the six northern counties and commencement of 'Operation Banner'; the first Ulster Volunteer Force (UVF) bombing in the Republic; the first casualty of a policeman related to the Troubles; and the creation of the Official and Provisional Republican Armies.

It was against the backdrop of these events that *An Taoiseach* Jack Lynch appeared on national television on 13 August denouncing the role of the RUC and British Army, announcing the establishment of field hospitals/nationalist refugee camps along the Irish border (following the burning of nationalist districts) and calling for the 'restoration of the historic unity of our country' (Lynch cited in Aldous 2007, 136).

Against the backdrop of such national sentiment, it is unsurprising the arrival of the Anglo-Normans, so frequently associated with '800 years' of English occupation, might not be celebrated at a national level. In a landscape like Wexford, however, where the conquest began, and where the Anglo-Norman presence left such an indelible mark in both the physical and the social landscape, how might the Anglo-Norman arrival be recalled, or might places such as Bannow Bay be commemorated?

To examine the eight-hundredth anniversary in Wexford we relied heavily on the archives of three local newspapers – *The Echo*, *The Free Press* and *The People* – after other avenues were exhausted. The papers indicate an initial local appetite to celebrate the Anglo-Norman landing. A meeting of the Tourist Development Committee of Wexford Chamber of Commerce (*The People*, 25 January) recorded that a 'Commemoration Committee' should be established from members of the County Corporation Tourist Development Society, the Festival and Fringe Events Committee and Old Wexford Tourists Development Office. A letter at that meeting, from John Small of Whites Hotel in Wexford town, gave an indication of the commemoration they hoped might materialise, which it was suggested could include:

- a pageant at the *Dun Mhuire* involving the county drama societies;
- a *son-et-lumière* at Selskar Abbey;
- a convention/function for people with Anglo-Norman surnames;

- a 'hand-across-the-sea' event through Normandy Ferries and/or through an exchange of mayors and Chambers of Commerce;
- lectures on the significance of Anglo-Norman landings for adults and children;
- outings to the actual Anglo-Norman landing sites, preferably guided by the Old Wexford Society;
- a 'Norman' cultural mini-festival.

The proposed commemoration had some initial local support, as indicated by a meeting of the Hook Tourist Development Association (*The People*, 1 February), which recorded their commitment to the commemoration plans.

The Commemoration Committee met in February 1969 when George Hadden was elected to the chair (*The People*, 15 February). Regional areas such as New Ross, Templetown, Wexford and Fethard were represented, although it was noted that many areas had not accepted an invitation to attend. It was recorded that the 'Bannow Group' were organising their own event, but that the group organiser (a Mrs Boggan) should be contacted to encourage them to join the county-wide initiative. No record of Bannow's event has been found and contact with the Bannow Historical Society has not yielded additional information. That the event proceeded is inferred by *The Free Press* of 14 March, which records a Mr Larry Devereux (cited as the last descendent of the original Devereuxs on Bannow Island) as looking forward to the Bannow commemorations of the Anglo-Norman landing.

Additional diverse ideas were suggested at the February Commemoration Committee meeting – from Anglo-Norman-themed pageants or plays, meetings of Anglo-Norman 'clans' (such as the Roches) to a 'Norman Fortnight'. Representatives from Fethard stated that they saw the celebration as a 1970 event, while others believed two full years were needed to work up a coherent policy or programme. In the end, Hadden concluded that the Old Wexford Society would organise a series of outings to commemorate the landing, with agreement reached with the New Ross Historical Society that they organise a lecture series. Hadden encouraged local groups to attend these outings and to formalise celebratory plans for future years.

'Commemorative' outings proceeded, as confirmed by the society proceedings of the *Journal of the Old Wexford Society* (vol. iii), which records fieldtrips between May and September 1969 to Bannow and Baginbun, Wexford town, Ferns, Dunbrody and Tintern abbeys, Ballyhack, Waterford and Rosslare. A second series of 'Festival Tours' led by Hadden to Bannow, Ferns, Dunbrody, Enniscorthy, Wexford town walls and Johnstown Castle are also recorded. *The Free Press* (18 June) documents at least some tours as having a large attendance, including from the New Ross Historical Society and Old Waterford Society. Other touring parties to Anglo-Norman landing sites were recorded that year, such as that of the Military History Society of Ireland, led by Richard Roche of the Irish Independent, to Bannow and other 'places of local interest' in June (*The People*, 31 May; *The Free Press*, 30 May).

12.1 Tintern Abbey, so long a popular tourist location, in January 2018

The lecture series by the New Ross Historical Society also proceeded, with Anglo-Norman-themed lectures recorded in the local press by Louis Cullen (Trinity College Dublin (TCD)) on 'The evolution of the Irish town' and by an un-named speaker on 'New Ross Bridge' (*The People*, 8 and 30 March). An earlier lecture in February by Mr R. Doran, to the Old Wexford Society, is also recorded in *The Free Press* (7 February) as coinciding with the eight-hundredth anniversary of the landing.

Aside from the tour outings and lectures, the original ambitions of the Commemoration Committee appear to have been curtailed as early as February, with only two of the seven original events proposed by Mr Small realised. The commemoration appears to have been driven by the Old Wexford Society, whose journal for that year (vol. ii) featured a distinctly Anglo-Norman feel (see Hadden 1969; FitzMaurice 1969; Roche 1969; Walsh 1969). Hadden's and Roche's papers were reported in the local press with the latter specifically mentioning their connection with the eight-hundredth anniversary of the landing (*The Echo*, 13 December; *The Free Press*, 28 March).

Other references to the Anglo-Normans in the 1969 Wexford press are largely incidental, but include: a 'Norman' article in *Ireland's Own* (*The People*, 11 October); Anglo-Norman Wexford being discussed on *Radio Éireann* (*The Echo*, 3 May); and a general-interest piece on Bannow and the landing (*The Free Press*, 14 March). Possible refurbishment of Roches' Castle (to include planting, a clean-up and floodlighting) in the hope of making it a focal point for outdoor dramas, pageants etc. was also reported in *The Free Press* (4 and 19 April). Having mistakenly identified the tower house as Carrick Castle, the piece notes the validity of such works in conjunction with the eight-hundredth anniversary of the Anglo-Norman landing. The social and tourist value of Anglo-Norman monuments was also reported in a piece entitled 'Vanishing Wexford' in *The Free Press* (28 February), which angrily proclaimed the need to safeguard and promote Anglo-Norman tourist attractions in order to grow tourism within the county.

Collectively, the press for the year 1969 indicates a good will among historical societies to celebrate the arrival of the Anglo-Normans. A successful tour and lecture series took place, but the occasion did not appear to engender enough public support to permit a wider programme of commemorative events. Much more telling on the attitudes of the wider public at this time may be the erection at Baginbun of a plaque to commemorate the eight-hundredth anniversary, which was vandalised within a week (Cosgrove 1990, 99). This event, coupled with the local press coverage during the year, certainly does not indicate widespread local support for recalling the Anglo-Norman landing. Some appetite evidently existed among historians, archaeologists and enthusiasts to commemorate the start of the colony; it was these groups and individuals who would be instrumental in encouraging a shift in public attitudes, which was reflected in Wexford in historical writings and the monumentalising of our built and archaeological heritage.

SHIFTING ATTITUDES IN WEXFORD, 1969–2019: A HISTORICAL PERSPECTIVE

The first piece of historical writing in Wexford (after the 1969 anniversary) appeared in 1970 from the pen of Richard Roche, a Wexford-born journalist working in Dublin. His book *The Norman invasion of Ireland* has seen numerous reprints (Roche 1970). As a work of writing, it contains none of the political attitudes embodied by Orpen or Hore but instead, and perhaps unsurprisingly, it makes reference to struggles between Ireland and England that lasted over eight hundred years. In this light, it is written more in a nationalist tone, and with vibrant prose, but crucially it embodies a sense of pride that the events related began in Co. Wexford.

At the very inception of the book, we get a sense of the author's view that the anniversaries of 1169, 1170 and 1171 were all being ignored by the government despite their importance 'in the entire history of Ireland' (Roche 1970, 9). As a member of a family descended from the Anglo-Norman invaders, there is a strong sense of pride in such a family history, indeed the author's preface is signed from Duncormick, Co. Wexford, 1 May 1970 – presumably to coincide with the precise

12.2 Ferns Castle during a visit by students from Carrick in June 2018

anniversary of the Bannow landings. There are frequent references in the text to the damaging role of England's involvement in Irish affairs (ibid., 9, 66, 111) and initially this appears to be in direct contradiction to the sense of pride that the author has for the first wave of Anglo-Norman invaders. Yet, this is neatly dealt with by seeing the visit of King Henry II to Ireland in 1171–2 as marking the end of a 'dream of an independent Norman state in Ireland' (ibid., 105). When 'the chances faded of a Norman-Irish state emerging [it] was the great tragedy of the entire adventure' (ibid., 110). While this book has been correctly criticised (Duffy 1996) for misinterpretations of fact, it remains, almost fifty years on, extremely readable as it was written in the engaging prose of a trained journalist. Moreover, the knowledge of the maritime landscape is impressive, with interpretations of landing sites and places of anchorage, which were clearly based on first-hand sailing experience. Intriguingly, while Roche felt that the Irish government was ignoring the invasion anniversaries, the government's Office of Public Works conducted a programme of archaeological excavations at the Anglo-Norman Ferns Castle during the period 1972–5 (see Sweetman 1979)(Figure 12.2).

Nicholas Furlong's (1973) *Dermot MacMurrough: king of Leinster and the foreigners* retains Roche's sense of pride in the central importance in a national narrative of places like Ferns, Bannow, Baginbun and Wexford town. As with Roche, the author's journalist background provided a lively writing style that richly sets the scene for personalities and places, for example:

> It was the first week of May in 1169 when up the dusty road to Ferns from the south rode a red-eyed Hy Kinsella man driving his horse into a foam of sweat. In through the lookout posts, past the houses, streaked with white dusty perspiration, on, on until at MacMurrough's castle he slackened rein. 'MacMurrough, they are here. The soldiers from Wales have come' (Furlong 1973, 128).

Equally interesting, Furlong's work sought to partly rehabilitate Diarmait Mac Murchada, not by denying his role or dark deeds but by putting them into the context of political power of the twelfth century. On his death, Mac Murchada is described as 'the scapegoat for our defeats' (ibid., 166), while the inside cover refers to his deeds in the words – 'It is a black picture. But it is also a false and unfair picture'.

The impression formed from looking at these publications in their original editions is that such historic events were being actively discussed in local societies and in the press but also that the context of the Irish state watching chaos and violence developing in Northern Ireland gave the events of eight hundred years ago an added currency. Both of these publications came from the pens of journalists writing from a local perspective, yet the distinguished medieval historian James Lydon of TCD concluded his book *The lordship of Ireland in the Middle Ages* on a similar bleak note about ongoing and unending conflict between both nations (Lydon 1972).

A decade later, the work of Billy Colfer, especially papers that reconstructed in detail the mosaic of Anglo-Norman settlement and its relationship with the Gaelic part of north Co. Wexford, began to appear with regularity – notably so from 1987 (Raftery 2016; see also ch. 1, above). Colfer's annual Anglo-Norman Connection conferences from 1992 onwards in Fethard did much to introduce scholars and locals to the medieval landscapes of Co. Wexford and significantly there was little political content to these discussions or in any of Colfer's publications. This feature of earlier writings was replaced by a strong knowledge of the landscape and of how Anglo-Norman settlement had integrated with it and equally shaped it through the carving out of knight's fees and manors, the density of tower houses and the extent of monastic lands. In many ways, Colfer's accounts, which are essentially published biographies of landscape, provided a local intellectual underpinning for the shift in how our heritage is now perceived – as a straightforward part of how Ireland has developed. O'Keeffe and Carey Bates (2016, 73) have commented that south Co. Wexford is a 'landscape

12.3 Bannow Church, now a valued local community resource

that evokes memories of the Anglo-Normans as no other Irish landscape does', yet it is hard to think of tensions that to this day arise over their historic meaning or their interpretation other than issues like planning, rural services and the use of natural resources. Places that might have been seen as difficult in any nationalist interpretation are hard to identify. Bannow Church, close to the May 1169 landing site and dating from the late twelfth century, is valued as a local cemetery and the church underwent conservation works at the instigation of the local community in recent years (Figure 12.3). Equally, Tintern Abbey, a Cistercian house founded by William and Isabella Marshal, is a well-used amenity run by the Office of Public Works and is seen as a means to encourage tourism and exercise in the local area. In New Ross, the development of the Ros Tapestry and ongoing conservation works on the medieval defences suggest a town at ease with its medieval heritage.

SHIFTING ATTITUDES IN WEXFORD, 1969–2019: AN ARCHAEOLOGICAL AND BUILT-HERITAGE PERSPECTIVE

The hostility toward the Anglo-Normans and negative connotations to England were initially as prevalent among Irish archaeologists as historians for much of the twentieth century. In 1928, R.A.S. Macalister, chair of Celtic Archaeology at University College Dublin (UCD), had commented in relation to Anglo-Norman achievements that 'such subjects … are a branch of English archaeology and even their extension to Ireland is much more a matter of English than of Irish interest'. Macalister continued to teach at UCD up until 1943 and was a major influence on generations of Irish archaeologists; indeed, the sentiment expressed in his comment appears to have held true until the later decades of the twentieth century. Kieran O'Conor, writing in 1998 on the history of medieval rural settlement studies in Ireland, points to a continuing disinterest bordering on antipathy towards the Anglo-Norman material right up to the mid-1980s (O'Conor 1998, 1–16). By that time, however, things were beginning to change quite significantly. Terry Barry saw this resulting in part at least from the state's growing involvement on the international stage in fora such as the United Nations (UN) and the European Union (EU), which encouraged a more varied interpretation of our past (Barry 1987, 1–2). Overall, Barry took the view that by 1987 there was an acknowledgment of the contributions of Vikings and Anglo-Normans to the development of Irish society (ibid., 2).

Interestingly, it was that same year that saw the establishment of the Irish National Heritage Park (INHP) in Wexford, undoubtedly one of the seminal moments in the public expression of Wexford's – and indeed Ireland's – diverse heritage (see also ch. 10, above). The brainchild of a small group of local enthusiasts, the name chosen for the new park signals a much greater, national ambition. In the context of the current discussion, however, what is interesting is that recognition of Ireland's Anglo-Norman heritage was part of the proposal from the very start. The germ of the idea for the park was contained in a proposal presented by Edward Culleton in 1983 (see ch. 10, above). This was just a few years after the famous 'Save Wood Quay' protest march, which took place on 23 September 1978, and which itself played such an important role in transforming public perception of our Viking heritage – up to then often perceived as alien to our 'native' Gaelic culture. The transformation of the public perception of the Vikings prepared the way for a revision of attitude towards the legacy of the Anglo-Normans, which in turn made the proposals for interpreting this legacy at the new INHP much more acceptable.

A study of archived material still held by the INHP shows the extent of the planning that was brought to bear on the creation of the new park, not least in terms of its philosophy, one objective of which was 'to educate Irish people, particularly young people, concerning their rich material heritage of which they are both heirs and guardians' (Culleton 1994). That this included their Anglo-Norman heritage was abundantly clear. The archived papers clearly show the detailed research being carried out into the forms of motte-and-bailey castles that might prove models for reconstructions onsite; indeed, the motte-and-bailey site, the ringfort and the crannog were the first three reconstructions planned. The wider context of Anglo-Norman heritage at or near Ferrycarrig was also very much a factor in selecting the preferred site for the park as a whole, with the Fitz Stephen earthwork, the later Anglo-Norman borough, the nearby church of St Nicholas of Myra and Roches' Castle all explicitly cited as reasons for establishing a heritage park here.

The very first visitor guide from 1987 presents a remarkably balanced view of Ireland's heritage, commenting:

> In Ireland you can find the last vestige of the once-powerful Celtic civilisation, the monasteries that Christianised much of Europe, the 1,000-year-old towns founded by the Vikings or the earthen ramparts of the early Norman colonisers.

Here we have the native Gaelic, Viking and Anglo-Norman traditions clearly stitched together to create a new, holistic view of what constituted Irish heritage. When the park was being promoted by Bord Fáilte at its international Trade Producer Workshop in the Burlington Hotel in Dublin in 1987, the central image on its promotional material was not the ringfort or the crannog, it was the motte-and-bailey castle. That same year, an article on the INHP by Máirín de Búrca in the *Sunday Times* (7 June) began with the sentences:

> It is not for nothing that Wexford is called the 'Model County'. The Normans must have realised its potential when they chose to land here and to this day it is home to some of the most civilised people on this island.

The almost gentle reference to the Anglo-Normans, and their clear place in creating the Wexford of today, marks a distinct softening of attitude towards what were often previously regarded as nothing more than alien invaders. The park's excellent student workbook from 1991 accords the Anglo-Normans equal standing with every other contributor to Irish culture, while one of the first promotional brochures (also from 1991) features Anglo-Norman knights prominently on the front cover.

Unfortunately, because of disagreement about the ultimate design of the motte-and-bailey castle, as well as direct criticism of what was eventually built, the Anglo-Norman site was never actually completed and the story of the Anglo-Normans ended up playing very little part in the overall narrative delivered to visitors. Elsewhere, however, Wexford's Anglo-Norman heritage was becoming increasingly recognised and indeed celebrated. One of the clearest ways of observing this is through the attitude displayed by the various community-run visitor attractions around the county, which can be seen as a barometer of wider public opinion. Hook Lighthouse has been to the fore in developing its Anglo-Norman story, which features strongly and positively in its visit narrative. Nearby Tintern also has an active community group seeking to highlight the site's Anglo-Norman heritage, in particular through the characters of William and Isabella Marshal. In New Ross, the remarkable Ros Tapestry, begun in 1998 and created by local volunteers, tells the story of the arrival of the Anglo-Normans, and the founding of the town by William Marshal. The tone of the tapestry

12.4 Students from Carrick visiting Hook Lighthouse in July 2018

is very much one of 'celebration'. More recently in Ferns, a very successful annual conference has been running since 2016, strongly focused on the interface between Gaelic and Anglo-Norman cultures, while the Anglo-Norman story dominates the narrative of the great castle of Ferns.

Shifting attitudes to the Anglo-Normans in Wexford were perhaps best expressed by the creation of the Norman Way in May 2017. Launched by Minister of State for Tourism and Transport, Patrick O'Donovan TD, the trail was developed by Wexford County Council, with support from Fáilte Ireland, with the objective of telling 'the compelling story of the Normans and their way of life over eight hundred years ago, [allowing people] to retrace the steps of their ancestors and celebrate the arrival of the Normans to Ireland, in the very landscape where it all began' (WCC 2017). Speaking at the launch, O'Donovan stated:

With a greater number of Norman castles and churches than any other county in Ireland, south Wexford has been left with an extraordinary legacy of Norman descent. The Norman Way aims to promote this rich heritage, both to our own and to visitors (ibid.).

An increasing awareness of the tourism value of this Anglo-Norman heritage has also been strongly evident among policy-makers and community alike, with the figure of William Marshal coming strongly to the fore as a unifying symbol. Indeed, there is a sense that Wexford needs to 'claim the space' in terms of Anglo-Norman heritage, using its rich store of built and cultural heritage to create a new and exciting visitor experience, while, in the figure of Marshal, Wexford very much claims the 'bones of the ancestors'.

CONCLUSION: WHAT FOR 2019?

While it is clear that an antipathy – or at best indifference – toward the Anglo-Normans existed in the fledgling Irish state in the early part of the twentieth century, it is slightly surprising how long this situation prevailed and how pervasive it was; although certainly it was encouraged and maintained by the politics surrounding the northern Troubles. Even in Wexford, where the Anglo-Normans so indelibly constructed both the physical and the cultural landscape, there was little support on an occasion as crucial as the eight-hundredth anniversary of their arrival. That any commemorations proceeded is a testament to the local historians and archaeologists of that day, as well as to those who preceded them.

Our national historiography undoubtedly changed from the 1970s onward, partly as 'modern' Ireland emerged as an EU state. This impacted firstly on our recollections of the Vikings, followed closely by those of the Anglo-Normans through the 1980s. As the theme of this chapter necessarily focuses on Wexford, what did changing national histographies mean within the county? Primarily, it saw a new suite of writing, much less political in tone, which itself helped foster local pride and celebration of Anglo-Norman 'spaces' – especially in terms of built heritage, where it held potential as touristic sites.

Much has changed in Ireland since 1969, and since the 1980s for that matter. Crucially, Ireland has witnessed more than twenty years of peacetime recovery, following the signing of the Good Friday Agreement on 10 April 1998. This and several other factors have contributed to a very gradual change in the psyche of much of the Irish public and in relations with the United Kingdom. Perhaps best exemplifying the measured speed, but also the considerable scale, of this change was the state visit of Queen Elizabeth II in May 2011 – a monumental occasion as it represented the first visit by a reigning British monarch in the history of the Republic of Ireland.

Within this new Ireland, how might the Anglo-Normans be recalled on the eight-hundred-and-fiftieth anniversary of their arrival in Wexford? As this chapter has been written in advance of 2019, it is impossible to elaborate significantly on the 2019 commemoration. Even this chapter and the volume at large, however, point toward a positive recollection of the Anglo-Norman landing. As stated, it was decided early in 2018 that the eight-hundred-and-fiftieth anniversary of the Carrick site should be memorialised in this volume, as well as through an international conference. An 'Anglo-Norman Landing' series of lectures is also planned, throughout the crucial summer months, which saw the first Anglo-Normans arrive eight-hundred-and-fifty years ago. Finally, the *Carrig Archaeological Centre* – a best-practice archaeological training centre, equipped for community outreach and experiential learning for children, and incorporating a 'live museum' – will be formally launched in the summer of 2019. The launch is the culmination of a year-long commitment by the INHP and the Irish Archaeology Field School (IAFS) to host an event to mark the arrival of the Anglo-Normans at Bannow Bay.

Elsewhere within the county, local history and community groups, as well as tourism providers and attractions, have begun to prepare for an ambitious programme of events and commemorations. At the time of writing, these include events at Hook, Tintern, the INHP and Ferns. A very welcome feature is how the various parties are working together to link these events to ensure a consistent programme emerges, offering something throughout the year for locals and visitors alike. Some of the plans that are already well advanced include medieval feasts, lectures and tours, a very interesting Brehon Law trial of Diarmait Mac Murchada in Ferns, and specially commissioned wooden sculptures of William and Isabella Marshal at Tintern. A bid for funding for a wider festival linking all areas including Baginbun, Bannow, Tintern, New Ross and Ferns has also been submitted to Fáilte Ireland.

All these planned events throughout the county indicate a climate of celebrating Wexford's Anglo-Norman history in 2019. At a time of radical political change, with the uncertainties of Brexit looming as we speak, commemorating our complicated but frequently shared histories has perhaps never been so important!

BIBLIOGRAPHY

Aldous, R. 2007. *Great Irish speeches*. London.
Barry, T. 1987. *The archaeology of medieval Ireland*. London and New York.
Casey, E. 2008. 'Place in landscape archaeology: a Western philosophical prelude'. In David, B. and Thomas, J. (eds), *Handbook of landscape archaeology*, 44–50. Walnut Creek.
Colfer, B. 2002. *Arrogant trespass: Anglo-Norman Wexford, 1169–1400*. Wexford.

Colfer, B. 2004. *The Hook Peninsula, County Wexford*. Cork.

Coogan, T. 1995. *The Troubles*. London.

Cooney, G. 1994. 'Sacred and secular Neolithic landscapes in Ireland'. In Carmichael, D., Hubert, J., Reeves, B. and Schanche, A. (eds), *Sacred sites, sacred places*, 32–43. London.

Cooney, G. 2000. *Landscapes of Neolithic Ireland*. London.

Cosgrove, A. 1990. 'The writing of Irish medieval history'. *Irish Historical Studies*, 27, 97–111.

Croucher, S. 2010. 'Cultural identity, and colonial and postcolonial archaeologies'. In Lydon, J. and Rizvi, U. (eds), *Handbook of postcolonial archaeology*, 351–64. Walnut Creek.

Culleton, E. 1994. 'Address to the World Archaeological Congress, Delhi, India, December 1994'. INHP archive.

David, B. and Barker, B. 2006. 'The social archaeology of indigenous Australia'. In David, B., Barker, B. and McNiven, I. (eds), *The social archaeology of Australian indigenous societies*, 2–19. Canberra.

De Búrca, M. 1987. [Title unknown]. *The Sunday Times*, 7 June.

Doyle, I. 2016. '"Telling the dancer from the dance": the archaeology of early medieval Wexford'. In Doyle, I. and Browne, B. (eds), *Medieval Wexford: essays in memory of Billy Colfer*, 35–61. Dublin.

Duffy, S. 1996. '*The Norman invasion of Ireland* by Richard Roche: review article'. *History Ireland*, 4:2, 6.

Duffy, S. 2000. 'Historical revisit: Goddard Henry Orpen, *Ireland under the Normans, 1169–1333*, 1911–20'. *Irish Historical Studies*, 32:126, 246–59.

FitzMaurice, G. 1969. 'Hervey de Montmorency'. *Journal of the Old Wexford Society*, 2, 19–26.

Foster, R. 1983. 'History and the Irish question'. *Journal of the Royal Historical Society*, 33, 169–92.

Furlong, N. 1973. *Dermot MacMurrough: king of Leinster and the foreigners*. Tralee.

Hadden, G. 1969. 'The origin and development of Wexford town, pt 3: the Norman period'. *Journal of the Old Wexford Society*, 2, 3–12.

Hall, S. 2006. 'New ethnicities'. In Ashcroft, B., Griffiths, G. and Tiffin, H. (eds), *The post-colonial studies reader*, 2nd ed., 199–202. London and New York.

Hore, P. 1900–11. *History of the town and county of Wexford*. 6 vols. London.

Johnson, M. 1999. *Archaeological theory: an introduction*. Oxford.

Lydon, J. 1972. *The lordship of Ireland in the Middle Ages*. Dublin.

Lydon, J. and Rizvi, U. 2010a. *Handbook of postcolonial archaeology*. Walnut Creek.

Lydon, J. and Rizvi, U. 2010b. 'Introduction: postcolonialism and archaeology'. In Lydon, J. and Rizvi, U. (eds), *Handbook of postcolonial archaeology*, 17–34. Walnut Creek.

Macalister, R. 1928 *The archaeology of Ireland*. London.

Macalister, R. 1930. 'Report of the council for 1930: excursions'. *Journal of the Royal Society of Antiquaries of Ireland*, 60, 79–81.

Meskell, L. 2010. 'Ethnographic interventions'. In Lydon, J. and Rizvi, U. (eds), *Handbook of postcolonial archaeology*, 445–8. Walnut Creek.

O'Conor, K. 1998. *The archaeology of medieval rural settlement in Ireland*. Dublin.

O'Keeffe, T. and Carey Bates, R. 2016. 'The abbey and cathedral of Ferns, 1111–1253'. In Doyle, I. and Browne, B. (eds), *Medieval Wexford: essays in memory of Billy Colfer*, 73–96. Dublin.

Orpen, G. 1968. *Ireland under the Normans*. 4 vols. Reprint. Oxford.

Raftery, C. 2016. 'Dr Billy Colfer: a bibliography'. In Doyle, I. and Browne, B. (eds), *Medieval Wexford: essays in memory of Billy Colfer*, 32–4. Dublin.

Roche, R. 1969. 'The Roches of Wexford'. *Journal of the Old Wexford Society*, 2, 39–49.

Roche, R. 1970. *The Norman invasion of Ireland*. Tralee.

Schama, S. 1995. *Landscape and memory*. London.

Strang, V. 2008. 'Uncommon ground: landscapes as a social geography'. In David, B. and Thomas, J. (eds), *Handbook of landscape archaeology*, 51–9. Walnut Creek.

Sweetman, D. 1979. 'Archaeological excavations at Ferns Castle, County Wexford'. *Proceedings of the Royal Irish Academy*, 79C10, 217–45.

Tamisari, F. and Wallace, J. 2006. 'Towards an experiential archaeology of place: from location to situation through the body'. In David, B., Barker, B. and McNiven, I. (eds), *The social archaeology of Australian indigenous societies*, 204–25. Canberra.

The Echo. 1969. '*Journal of the Old Wexford Society*', 13 December.

The Echo. 1969. 'Wexford town features on Radio Éireann', 3 May.

The Free Press. 1969. 'Devereux have survived since 1169', 14 March.

The Free Press. 1969. '*Old Wexford Journal*', 14 March.

The Free Press. 1969. 'On lonely Bannow Strand', 14 March.

The Free Press. 1969. 'Wexford landmarks: Ferrycarrig Castle rich in history', 18 April.

The Free Press. 1969. 'District notes: Wexford Norman tour', 18 June.

The Free Press. 1969. 'Vanishing Wexford', 28 February.

The Free Press. 1969. 'Historians to visit Norman sites', 30 May.

The Free Press. 1969. 'Our ancestors', 7 February.

The People. 1969. 'Hook Tourist Development Association', 1 February.

The People. 1969. 'Why the Normans came', 11 October.

The People. 1969. 'Norman landings', 15 February.

The People. 1969. 'County Wexford and tourism', 25 January.

The People. 1969. 'Seven bridges in 750 years', 30 August.

The People. 1969. 'Military History Society outing', 31 May.

Thomas, N. 1981. 'Social theory, ecology and epistemology: theoretical issues in Australian prehistory'. *Mankind*, 132, 165–77.

Tilley, C. 2008. 'Phenomenological approaches to landscape archaeology'. In David, B. and Thomas, J. (eds), *Handbook of landscape archaeology*, 271–6. Walnut Creek.

Van Dyke, R. 2008. 'Memory, place and the memorialization of landscape'. In David, B. and Thomas, J. (eds), *Handbook of landscape archaeology*, 277–84. Walnut Creek.

Walsh, D. 1969. 'Ferrycarrig Castle scheme must go on'. *The Free Press*, 4 April.

Walsh, T. 1969. 'The Knights of the Temple'. *Journal of the Old Wexford Society*, 2, 13–19.

WCC, 2017. 'Press release on official launch of the Norman Way heritage and cycling trail' (www.wexfordcoco.ie/news/2017/05/26/official-launch-of-the-norman-way-heritage-and-cycling-trail, 26 May 2017; accessed 27 August 2018).

Index

compiled by Michael Ann Bevivino